CHRIST STOPPED AT EBOLI

CHRIST STOPPED AT EBOLI

The Story of a Year   by CARLO LEVI

TRANSLATED FROM THE ITALIAN BY FRANCES FRENAYE

 TIME Reading Program Special Edition

Time-Life Books Inc., Alexandria, Virginia

Time-Life Books, Inc.
is a wholly owned subsidiary of
TIME INCORPORATED

TIME Reading Program: *Editor*, Max Gissen

For information about any Time-Life book, please write:
Reader Information, Time-Life Books,
541 North Fairbanks Court, Chicago, Illinois 60611

THE MOST FASCINATING WORK of literature to come out of Italy in the years following World War II was created by a man who was then unknown as a writer and, indeed, did not view himself as a literary person. Carlo Levi, the author of *Christ Stopped at Eboli,* had been trained in medicine and had won considerable acclaim as a painter. But up to the time this extraordinary book appeared, his only published works had been some newspaper and magazine articles, mostly polemics against Italy's Fascist regime. *Christ Stopped at Eboli* brought him swift acclaim. He was hailed as one of the great literary stylists of the era, and the book was immediately established as one of the classics of modern Italian literature.

To anyone who has read *Christ Stopped at Eboli,* this enthusiasm is not hard to understand, but it caused some confusion at the time. The book was modest in scope, and the reviewers had some difficulty conveying the nature of its special qualities. They even had some difficulty classifying the book: it was called a novel, a memoir, an album of sketches, a study in sociology. It is all of these in some degree. Ostensibly, it is simply a true account of a year that the author spent in a backward, malaria-ridden southern Italian village, Gagliano, in the province of Lucania. Levi had been exiled there in 1935, after a period of imprisonment for opposing the Mussolini dictatorship. The book ends with the author's return to northern Italy in 1936, after he was freed in a political amnesty.

Levi's stay in Gagliano was not, on the face of it, especially eventful. The tales of brutality or persecution that we might anticipate from an oppositionist apprehended by the police in a modern totalitarian state are entirely lacking in this account. Most American readers will, in fact, be surprised at the relaxed and easygoing treatment the regime accorded one of its most uncompromising critics. Levi was obliged to stay within fairly narrow geographical limits while he was in Gagliano, but otherwise there were scarcely any restrictions on him, and the peasants, the townspeople and even the local officials and Fascist party leaders were friendly to him. Indeed, Fascism was not much of an issue in the town. What really set Levi apart from Gagliano's people was not so much his anti-Fascist views as the fact that he had any views at all, that he was a man of some culture, with an interest in the affairs of the 20th Century. The men and women around him, by contrast, had a mode of thinking and a style of life not much different from what it had been a hundred—or for that matter, 300—years earlier. Levi's portraits of these simple souls constitute the main ingredient of his book.

Why should anyone care about the people who lived in Gagliano in 1935? One might answer plausibly that the existence of such poverty, illiteracy and superstition in that year was a compelling indictment of the Fascist regime and that the book is an effective answer to the neo-Fascist ideologies trying to envelop the Mussolini years in a legend of national grandeur. Levi's testimony on the "grandeur" of those years is certainly devastating. The people of Gagliano were utterly indifferent to the appeals of Fascism, stone deaf to the bombast of their local leaders, unconcerned about the success of Italy's attack on Ethiopia that year.

But Levi is not primarily interested in proving again the phoniness of Fascist claims, and he makes it clear that the peasants would have felt pretty much the same about any kind of rule from Rome. Any government would have seemed alien to their own interests and preoccupations; they viewed the state itself as a kind of scourge, like malaria. As Levi says:

> For this reason, quite naturally, they have no conception of a political struggle; they think of it as a personal quarrel among the "fellows in Rome." They were not concerned with the views of the political prisoners who were in compulsory residence among them, or with the motives for their coming. They looked at them kindly and treated them like brothers because they too, for some inexplicable reason, were victims of fate. During the first days of my stay whenever I happened to meet along one of the paths outside the village an old peasant who did not know me, he would stop his donkey to greet me and ask in dialect: "Who are you? Where are you going?" "Just for a walk; I'm a political prisoner," I would answer. "An exile? (They always said exile instead of prisoner.) Too bad! Someone in Rome must have had it in for you." And he would say no more, but smile at me in a brotherly fashion as he prodded his mount into motion.

Levi himself has been described as an anarchist—from time to time he has engaged in the politics of the far Left—and his own hostility to the state certainly has some roots in his observations of life in Gagliano. But he is not telling us about its people just to argue the anarchist position. The people of Gagliano, he makes it clear, are a very special case, and he is writing about them precisely for that reason.

They are, we quickly perceive, the forsaken of the earth. The title of the book refers to a saying among them, "Christ stopped short of here, at Eboli," which means, in effect, that they have been bypassed by Christianity, by morality, by history itself—that they have somehow been excluded from the human experience. To their hopeless lot they can bring only one of two attitudes. The usual one is a "gloomy resignation, alleviated by no hope of paradise, that bows their shoulders under the scourges of nature." Alternating with this attitude is a furious defiance, manifesting itself historically in irrational (and hopeless) outbreaks of violence. The most recent eruption of this sort had been some outbreaks of brigandage in the mid-19th Century; these outbreaks, directed against the Italian social order of that period, had been put down in 1865, but tales of the brigand days were still common among the peasants. Levi actually met one survivor of that epoch, who told him proudly how the brigands had kidnaped a wealthy landowner and mailed one of his ears to his wife when she was slow paying the ransom. Such tales were the closest the peasants came to having anything like a historical tradition of their own. Many of the men of Gagliano had fought, and some had died, in World War I, but Levi says he never heard tales of this experience; it was evidently viewed by the peasants as just another of nature's gratuitous insults.

The extraordinary readability of the book stems from the fact that it introduces the reader to these bypassed people of

Gagliano as individuals, with the introductions performed by a master of characterization. Levi's gallery of portraits is a fantastic one. There is his maid, Giulia, matter-of-factly identified (by herself as well as by others) as a witch, able to cast spells and mix love philters, even to "bring about the death of anyone she chose by uttering terrible incantations." There is a forlorn, drunken village priest, half-crazy with loneliness. There is Donna Caterina, wife of the local Fascist leader and sister of the mayor and, inevitably, a power in the village. Herself a mistress of intrigue, she is convinced that her husband has been bewitched and is the lover of the druggist's daughter, a sinuous local beauty who, Donna Caterina is certain, plans to poison her.

> As to her husband, Donna Caterina knew how to handle him. There was to be no scandal, no one must have the slightest suspicion. In the privacy of their own four walls Donna Caterina accused him every day of adultery and murder, and forbade him access to her bed. The powerful and feared Party leader of Gagliano lost every bit of his arrogance as soon as he entered his own house, where in the darting black eyes of his wife he was a hopeless reprobate and unforgivable sinner, and he had to settle down to a solitary sleep on a couch in the drawing room. This sad life went on for six months until there appeared a last chance for redemption: the war with Abyssinia. The humiliated sinner enrolled as a volunteer. . . .

There are also several "Americans" in Gagliano—a barber, a tailor and others. These are men who have been to America and returned, usually planning to visit just for a while and then return to New York. But many of them have never gone back; they squandered their savings, settled back to life in Gagliano, and were soon indistinguishable from their neighbors. "Along with poverty they regain their agelong patience and resignation and all their former peasant habits."

These "Americans" are in a way the sorriest of the lot, because they have had a vision of the promised land. There is no doubt about what that land is. For the people of Levi's Gagliano, Rome is a hostile and alien oppressor, but New York represents at least some faint distant vision of betterment, and to the extent that they are religious at all, America is a major ingredient of their faith. Levi describes a remarkable scene that he observed in just about every bedroom.

> On one side was the black, scowling face, with its large, inhuman eyes, of the Madonna of Viggiano; on the other a colored print of the sparkling eyes, behind gleaming glasses, and the hearty grin of President Roosevelt. I never saw other pictures or images than these: not the King nor the Duce, nor even Garibaldi; no famous Italian of any kind, nor any one of the appropriate saints; only Roosevelt and the Madonna of Viggiano never failed to be present. To see them there, one facing the other, in cheap prints, they seemed the two faces of the power that has divided the universe between them. But here their roles were, quite rightly, reversed. The Madonna appeared to be a fierce, pitiless, mysterious, ancient earth goddess, the Saturnian mistress of this world; the President a sort of all-powerful Zeus, the benevolent and smiling master of a higher sphere.

Levi wrote *Christ Stopped at Eboli* some eight years after the events he described, in 1943-1944, when he was living in Florence as a hunted member of the Underground. Some months later, in 1944-1945, he served as editor of a Resistance newspaper, *La Nazione del Popolo*. Early in 1945 he went to Rome and edited another Resistance newspaper there. *Christ Stopped at Eboli* was published that year.

After the war years, Levi wrote several other books. All of them were well enough received to make it clear that his first was no fluke, but none had the success or the impact of *Christ Stopped at Eboli*. There are undoubtedly many reasons for this—including the inability of the author to find another cast of characters even remotely as interesting as the people of Gagliano. But there is another reason that is probably more to the point: *Christ Stopped at Eboli* comes close to being a literary masterpiece; not many authors could produce two like it. Levi died in Rome in 1975.

—THE EDITORS

CHAPTER ONE

MANY YEARS HAVE GONE
by, years of war and of what men call History. Buffeted here
and there at random I have not been able to return to my
peasants as I promised when I left them, and I do not know
when, if ever, I can keep my promise. But closed in one room,
in a world apart, I am glad to travel in my memory to that
other world, hedged in by custom and sorrow, cut off from
History and the State, eternally patient, to that land without
comfort or solace, where the peasant lives out his motionless
civilization on barren ground in remote poverty, and in the
presence of death.

"We're not Christians," they say. "Christ stopped short of
here, at Eboli." "Christian," in their way of speaking means
"human being," and this almost proverbial phrase that I have
so often heard them repeat may be no more than the expression of a hopeless feeling of inferiority. We're not Christians,

we're not human beings; we're not thought of as men but simply as beasts, beasts of burden, or even less than beasts, mere creatures of the wild. They at least live for better or for worse, like angels or demons, in a world of their own, while we have to submit to the world of Christians, beyond the horizon, to carry its weight and to stand comparison with it. But the phrase has a much deeper meaning and, as is the way of symbols, this is the literal one. Christ did stop at Eboli, where the road and the railway leave the coast of Salerno and turn into the desolate reaches of Lucania. Christ never came this far, nor did time, nor the individual soul, nor hope, nor the relation of cause to effect, nor reason nor history. Christ never came, just as the Romans never came, content to garrison the highways without penetrating the mountains and forests, nor the Greeks, who flourished beside the Gulf of Taranto. None of the pioneers of Western civilization brought here his sense of the passage of time, his deification of the State or that ceaseless activity which feeds upon itself. No one has come to this land except as an enemy, a conqueror, or a visitor devoid of understanding. The seasons pass today over the toil of the peasants, just as they did three thousand years before Christ; no message, human or divine, has reached this stubborn poverty. We speak a different language, and here our tongue is incomprehensible. The greatest travelers have not gone beyond the limits of their own world; they have trodden the paths of their own souls, of good and evil, of morality and redemption. Christ descended into the underground hell of Hebrew moral principle in order to break down its doors in time and to seal them up into eternity. But to this shadowy land, that knows neither sin nor redemption from sin, where evil is not moral but is only the pain residing forever in earthly things, Christ did not come. Christ stopped at Eboli.

Chapter Two

I ARRIVED AT GAGLIANO ONE August afternoon in a rattling little car. I was wearing handcuffs and I was escorted by two stalwart servants of the State with vertical red bands on their trousers, and expressionless faces. I arrived reluctantly and ready for the worst, because sudden orders had caused me to leave Grassano where I had been living and where I had learned to know the region of Lucania. It had been hard at first. Grassano, like all the villages hereabouts, is a streak of white at the summit of a bare hill, a sort of miniature imaginary Jerusalem in the solitude of the desert. I liked to climb to the highest point of the village, to the wind-beaten church, where the eye can sweep over an endless expanse in every direction, identical in character all the way around the circle. It is like being on a sea of chalk, monotonous and without trees. There are other villages, white and far away on the tops of their hills, Irsina, Craco, Montal-

3

bano, Salandra, Pisticci, Grottole, Ferrandina, the haunts and caves of the brigands; and beyond the reach of vision lies the sea, and Metaponto, and Taranto. I felt that I had come to understand the hidden virtues of this bare land and to love it; I had no mind to change. I am by nature sensitive to the pangs of separation and for this reason I was anything but well disposed toward the new village where I had to adapt myself to living. I looked forward, however, to the trip from one locality to the other and to the chance of seeing places I had heard so much about, and had pictured in fancy, beyond the mountains hemming in the Basento Valley. We went by the precipice where a year earlier the village band of Grassano, on the way back late at night from playing in the square at Accettura, had been lost. Ever since that night the dead band-players meet at midnight at the foot of the precipice to blow their horns, and shepherds skirt the neighborhood in holy terror. But we passed by in broad daylight; the sun was bright, a wind from Africa scorched the earth, and not a sound came from the wastes of clay below.

At San Mauro Forte, just a little higher up on the mountain, I saw on the outskirts of the village the poles where for years the heads of brigands were exposed to view, and then we entered the Accettura Forest, one of the few bits left of the wooded land that once included all of Lucania. The definition of *Lucus a non lucendo* really holds true today when Lucania, the woodland, is quite bare. To see trees again at last, and fresh undergrowth, and green grass, and to smell the leaves was for me like a visit to fairyland. This was the kingdom of the brigands, and the mere remote memory of them causes the traveler to cross it even today with a mixture of fear and curiosity. But the kingdom is a narrow one and we soon left it behind as we went up to Stigliano, where Mark, the ancient crow, has been for centuries in the village square, like a local

4

god, spreading his black wings above the cobblestones. After Stigliano we went down into the valley of the Sauro River with its bed of white stones and an island, now renowned for Prince Colonna's fine olive trees, where a battalion of *bersaglieri* troops was wiped out when the brigands of Boryes marched on Potenza. Here, at a crossroads, we left the route to the Agri Valley and turned to the left on a recently built narrow road.

Farewell, Grassano; farewell, country seen from afar or in the imagination! We had crossed to the other side of the mountains and were leaping up to Gagliano, where only a short time before the wheel of no vehicle had ever come. At Gagliano the road ends. My impression was an unpleasant one. At first sight the village did not seem to be a village at all, but merely a group of scattered white houses, slightly pretentious in their poverty. It was not on the summit of a hill, like the others, but perched on a sort of jagged saddle rising among picturesque ravines; as I first saw it there was lacking the severe and terrible aspect typical of the settlements in these parts. There were a few trees and a spot of green by the way where we had come in, and this very softening of character was displeasing to me. I was accustomed by now to the bare and dramatic austerity of Grassano, to its creviced plaster walls and its mysterious and meditative silence. The country air apparently hanging over Gagliano seemed to me to strike a false note in this land which had nothing of the countryside about it. And then, perhaps out of vanity, it seemed to me inappropriate that the place where I was condemned to live should not appear shut in, but spread out and almost welcoming. A prisoner may find greater consolation in a cell with romantic, heavy iron bars than in one that superficially resembles a normal room. But my first impression was only in part correct.

I was unloaded from the car and turned over to the village

clerk, a spare man, hard of hearing, with pointed black whiskers on a yellowish face, who wore a hunter's jacket. When I had been presented to the mayor and to the sergeant of the *carabinieri* police and had said goodbye to my guards, who were anxious to be on their way, I found myself alone in the middle of the road. It was then that I became aware that I had not properly seen the village upon my arrival, because it wound its way like a worm on either side of the single street, which sloped abruptly down the narrow ridge between two ravines, then climbed up and down again between two other ravines, and came to an abrupt end. The countryside which I thought I had seen at the very beginning was no longer visible. At every turn there were steep slopes of white clay with houses hanging from them as if they were poised in the air, and all around there was still more white clay, with neither trees nor grass growing upon it, eroded into a pattern of holes and hillocks like a landscape on the moon. Almost all the houses appeared to teeter over the abyss, their walls cracked and an air of general fragility about them. Their doors were framed with black pennants, some new, others faded by sun and rain, so that the whole village looked as if it were in mourning or decked out for an All Souls' Day. I found out later that it was customary to drape with these pennants the door of a house where someone had died and that they are left hanging until time and the weather fade them out altogether.

There are no shops, properly speaking, in the village, and no hotel. The clerk had directed me, until I should find lodgings of my own, to his widowed sister-in-law, who had a room for occasional visitors and would give me my meals as well. Her house was near the entrance to the village, only a few steps from the town hall. Before examining my new residence more carefully, I entered the black-framed door of the widow's house, carrying my bags and followed by my dog Barone, and sat down in the kitchen.

The air was black with thousands of flies, and other thousands covered the walls; an old yellow dog was stretched out on the floor with an air of infinite boredom. The same boredom and a sort of disgust, born of the experience of injustice and horror, were reflected on the widow's pale face. She was a middle-aged woman, dressed not as a peasant but in the manner of the fairly well-to-do, with a black veil on her head. Her husband had come to a bad end three years before. A peasant witch-woman had drawn him into her toils by means of love potions, and he had become her lover. A child was born to them, and because at this point he wished to break off their sinful relationship she had given him poison. His illness was long and mysterious; the doctors found no name for it. Gradually his strength melted away; his face grew dark until the skin was the color of bronze and finally quite black; then, at last, he died. His widow was left with a ten-year-old son and very little money, and so she rented a room to strangers. Her position was midway between that of the peasants and that of the gentry; she displayed the poverty of the one class and the good manners of the other. The boy had been sent to a seminary in Potenza for his schooling. When I came, he was at home for a holiday, a silent, gentle, and obedient lad, already set apart by his religious education, with his head shaved and a gray school uniform buttoned up around his neck.

I had been only a short time in the widow's kitchen and had just begun to question her about the village when there was a knock at the door and a group of peasants asked timidly if they might come in. There were seven or eight of them, wearing black hats and with an unusual seriousness in their dark eyes.

"Are you the doctor that has just arrived?" they asked me. "Come, there is someone in a bad way."

7

They had learned of my arrival at the town hall and had heard that I was a doctor. I told them that I was a doctor, to be sure, but I had not practiced for many years, that there must be a doctor on call in the village and that for this reason I must refuse them. They answered that there was no doctor and that their friend was dying.

"Is it possible that there's no doctor?"

"None."

I was greatly embarrassed and uncertain whether, after so many years away from medicine, I could be useful. But how was I to resist their pleas? One of them, an old man with white hair, came close to me and took my hand as if to kiss it. I drew back and blushed with shame, as I was to do on many more occasions during the following year when other peasants made the same gesture. Was this an entreaty or a remnant of feudalism? I got up and followed them to where the sick man lay.

The house was near at hand. The patient was lying on a sort of stretcher near the door, completely dressed, with his hat and shoes on. The room was dark and I could just make out in the shadows the figures of weeping women. A small crowd of men, women, and children followed me in from the street and stood in a circle around me. From their broken sentences I gathered that the man had just been brought back into the house after they had taken him fifteen miles on a donkey to Stigliano to see a doctor. There were doctors at Gagliano but they were not decent Christians, they said. The doctor at Stigliano had told him to go back and die in his own house. Here he was and I should try to save him. But there was nothing I could do, for he was very near the end. The hypodermics I had found at the widow's house were of no avail, although, in order to satisfy my conscience, I tried hopelessly to revive him. He had suffered an acute attack of malaria, the fever had

8

soared above every limit, and his body could endure no more. With his face an earthy color he lay limp on the stretcher, breathing with difficulty, and unable to speak, surrounded by the wailing of his friends. In a little while he was dead. The onlookers made way for me and I went out alone to the square where the view widens over ridges and valleys in the direction of Sant' Arcangelo. The sun was setting behind the mountains of Calabria and, as the shadows overtook them, the peasants, dwarfed by distance, scurried along paths cut through the clay toward their homes.

Chapter Three

THE SQUARE WAS NO MORE than a widening of the single street at the level stretch that marked the end of Upper Gagliano, the higher part of the village. After this stretch came a short ascent and then another downward slope through a smaller square to Lower Gagliano, which ended on the edge of a landslide. There were houses on only one side of the main square; the other side was bounded by a low wall over a precipice known as the Fossa del Bersagliere, because in earlier days a captured *bersagliere* from Piedmont had been thrown down into the ditch by brigands.

It was dusk, crows were flying across the sky, and the gentry were arriving in the square for their customary gossip. Here they strolled up and down every day at this time, stopping to sit on the wall with their backs to the dying rays of the sun while they smoked cheap cigarettes and waited for the evening breeze. On the other side, leaning up against their houses, stood the peasants back from the fields, but the sound of their voices did not cross the square.

The mayor recognized me and called me over. He was an overgrown, corpulent young man with a lock of oily black hair tumbling over his forehead, a yellowish, beardless face and darting black eyes both insincere and self-satisfied in expression. He wore high boots, checked riding breeches, and a short jacket, and his hands were toying with a small whip. He was known as "Professor" Luigi Magalone, but he was only an elementary school teacher, and his chief job was to watch over the political prisoners sentenced to compulsory residence in Gagliano. This job he performed with gusto and zeal, as I soon had a chance to observe. Had he not been described by His Excellency the Prefect (he lost no time in telling me this in the emasculated falsetto voice that issued in a complacent squeak from his immense body) as the youngest and most Fascist mayor in the province of Matera? Upon this I had to congratulate the professor, and he in turn told me something about the village and advised me how to behave. There were quite a few political prisoners here, a dozen in all. I was not to see them; this was forbidden. Anyhow they were of no account, workers and such, whereas it was plain to see that I was a gentleman.

I realized that the professor was proud to exercise his authority for the first time over a gentleman, a painter, a doctor, a man of some culture. He too was cultivated, he hastened to assure me; he wanted to treat me well because we were of the same class. But how in the world had I got myself arrested? And this year, of all years, when our country was on the road to greatness? There was a slight hesitation in this last statement, for the war against Abyssinia had hardly begun. "Let us hope that all goes well." "Yes, let us hope so." But I should be comfortable here; the village was healthful and prosperous. There was only a bit of malaria, nothing to speak of. Most of the peasants owned their land and very few of them were listed as indigent. The village was one of the richest in all the province. But I must be very wary; there were many evil tongues. I had better trust no one. He, himself, had many enemies. He had heard that I had taken care of a certain peasant. My coming was a stroke of luck since I could act as a doctor. I would prefer not to do so? I must, absolutely. His old uncle, Dr. Milillo, was just walking up from the other end of the square; he was the official practitioner. But I need not worry; he would see to it that his uncle did not object to my competing with him. His uncle was of no importance anyhow. I should look out, rather, for the other doctor who was pacing up and down some distance away; he was quite unscrupulous. It would be a good thing if I were to take all his patients away from him; the professor would stand up for me.

Dr. Milillo approached timidly. He appeared to be a little under seventy, with the flabby cheeks and kind watery eyes of an old hunting dog. There was an awkwardness in his movements that was natural rather than the result of his age. His hands shook and words came out brokenly between his upper lip, which was exaggeratedly long, and the hanging lower one. My first impression was that he was a good man gone completely to seed. It was obvious that he was not very happy over my arrival, and I sought to reassure him. I had no intention of practicing medicine; I had gone today to the dying man because his case was desperate and I knew nothing of the local doctors. The doctor was visibly cheered by what I said and, like his nephew, he felt obliged to make a show of his culture, searching the corners of his mind for outdated medical terms left over from his years at the university. They were like war trophies forgotten in an attic. Only one thing was clear from his stammerings: that he no longer had the slightest knowledge of medicine, if he had ever had any. The glorious teachings of the Neapolitan School had faded away from his memory and melted into the monotony of a prolonged everyday indifference. Remnants of his lost ability floated senselessly amid the wreckage of his lassitude, on an ocean of quinine, the sovereign remedy for every ill. I rescued him from the dangerous subject of science and questioned him about the village, its inhabitants and the life they led.

"Good people, but primitive. Above all look out for the women. You're a young man and a handsome one. Don't take anything from a woman. Neither wine nor coffee; nothing to eat or drink. They would be sure to put a philter or love potion in it. The women here will certainly take a fancy to you and all of them will make you such philters. Don't accept anything from the peasant women. The mayor knows I'm right. These potions are dangerous. Unpleasant to the taste, in fact disgusting. Do you want to know what they are made of?" And the doctor, overjoyed to have at last remembered a correct scientific term, bent over to whisper stammeringly into my ear: "Blood, ca-ta-menial b-blood." The mayor laughed in his throat, like a chicken. "They put herbs into it and murmur some abracadabra, but that's the main ingredient. They're just ignorant women. They put it everywhere, in drinks, in chocolate, in sausages, perhaps even in their bread. Yes, catamenial. Take care!"

Alas, how many philters did I unwittingly drink during the year! Of course I didn't take the advice of either uncle or nephew; every day I braved the peasants' coffee and their wine, even if a woman made them ready for me. If there were philters in it they must have counteracted each other. Certainly they did me no harm; perhaps in some mysterious way they helped me to penetrate that closed world, shrouded in black veils, bloody and earthy, that other world where the peasants live and which no one can enter without a magic key.

The evening shadows came down from Mount Pollino. All the peasants had come back to the village, fires were lit in the houses, and from all around there were voices and the noise of goats and donkeys. By now the gentry had completely filled the square. The solitary doctor, the mayor's enemy, was consumed with a desire to make my acquaintance. He walked in ever smaller circles around and around us, like a diabolical black poodle. He was an elderly man, stout but of erect carriage, with a pointed gray beard and a moustache that came down over a wide mouth full of irregular yellow teeth. The expression on his face was one of spiteful mistrust and chronic ill-concealed anger. He wore glasses, a sort of black top hat, a worn black frock coat, and frayed black trousers. He was swinging a huge black cotton umbrella which I often saw him carrying later, with great dignity, in winter and summer, sunshine and rain, open straight above his head, like a canopy over the tabernacle of his authority. Dr. Gibilisco was furious and his authority, alas, seemed considerably shaken.

"The peasants pay no attention to us. They don't even call us when they are sick," he said, with the bitter and choleric tone of a pontiff denouncing a new heresy. "Or else they won't pay. They want to be looked after and not to pay for it. But they'll find out. You saw the fellow today who wouldn't call us? He went to Stigliano. He called you. Then he died, and it's a good thing he did."

On this point Dr. Milillo agreed, with moderation:

"They're stubborn as mules. Ah, yes. They like their own way better. We give them quinine and more quinine, but they won't take it. There's no cure for their mulishness."

I tried to persuade Dr. Gibilisco that I had no intention of setting myself up as his rival, but his eyes were doubtful and suspicious, and his anger did not cool.

"They don't trust us. They don't trust the pharmacy. Of course there's not a complete stock of drugs, but we can make one thing do for another. If there's no morphine, then we use apomorphine."

Gibilisco, too, was eager to display his knowledge. But I soon reached the conclusion that his ignorance was even deeper than that of old Milillo. He knew nothing at all and was talking at random. One thing he did know: the peasants existed merely in order that Gibilisco should visit them and succeed in getting money and food for his visits. Those on whom he laid his hands must pay for those who escaped him. The science of medicine was to him a privilege or *jus neca-tionis*, a feudal right over the life and death of the peasants, and because his poor patients rebelled against this, he was devoured by a continuous and bestial rage against their tribe. If the consequences were not always fatal it was not for any lack of good intentions on his part, but merely because, in order to do a Christian to death with artistry, a smattering of science is necessary. The use of one medicine rather than another was indifferent to him; medicines he neither knew nor cared to know, regarding them simply as weapons for defending his privilege. A warrior may arm himself, in order to be feared, with what weapons he chooses: crossbows, swords, scimitars, pistols, or even Malayan daggers. Gibilisco's privilege was an hereditary one; his father and his grandfather before him had been doctors. His brother, who had died the previous year, was, as a matter of course, the druggist. There was no one to take over the pharmacy and it should rightly have been closed. But through the offices of a friend at the prefecture of Matera, permission had been obtained to keep it open for the welfare of the local population, until its reserves of drugs should be exhausted. In charge were the druggist's two daughters, who had not studied pharmaceuticals and could not be licensed to dispense poisons. The reserves, of course, would never come to an end; some powder or other would replenish the half-empty boxes, and there would be less danger attached to an error in measuring out the prescriptions. But the peasants were stubborn and mistrustful. They would go neither to the pharmacy nor to the doctor; they did not recognize the feudal right. And malaria, quite rightly, killed them off.

I found out something about the gentlemen who were strolling about or sitting silently on the wall. The glittering sergeant of the *carabinieri* passed by. He was a handsome young fellow from Apulia, with pomaded hair and an unpleasant face, dressed in a close-fitting, narrow-waisted uniform and highly polished shoes, perfumed, always hurried and disdainful. I had little to do with him; he looked at me from a distance as if I were a dangerous criminal. He had been here three years, they told me, and already he had salted away forty thousand lire. He earned ten lire at a time by the prudent assertion of his authority over the peasants. His mistress was the midwife, a tall thin woman, slightly twisted to one side, with large, bright, languorous, romantic eyes and a long horselike face. She had the air of being constantly busy, and her speech and gestures were sentimental and overdone like those of a small-town café singer. The sergeant, who was the mayor's right-hand man, stopped to talk to him for a moment. I was to see them often in lengthy and mysterious consultation, perhaps upon the best means of keeping order and increasing the majesty of the law. Then he walked away, looking straight

16

through us, and went toward the house of his mistress, down the way.

Or perhaps he went instead to the beautiful *maffiosa*, the woman bandit from Sicily, who lived in forced residence in the house behind the midwife's. She was a splendid creature, dusky and rose-colored, whom no one ever saw because, in accordance with her native customs, she hid her beauty indoors and, the better to shield her modesty, she managed to go only once a week instead of every day to sign her name at the town hall. The sergeant, it appeared, paid her court in a manner as gallant as it was threatening. Although the chaste Sicilian was reputed to be invincible, and rumor had it that many a man in Sicily was ready to defend her honor, her veiled beauty was hard put to it to withstand the power of the law in person.

The three gentlemen in the middle of the square, wearing old-fashioned, black, double-breasted waistcoats and smoking silently with an air of mournful dignity about them, were landowners. And the slender old man with an intelligent face, standing alone, was Mr. S., a lawyer and the richest man in the village, a good man with an air of melancholy tinged with mistrust and scorn of the world he had to live in. His only son had died the year before, and from that day on his beautiful daughters, Concetta and Maria, had not set foot outside the house, not even to go to mass. It is the custom hereabouts, at least in the upper class, for girls to stay shut up three years for the death of a father and one for that of a brother. The old man with a long white beard hanging down over his chest, next to the lawyer, was the retired postmaster, a crony of Dr. Gibilisco. His name was Poerio, and he was the only survivor of a branch native to Gagliano of the famous patriot family. He was deaf and very ill, unable to pass water and grown extremely thin. He was apparently very close to death.

These bits of information were furnished me by P., a cheerful young lawyer who had joined our group. He told me right away that he had taken his degree a few years before at the University of Bologna. Not that he was a studious boy or was consumed by professional ambition. Quite the contrary. But an uncle had left him his house and lands on the condition that he study at the university, and this was how he came to go to Bologna. Those student days had been the great adventure of his life. After he had taken his degree and come back to the village to enjoy his inheritance he had married an older woman and found himself unable to get away again. All that he did the whole day long was to try to continue his student life in these peasant surroundings. How was he to while away his hours and days? With card games, gambling for drinks, chatting in the square, and evenings spent in various wine cellars. He had lost most of the money left him by his uncle at gambling while he was still at Bologna, before it was really his; now his lands were mortgaged, his income meager, and his family growing. But he was still the student of Bologna, rakish and gay. The noisy fellow on the other side of the square was his companion at drinking and cards, the substitute schoolteacher. This evening he was quite drunk, and such was his usual condition from early morning through the day. But he carried his wine badly and soon became choleric and quarrelsome. When he held forth at the school his shouting could be heard from one end of the village to the other.

All of a sudden everyone rose and moved toward the post office. The old woman letter-carrier appeared on the crest of the road with the sack of letters and papers that she fetched every day with a mule from the crossroad at the Sauro River where, after a series of jolts and hairpin turns, a rattling bus deposited travelers from faraway Matera to the Agri Valley. To the post office, then, went all those who had crowded the square, to wait for Don Cosimino, a keen-faced hunchback, to open the sacks and distribute the mail. This was the evening ceremony, which no one ever missed and in which I, too, was to participate every day the year around. The little crowd waited outside while the mayor and the sergeant, with the excuse of official business, went in and looked with curiosity at everyone's letters. On this, my first evening, however, the mail was late. Night was falling and I was not allowed to stay out after dark. I saw the priest arrive, limping, a thin little man with a large red tassel on his hat. No one greeted him. Then I really had to go. I whistled to Barone, my dog, who frisked ahead of me, in ecstasy over the smells of the dogs, sheep, goats and birds of his new home, and walked slowly up toward the widow's house.

The Fossa del Bersagliere was filled with shadows, and darkness shrouded the purple and black mountains that on every side embraced the horizon. The first stars were out and beyond the Agri shone the lights of Sant' Arcangelo and, farther away and barely visible, those of some other village, Noepoli, perhaps, or Senise. The path was narrow and in the doorways the peasants sat among the enveloping shadows. From the dead man's house came the wails of women. An indistinct murmur spun around me in wide circles; beyond lay a deep silence. I felt as if I had fallen from the sky, like a stone into a pond.

CHAPTER FOUR

So the people of this village are *decent* people!" I thought to myself while I waited in the widow's house for my supper. The good woman had lit a fire under the saucepan because she thought I must be tired from my trip and in need of something hot. Even the rich seldom made a fire in the evening, but contented themselves with left-overs from their noon dinner, a little bread and cheese, a few olives, and the usual dried figs. As for the poor, they ate plain bread the whole year around, spiced occasionally with a carefully crushed raw tomato, or a little garlic and oil, or a Spanish pepper with such a devilish bite to it that it is known as a *diavolesco*.

"The people of this village are *decent* people." My first impressions were not quite clear and I had not yet penetrated all the secrets of local politics and passions. But I had been struck by the gravity of the gentry assembled in the square and by the rancor, scorn, and mistrust inherent in their conversation. Because they had freely revealed their primitive hates, with none of the reserve they might have been expected to maintain in the presence of a stranger, I had been immediately informed of the vices and weaknesses of their fellows. Although I could not yet be quite sure, it appeared that here, as in Grassano, the hate they felt for each other divided them into two factions. And as in Grassano, and everywhere else in Lucania where the upper classes had been held back by ineptness or poverty or premature marriage or family interests or some other fateful necessity from emigrating to the paradise of Naples or Rome, they had funneled their disappointment and their mortal boredom into a generic rage, a ceaseless hate.

Their life was a continuous renewal of old resentments and a constant struggle to assert their power over all those who shared the parcel of land where they had to stay. Gagliano was a tiny village far from the traffic of men; the passions that reigned there were simpler and more primitive but no less intense than those of the world without. It should not be very difficult, I thought to myself, to find the key to them.

Grassano was a larger place, on a main thoroughfare, not far from the capital of the province. There was not the same everyday rubbing of shoulders among the inhabitants, and passions were better hidden, more moderate in appearance, and involved in greater complexities. The secrets of Grassano had been revealed to me from the very beginning of my stay there by one of their most ardent participants. How should I come to know the secrets of Gagliano? I was to live there three years, a time bordering on infinity. It was a closed world, in which the rivalries and hates of the gentry made up the sum of daily events. Already I had seen in their faces how deep and violent these were; they were at the same time paltry and intense, like the motives of a Greek tragedy. Like Stendhal's heroes, I had to lay my plans so as not to expose myself to error. In Grassano my mentor had been the head of the Fascist Militia, Lieutenant Decunto. Who would be his counterpart in Gagliano?

When Lieutenant Decunto, the local commander of the Militia, had summoned me peremptorily the day after my arrival from Regina Coeli, the prison in Rome, I was afraid that new troubles were in store for me. I had hardly seen my surroundings and I did not know what was happening in the world at large or how high feeling ran in Grassano in regard to the imminent war with Abyssinia. In the tiny room that served him as an office, I found a short, blond, courteous young fellow with a bitter expression around his mouth and evasive light-blue eyes that waywardly refused to look straight at anything, not because their owner was afraid, but because he was either ashamed or disgusted. He had called me simply because, like himself, I was a reserve army officer and he wanted to know me. He hastened to tell me that although he commanded the Militia he had nothing to do with the police, the *carabinieri*, the mayor, or the local Fascist Party leader. This last was a criminal and the rest fit companions. Life in Grassano was impossible, but there was nothing to be done about it. Everyone was ambitious, thieving, dishonest, and violent. He *must* get away from here, or else he would die. He had applied for enlistment as a volunteer in Africa. Never mind if the whole venture turned out badly; he had little to lose.

"We're playing for all or nothing," he said, looking beyond me. "This is the end, do you understand? The end. If we win, things may improve, who knows. But England won't allow it. We'll break our head against a stone wall. This is our last card. And if our luck doesn't turn . . ." Here he made a gesture descriptive of the end of the world. "We shan't succeed; you'll see. But it doesn't matter. We can't go on like this. You're to be here some time. You're a stranger to local conditions and you can judge for yourself. After you've seen what life here is like, you'll concede that I was right. . . ."

I remained silent and unconvinced. But later I had to admit that, even if it was Lieutenant Decunto's job to watch over me, he was sincere and his pessimism was by no means an affectation. He took a liking to me because I was an outsider and to me he could freely express his resentments. Every time that I climbed up to the church at the summit of the village and stood in the wind to contemplate the desolate landscape, he would appear at my side. His light hair and gray uniform gave him the air of a ghost. Without looking at me he would begin to talk. He was, he said, only the last link in a chain of hates that went back for generations, a hundred years, two hundred years, or more, perhaps forever. He was bound up in these inherited passions. There was nothing he could do about it except to eat his heart out. Here they had hated each other for centuries and would go on hating, among the same houses, before the same white stones of the Basento Valley and the same caves of Irsina. Now, of course, they were all Fascists. But that meant nothing. Once they had all been partisans of Nitti or Salandra, for or against Giolitti, of the Right or of the Left, for the brigands or against the brigands, followers of the Bourbons or liberals, and in times still more remote, divided in other ways. But in the very beginning there were the decent people and there were the brigands; the sons of the decent people and the sons of the brigands. Fascism had not made much of a change. In fact, before Fascism, when there were various parties, the respectable could stick together under one flag, set themselves apart from the others and wage a political battle. Now they could have recourse only to anonymous letters, corruption, and the exercise of pressure on the prefecture. For all of them were bound up with Fascism.

"You see, I come from a family of liberals; my great-grandfather was in prison under the Bourbons. But do you know who the local Fascist Party leader is? He's the son of a brigand. Yes, the son of a brigand. And the band of his supporters, who rule over the village, is of the same caliber. It's the same thing at Matera. N., the National Councillor, is of a family that supported the brigands. And Baron Collefusco, the great landowner and proprietor of the palace in the main square, who is he? He lives in Naples, as everyone knows, and never comes to these parts. You don't know him? The barons of Collefusco in 1860 were the real brigand leaders. They paid the brigands and armed them." His narrow blue eyes sparkled with hate. "I see you sitting very often on the stone bench in front of the palace. A hundred years ago or more the baron's great-grandfather used to sit on that same bench, taking the air every evening, just as you do. He used to hold a small child in his arms, the baron's grandfather, who became a deputy to Parliament and a supporter of the brigands in his turn. On that bench the old man was murdered, by a relative of my great-grandfather. He was a druggist by the name of Palese, the brother of a doctor. There are still some of the doctor's great-grandsons in Potenza, and here in Grassano we Decuntos are of the same family.

"This is how it happened. At that time there was a group of *carbonari*, or liberal conspirators, among them the two Palese brothers, a Lasala, of the same family as the carpenter whom you know, a Ruggiero, a Bonelli, and a number of others. Baron Collefusco, the pretended liberal, belonged to it, too. But the baron was a spy; he had joined the group only in order to report on it to the police. One fine day they held a meeting to plan a future course of action. As soon as the meeting was over, the baron went home, called a trusted servant, mounted him on his best horse, and sent him with a letter containing the names of all the conspirators to the Governor of Potenza. But the servant was seen as he rode away. They had reason to suspect him: what could he be up to on the road to Potenza at that hour on the fastest horse in the village? There was no time to be lost; they must follow him and stop him in order to ascertain whether they had been betrayed.

"Four *carbonari* set off on horseback but the baron's horse was better than theirs and had an hour's head start. The four of them took narrow paths and short cuts and they galloped so hard all night long that they overtook the servant just at the gates of Potenza by the edge of a wood. They shot at his horse from a distance while they were still in the saddle, and the horse fell. They took the servant, tied him to a tree, searched him and found the baron's letter. Then they left him there, tied up, without killing him, and returned at full speed to Grassano. The traitor must be punished. The *carbonari* held a meeting and drew lots to see who should kill the baron. The job fell to Doctor Palese, but his brother, the druggist, who was a better shot and a bachelor, asked to replace him. In those days there were no houses opposite the palace, only a tall oak tree at the edge of a field. It was evening. The druggist hid with his gun behind the oak and waited for the baron to come out for a breath of air. There was a full moon in the sky. The baron appeared, but he had the child in his arms, and he sat down on the stone bench in order to bounce him up and down on his knees. The druggist held fire, unwilling to hit the innocent child, but when he saw that the child was going to stay, he had to make up his mind. He was a first-rate shot and he hit the baron in the center of his forehead at the very moment when the child was hugging him. Of course the liberals all went into hiding, but they were arrested and sentenced. The druggist died in prison in Potenza.

"The doctor also was in prison for many years and might have died there, too, had it not come about that the Governor's wife suffered complications in childbirth and was near death. None of the doctors in Potenza could help her, but finally someone thought of calling the doctor who lay there in prison. He came and saved both the Governor's wife and her infant son. As soon as she was well, she went to Naples and threw herself at the feet of the Queen. The doctor received a pardon, but rather than return to Grassano he chose to stay in Potenza, and there his descendants are living today. The little boy whom the druggist took such good care to miss became later, as I have told you, Grassano's first deputy to Parliament. He, too, pretended to be a liberal while at the same time he lent a hand to the brigands. His son, the present baron, never comes here, but he is the secret protector in Rome of the ruling clique of Grassano, all of them sons of brigands."

I never found out whether the details of this story were true. It ennobled, after a fashion, the feuds still extant among the first families of Grassano, by tracing their origin back to remote times and endowing them with causes to some extent idealistic. But their real significance did not lie here. The rivalries of the gentry did not derive from an hereditary motive of *vendetta*, nor was the struggle at bottom a political one between conservative and progressive elements, although at times it took on this form. Each side, of course, accused the other of the worst crimes. Lieutenant Decunto's stories were repeated to me, with a quite different emphasis, by members of the faction in power.

The truth is that the internecine war among the gentry is the same in every village of Lucania. The upper classes have not the means to live with decorum and self-respect. The young men of promise, and even those barely able to make their way, leave the village. The most adventurous go off to America, as the peasants do, and the others to Naples or Rome; none return. Those who are left in the villages are the discarded, who have no talents, the physically deformed, the inept and the lazy; greed and boredom combine to dispose them to evil. Small parcels of farm land do not assure them a living and, in order to survive, these misfits must dominate the peasants and secure for themselves the well-paid posts of druggist, priest, marshal of the *carabinieri*, and so on. It is, therefore, a matter of life and death to have the rule in their own hands, to hoist themselves or their relatives and friends into top jobs. This is the root of the endless struggle to obtain power and to keep it from others, a struggle which the narrowness of their surroundings, enforced idleness, and a mixture of personal and political motives render continuous and savage. Every day anonymous letters from every village of Lucania arrived at the prefecture. And at the prefecture, they were, apparently, far from dissatisfied with this state of affairs, even if they said the contrary.

"In Matera they pretend that they wish to moderate our quarrels," Lieutenant Decunto told me. "But in reality they do all they can to foment them. Such are the instructions they have from Rome. In this way they hold us all through either hope or fear in the palm of their hands. But what have we to hope for?" Here he made his characteristic gesture signifying absolute nothingness. "This is no place to live. A man must get away. Now we are going into Africa. It's our last chance."

The lieutenant's face turned gray when he spoke in this vein, and his evasive eyes were white with impotent rage, their expression became desperate and evil. He belonged completely to these people, to their hates and passions, he was

27

one of them and he was eating his heart away. There was in him a grain of conscience and of dismay. Like all the rest he believed in the African adventure, in the "living space" necessary to a degenerate dominating class. At the same time he was aware, in a primitive and sentimental fashion, of the decay and spiritual poverty around him, and he saw the war as an escape, an escape into a world of destruction. At bottom what drew him most to the adventure was his premonition of defeat and annihilation. This was clear from the tone in which he repeated: "It's our last card." The gleam of conscience that set him apart from his fellow-citizens was manifest only in a deep and shameful contempt for himself. To the hates of the gentry he added self-hate and it was clear to anyone observing him closely that this made him more spiteful and bitter than the rest, capable, indeed, of any evil. It was not out of keeping with the naïve and over-simplified views of this young man of good family that he should rob, kill, play the part of a spy, and perhaps even die as a hero, because of his fundamental despair. Here lay the meaning to him of the war in Africa. If it ended badly, what did it matter? Let the whole world perish in order to efface even the memory of Grassano, white on the mountain top, with its gentry and its brigands.

CHAPTER FIVE

BUT THE FLICKERING, BALE-
ful light of conscience in Lieutenant Decunto," I thought
to myself while I waited in the widow's kitchen for my supper,
"is something rare, perhaps even unique." I had not seen it
reflected in any of the dull, malicious, and greedily self-satisfied faces of my new acquaintances in the square. Their
passions, it was plain to see, were not rooted in history; they
did not extend beyond the village, encircled by malaria-ridden
clay; they were multiplied within the enclosure of half a dozen
houses. They had an urgent and miserable character born of
the daily need for food and money, and they strove futilely to
cloak themselves in the genteel tradition. Penned up in petty
souls and desolate surroundings, they seethed like the steam
pressing against the lid of the widow's saucepan where a thin
broth was whistling and grumbling over a low wood fire. I
looked into the fire, thinking of the endless chain of days that

29

lay ahead of me when my horizon, too, would be bounded by these dark emotions.

The widow, meanwhile, put bread and a jar of water on the table. The bread was of the characteristic black variety made of hard wheat in great loaves weighing five or ten pounds. They lasted a whole week, the mainstay of rich and poor alike, round like the sun or like a Mexican calendar-stone. I began to slice it, with a gesture I had already learned, holding it against my chest and drawing the sharp knife toward me, taking care not to cut my chin. The jar, like those in use at Grassano, was of the amphora type made in Ferrandina that the peasant women carry on their heads, of reddish yellow terra cotta with curves like those of an archaic figurine of a woman, with a narrow waist, rounded breast and hips, and handles like two small arms.

I sat alone at the table in front of the heavy hand-woven linen cloth, but the room was not empty. Every now and then the door on the street opened and neighbor women came in. They came on various pretexts, to bring water or to ask whether they should take the widow's washing to the river the next day. They stayed far away from my table, near the door, close to one another, all twittering together like birds. They were pretending not to look at me but every now and then their black eyes darted a curious glance from under their veils in my direction and then darted away again like woodland animals. Because I was not yet used to their dress (a poor sort of costume in no way equal to the famous varieties worn at Pietragalla and Pisticci) they seemed to me all alike, with their faces framed by a veil folded several times and falling over their shoulders, plain cotton blouses, wide, dark bell-shaped skirts that went halfway down their legs, and high boots. They stood erect with the stately posture of those accustomed to balancing heavy weights on their heads, and their faces had an expression of primitive solemnity. Their motions were grave but without womanly grace, like the weighty glances cast by their curious black eyes. They did not seem to me like women, but like the soldiers of a strange army, or rather like a fleet of dark round boats waiting all together for the wind to inflate their white sails. As I was looking at them and trying to understand what they were saying in a dialect that was new to me, there was a knock at the door, whereupon they took leave amid an undulating movement of veils and skirts, and a new figure entered the kitchen.

This was a young man with a small red moustache, carrying a long case in brown leather. He was badly dressed and his shoes were covered with dust, but he wore a shirt and tie and on his head a strange high-crowned cap with an oil-cloth visor, of the kind once worn by academicians. Against its gray background were sewn two conspicuous letters cut out of orange felt: U.E. for *Ufficiale Esattoriale* or tax collector, as he told me when I asked him their meaning. He put the leather case down carefully, sat down at my table, took some bread and cheese out of his pocket, asked the widow for a glass of wine, and began to eat his dinner. His office was in Stigliano, but he came often to Gagliano to discharge his duties.

This evening he was late and he had to spend the night at the widow's, as he had more work to do in the neighborhood the next day. He was reluctant to speak of his business, but he took pleasure in showing me immediately what was in his leather case. It was a clarinet. He could never be parted from it but always carried it with him when he went in pursuit of the peasants' money. He had to make a living and this was his job, but his heart was elsewhere, in his music. He was not yet perfect, for he had studied only a year, but he practiced continually. Yes, he would play me a piece, because he could see that I was a connoisseur, but only one; it was late and he wanted to call on an old friend. The bread and cheese were finished and there was nothing more to eat. The clarinet gave forth the fragile and indecisive notes of a current song and the dogs supplied a rumbling accompaniment.

As soon as the musical tax collector had gone out and we were alone, the widow made abundant excuses for the necessity of sharing my room with a stranger. There was no other choice. "But he's a decent fellow; he's clean and not a peasant." I assured her that I should make out perfectly well in his company. By now I was used to such random roommates. At Grassano, when I lived at Prisco's inn, I had a different one almost every night. There were two rooms in all, and when one was full mine was on call. Many strangers stopped for the night because Grassano was on the main road and Prisco's inn was known as the best in the province. In fact, travelers with business at Tricarico chose to come all the way back to Grassano at night rather than stay at the miserable tavern of that episcopal seat.

I had, then, in my room traveling salesmen from Apulia, Neapolitan pear-growers, teamsters, and all sorts of others. Very late one night, when I was already in bed, I heard the unaccustomed roar of a motorcycle, and when the rider appeared in my room, his cap covered with dust, he turned out to be Baron Nicola Rotunno of Avellino, one of the richest landowners of the province. With his lawyer-brother he owned extensive tracts of land around Grassano, Tricarico, Grottole, and many other townships of the Matera region, and he went about on a motorcycle to collect from his agents the money yielded by the sale of the crops and to press the peasants for the payment of their debts, debts which they contracted in order to get through the year, but which amounted to far more than their yearly earnings and which piled up until no season was favorable enough to liquidate them. The baron, a thin, beardless young man with a pince-nez, shared his brother's reputation for ruthlessness. He would go after a peasant for a debt of a few lire; he drove a hard bargain, knew how to choose land agents faithful to his interests, and wasted pity on no one. He was a devout churchman and wore in his buttonhole, instead of the usual Fascist Party emblem, the round badge of Catholic Action. To me he was exceedingly kind. When he heard that I was a political prisoner, he immediately offered to obtain my freedom through the good offices of a lady intimate with Senator Bocchini, the head of the national police. This lady, like himself, came from Avellino, and she shared his particular devotion to the Madonna worshiped in a famous shrine near this city.

We began to talk of saints and shrines, especially of San Rocco di Tolve, whose powers I had come to know by personal experience of his favors. Tolve is a village near Potenza, and the pilgrimage directed there every August had just recently taken place. Men, women, and children came from the neighboring provinces on foot or by donkey, walking day and night. San Rocco awaited them, poised in midair, above the church. "Tolve is mine and I will protect it," he says in a popular print, which shows him dressed in brown with a halo of gold against the blue sky over the village.

Grassano, too, had a kindly saint for a patron, a resplendent San Maurizio in the lower church, armed to the teeth, a magnificent warrior in papier-mâché of the sort still made so skilfully today in Bari. From San Maurizio, we passed to the companion of his warlike exploits and of his beatitude and to other saints, including Saint Augustine and his *City of God*, and finally to talk of the Gospels. The baron appeared to be surprised and pleased at my knowledge of matters with which he had not supposed I was acquainted. It was very late, and my eyes were half-shut with sleepiness when I saw the

33

baron rise up suddenly in his bed, take his pince-nez from his bed-table and thrust it upon his nose, jump down to the floor, and silently approach my bed, enshrouded, like a ghost, in a long white nightshirt which came down almost to his bare feet. When he was close to me he made a great sign of the cross over me with his hand and said in a solemn and emotional voice: "I bless you in the name of the Child Jesus. Good night." With which he made the sign of the cross again, got back into bed, and put out the light. Protected by the unexpected blessing of the wealthy baron, I fell asleep promptly, only to wake up at dawn as usual, to the angelic sound of the bells on the sheep going to pasture and the diabolical noise made by Prisco, the landlord, as he roused in stentorian tones his drowsy offspring.

The widow's spare room, which I was to share that night with the tax collector, was far gloomier than the one I had occupied at Prisco's inn. It was long, narrow, and dark with a small window at one end, and the plastered walls were gray and encrusted with dirt. There were three cots, a chipped basin and jug in one corner, and an unsteady chest of drawers opposite the beds. A light bulb black with the traces of flies emitted a pale yellow gleam. Flies swarmed everywhere in the suffocating heat. The window was closed in order to keep out the mosquitoes but I had hardly laid my head on the pillow when I heard them hissing on every side, a frightening sound in this malarial country.

Meanwhile my roommate arrived, hung his cap on a nail opposite my bed, put his clarinet case on the chest of drawers, and undressed. I asked him about the progress of his work here in Gagliano.

"Very bad," he said. "Today I came to make seizures. They don't pay their taxes. And when I come to seize their chattels, there's nothing to be had. I went to three houses and there was no furniture in any of them, except for beds, and we can't touch them. I had to be satisfied with a goat and a few pigeons. They haven't enough to pay for even the revenue stamps on the change of title. Tomorrow I've two other places to go; here's hoping I've better luck. It's a disgrace, the peasants simply don't want to pay. Most of them here in Gagliano own a bit of land, even if it's two or three hours' walking distance from the village; sometimes, of course, it's poor soil and yields them practically nothing. The taxes are heavy, it's true, but that's not my affair; I didn't lay down the taxes, my job's merely to collect them. You know how the peasants are, they claim that every year's a bad one. They're loaded down with debts, they have malaria and they've no food. But I'd be in a pretty fix if I listened to them. I have a job to do. Well, they don't pay, and I have to seize what I can lay my hands on, stuff that's quite worthless. Sometimes I come all the way for a few bottles of oil and a little flour. And with that they scowl at me; there's hate in their eyes. Two years ago, at Missanello, they shot at me. Mine's an ugly business. But a man's got to live."

I saw that the subject was distasteful to him and by way of consolation I began to speak of music. He wanted to write songs, to enter them in a competition, and, if he won a prize, to leave the business of tax-collecting. Meanwhile he played the clarinet in the band at Stigliano. I asked him about the folk songs of the region, whether he could teach me any of them, or with his talent, write them down for me. He asked me if I wanted to hear "Little Black Face,"* or some other tune of the day. No, I was after the peasants' songs. He stopped to think, as if the idea were new to him. He could write down the notes of a song for me if he picked them out one by one on

* Song in vogue during the Abyssinian War.

the clarinet. But he couldn't remember ever having heard the peasants sing. At Viggiano they sang and made music, but not in these parts. There might be some church song; he would find out. Indeed, I myself noticed the same lack. No voice broke the silence of the land, either in the morning when the peasants went off to work, or under the noon sun, or in the evening when the long black lines of them made their way back to their homes in the hills with their donkeys and goats. Only once, in the direction of the Basento River, I heard the wail of a reed pipe, to which another made answer from the mountain opposite. Two shepherds from a distant region were going with their flock from village to village and calling to each other. Here the peasants did not sing.

My companion made no further response; I could hear the regular whistle of his breathing against the ceaseless buzz of the flies, made restless by the heat. A narrow ray of light filtered through the closed window from the crescent moon. It struck the letters U.E. on the cap hanging on the wall opposite my bed, and I stared at them through the darkness until my eyes closed and I was asleep.

CHAPTER SIX

I WAS NOT AWAKENED EARLY
in the morning by the sheep bells as I had been at Grassano,
because here there were neither shepherds nor pastures, but
by the beat of donkey hoofs on the paving stones and the
bleating of goats. This was the daily pilgrimage, and the
peasants got up while it was still dark to travel three or four
hours to their fields, in the direction of the malarial banks of
the Agri and the Sauro or the slopes of faraway hills. The room
was flooded with light and the initialed cap was gone. My
roommate must have left at dawn to bring the comforts of the
Law to the peasants' homes before their owners left for the
fields; perhaps by this time he was already on the way back to
Stigliano, with the visor of his cap glistening in the sun, his
clarinet in one hand and a goat trailing on a leash behind him.

From the door I could hear a sound of women's voices and
the crying of a child. A dozen women with children in their

arms or standing beside them were waiting patiently for me to get up. They wanted to show me their offspring and have me attend to them. The children were pale and thin with big, sad black eyes, waxen faces, and swollen stomachs drawn tight like drums above their thin, crooked legs. Malaria, which spared no one in these parts, had already made its way into their underfed rickety bodies.

I was anxious to avoid looking after the sick because this was not my profession and I was aware of my deficiencies. I realized, moreover, that to do so would draw me into involuntary conflict with the already established and jealously guarded world of interests of the local gentry. But this morning I saw that it would be difficult for me to resist. The scene of the day before began all over again. The women supplicated me, calling down blessings on my head and kissing my hands. Their faith and hope in me were absolute and I could only wonder at them. The sick man of the preceding day had died and I had been powerless to help him, yet the women claimed to see that I was not a fifth-rate doctor like the others but a good Christian who could help their children. Perhaps I owed their esteem to the natural prestige of a stranger whose faraway origin makes him a sort of god, or else to their perception that, in spite of the hopelessness of his case, I had really tried to do something for the dying man and that I had looked at him first with real interest and later with genuine sorrow. I was astonished and shamed by their confidence, which was as complete as it was undeserved. Finally I sent them away with a few words of advice and followed them out of the dark house into the dazzling morning sunlight. The shadows cast by the village houses were black and still, the hot wind blowing through the ravines raised clouds of dust, and in the dust dogs lay scratching their fleas.

I wanted to take stock of the limits beyond which I was not

allowed to go, although I already knew that they coincided with the boundaries of the village; to reconnoiter my island, since the surrounding lands were forbidden territory, beyond the pillars of Hercules. The widow's house lay at the upper end of the village where the road widened and came to an end in front of the church, a little white church hardly larger than the houses around it. The priest stood at the door threatening with his stick a group of boys a few steps away who were ridiculing him and making faces at him, while some of them leaned over to pick up stones which they plainly intended to throw in his direction. Upon my arrival, the boys scattered like sparrows. The priest cast an irate look after them, brandishing his stick and shouting: "Cursed, heathen boys, I'll excommunicate you!"

"There's no grace of God in this village," he said, turning toward me. "No one comes to church but the boys, and they come to play. You saw them, didn't you? I say my mass to empty benches. The people are not even baptized. And there's no way of getting them to pay a penny from the yield of their miserable fields. I've not yet had the tithes from last year. Yes, they're a fine decent lot, the people of this village; you'll see that for yourself."

He was a thin little old man with steel-rimmed glasses hanging over a pointed nose, overshadowed by the red tassel which hung from his hat. Behind the glasses were sharp eyes which passed quickly from an obsessed stare to a keen sparkle. His thin lips were turned down in an expression of habitual bitterness. Below his rumpled, dirty habit, half unbuttoned and covered with spots, he wore dusty, down-at-the-heel boots. There was an air about him of weariness and ill-tolerated poverty, like the ruins of a burned hovel, charred and overgrown with weeds. Don Giuseppe Trajella was not loved by anyone in the village, and the evening before I had heard the local gentry curse at him roundly. They abused and reviled him, set the urchins against him, and complained of him to the prefect and the bishop.

"Look out for the priest!" the mayor had told me. "He's a disgrace to the village and a living profanation of the House of God. He's perpetually drunk. We haven't yet managed to get rid of him, but we hope to throw him out soon, or at least to have him shifted to Gaglianello, another area of the township, which is his real parish. He's been here for some years, as a penance. He was a professor at the seminary and they sent him to Gaglianello to punish him for taking certain liberties—you know what I mean—with his students. He has no real right to be at Gagliano, but we've no other priest. The punishment, you might say, is visited upon *us*."

Poor Don Trajella! Even if the devil himself had tempted him when he was young, that time was long past and forgotten. Now he could hardly stand on his feet; he was only a poor persecuted and embittered old man, a stricken sheep beset by a pack of wolves. But even in his decay it was apparent that in the days when he taught theology at the seminaries of Melfi and Naples, Don Giuseppe Trajella of Tricarico must have been a good, intelligent, witty, and resourceful man. He had written lives of the saints, made paintings and sculptures, and taken a lively interest in what was going on in the world, when sudden disgrace struck him, cut him off from everything, and cast him like a shipwreck upon this remote and inhospitable shore. He had let himself go with a vengeance, taking a bitter delight in increasing his misery. He had never touched a book or a paintbrush again. With the passing of the years only one of his former passions, rancor, remained, and this had become a veritable fixation. Trajella hated the world because the world persecuted him. He lived alone, speaking to no one, with his mother, an old woman of ninety, now weak-minded and helpless. His only consolation—beside, perhaps, the bottle—was to write Latin epigrams against the mayor, the *carabinieri*, the authorities in general, and the peasants.

"The people here are donkeys, not Christians," he said, beckoning me to enter the church. "You know Latin, of course, don't you?"

> *Gallianus, Gallianellus*
> *Asinus et asellus*
> *Nihil aliud in sella*
> *Nisi Joseph Trajella*

> Gagliano and Gaglianello
> Are a donkey and its young;
> On a saddle between them
> Joseph Trajella is hung.

The church was merely a large room with plastered walls, dirty and neglected, with an unadorned altar on a wooden platform at one end and a small pulpit on the side. The cracked walls were covered with seventeenth-century paintings on peeled and torn canvas, hung with no apparent pattern in several irregular rows.

"These come from the old church; they were all we could save. Look at them, since you're a painter. But they're not worth much. The present church was only a chapel then. The real church, the Madonna of the Angels, was at the other end of the village, where you can still see the landslide. The church gave way suddenly and caved in three years ago. Luckily it was night; we had a narrow escape. Here there are landslides all the time. When it rains the ground gives way and starts to slide, and the houses fall down. Some fall every year. People make me laugh with their talk of supporting walls. In a few years this village will have ceased to exist; it will all be carried away. It had rained for three days when the church went. But it's the same thing every winter, some disaster, great or small, overtakes this village and every other one in the province. There are no trees and no rocks; the clay simply melts and pours down like a rushing stream, carrying everything with it. This winter you'll see for yourself. But for your sake I hope you won't still be here. The people are worse than the soil. I hate the mob. *Odi profanum vulgas . . ."* The priest's eyes shone behind his glasses. "Well, we've had to make out with this old chapel. There's no bell-tower; the bell is outside, attached to a post. The roof needs repairs; the rain comes in. Already we've had to stave it up. Do you see the cracks in the walls? But where am I to get the money? The church is poor and the village is poorer. Besides, they're not Christians; they've no religion at all. They don't even bring me the customary tribute, much less the money for a bell-tower. The mayor, Don Luigi, and the others agree that nothing should be done. Druggists, they call themselves. You'll see the public works they go in for! You'll see!"

My dog, Barone, unaware of the holiness of the place, and tired of waiting for me, stuck his head in the door and barked happily. I could neither quiet him nor chase him away. I took leave of Don Trajella and made my way along the road running to the left of the church, by which I had traveled the day before, toward a few outlying houses at the extremity of the village. This was the region whose green trees had seemed to me mild and welcoming as we passed rapidly by in a car, but now under the fierce morning sun the green appeared to have melted into the dazzling gray of walls and earth. A group of houses stood in untidy fashion on either side of the road, surrounded by shabby vegetable gardens and a few sparse olive trees. The houses were nearly all of only one room, with no windows, drawing their light from the door. The doors were latched because the men were in the fields; in the doorways young women dandled their babies or old women spun wool. They waved and looked after me with wide-open eyes. Here and there was a house with a second story and a balcony, where the front door was not made of worn black wood, but had a conspicuous coat of shiny varnish and was decked out with a brass doorknob. Such houses belonged to the "Americans." Among the peasants' shacks stood one narrow, long, single-story building of recent construction, in so-called modern or suburban style. This was the barracks of the *carabinieri*. Around the houses and on the road, several sows, surrounded by their progeny of piglets, with the wizened faces of greedy and lustful old men, grubbed suspiciously and savagely in piles of rubbage and garbage. Barone drew back, growling and curling his lips, his hair standing on end in a sort of strange horror.

Beyond the last house of the village, where the road, after a brief rise, began to go down to the Sauro Valley, there was an uneven open space spotted with melancholy yellow grass. This was the sports field, instituted by the mayor, Magalone. Here the Fascist Scout organization was supposed to exercise, and the general population to hold patriotic gatherings. To the left a path wound up an adjacent olive-covered slope to an iron gate between two pillars, which marked either side of the beginning of a low brick wall. Behind the wall stood two slender cypress trees and through the gate one could see tombstones, white in the sun. The cemetery was the highest point of the territory where I was allowed to circulate. Here the view was wider and less squalid than from any other place. I could not see all of Gagliano, which lay hidden like a long snake stretched out among the stones, but the yellowish-red roofs of the higher part of the village, seen among the gray leaves of the olive trees as they moved in the breeze, appeared less motionless than usual and almost alive. Behind this colorful foreground the wide desolate stretches of clay seemed to wave in the heat, as if they were suspended in mid-air, and above their monotonous whiteness passed the shifting shadows of the summer clouds. Lizards lay without moving on the sunny wall and two grasshoppers answered each other fitfully, as if they were practicing the parts of a song, and then suddenly fell silent.

Since I was not allowed to go beyond this point, I went back to the village by the same way I had come. I passed in front of the church and the widow's house, and went on down to the post office and the Fossa del Bersagliere. The mayor and schoolmaster was at this moment exercising his teaching function. He was sitting on a balcony just off the classroom and having a smoke while he looked at the people in the square below and democratically hailed the passers-by. He had a long cane in his hand, and, without moving from his chair, he restored order within by striking through the window with astonishing accuracy at the heads or hands of such boys as had taken advantage of his absence to make a rumpus.

"A fine day, Doctor!" he shouted to me when he saw me appear in the square. From his vantage point on the balcony with the cane in his hand he had reason to feel that he was the ruler of the village, a kindly, popular and just ruler, who missed nothing of what was going on.

"I didn't see you this morning. Where have you been? For a walk? Up to the cemetery? Good for you; get on with your walk! Amuse yourself as best you can! And come here to the square this afternoon about half-past five. I dare say you'll have a nap first. I want you to meet my sister. Where are you going? To the lower part of the village? Are you looking for lodgings there? My sister will find you something; have no fear. A man like you can't do with just a peasant house. We'll turn up something better than that, Doctor! Here's wishing you a pleasant walk!"

After the square, the road rose to a slight elevation and then went down to another much smaller square surrounded by low houses. In the middle of this square there was a strange monument, almost as high as the houses around it and endowed by the narrowness of the place with a certain solemnity. It was the public toilet, the most modern, sumptuous, and monumental toilet that can be imagined, built of concrete, with four compartments and a weatherproof overhanging roof, of the type that has only recently been put up in the big cities. On one wall stood out in huge block letters an inscription of the makers' name, familiar to city-dwellers: "Renzi & Co., Turin." What strange circumstances, what magician or fairy had borne this marvelous object through the air from the faraway North and let it fall like a meteorite directly in the middle of this village square, in a land where for hundreds of miles around there was no water and no sanitary equipment of any kind? It was a by-product of the Fascist government and of the mayor, Magalone, and, judging by its size, it must have cost the yield of several years of local taxes. I looked inside: a pig was drinking the stagnant water at the bottom of one receptacle; two children were floating paper boats in another. In the course of the year I never saw it serve any other function. I saw no one enter it but pigs, dogs, chickens, and children except on the evening of a feast day in September, when a few peasants climbed up on the roof to get a better view of the fireworks. Only one person put it to the use for which it was intended, and that was myself. Even so I must confess that I did so less from necessity than on account of a certain homesickness.

In one corner of the square, which barely escaped falling within the long shadow cast by the monument, a lame man, dressed in black with a wizened, solemn, almost priestly face, as thin as that of a polecat, was blowing like a pair of bellows into the body of a dead goat. I stopped to look at him. The goat had been killed shortly before right in the square and laid out on a board supported by two wooden trestles. The lame man had made only one incision in the skin, on a hind-leg just above the foot. Here he had set his lips and was blowing with all his might and main while he pulled the skin away from the flesh. To see him attached in this way to the animal, whose form was gradually inflated, while he seemed silently to grow thinner and thinner as he emptied himself of his breath recalled some strange sort of metamorphosis whereby a man is changed into a beast. When the goat was swollen up like a balloon the lame man held the leg tightly in one hand, removed his mouth from the foot and wiped it with his sleeve, then quickly peeled off the skin as if it were a glove until the goat was left stripped and naked on its board, like a saint, looking up at the sky.

"This way the skin can be preserved and made into a flask," the lame man explained gravely while his nephew, a gentle and taciturn boy, helped him to quarter the animal. "This year there's plenty to do. The peasants are slaughtering all their goats. They've no other choice, since they can't pay the tax on them."

The government, it seems, had just discovered that goats were harmful to the crops because they had a way of nibbling at growing things, and a law had been made covering every town and village in the nation which set a tax on goats equivalent almost to their market value. Thus the goats were smitten while the crops were saved. But around Gagliano, for instance, there was no farming, and the goats were the peasants' only source of revenue, because they lived off nothing, leaped over the banks of bare clay, browsed on thorny bushes, and did without the pastures essential to cattle and sheep. The goat tax then, was a catastrophe, and because the peasants had no money to pay it there was nothing they could do about it. They could only kill off the goats and that left them without milk and cheese. The lame man was an impoverished landowner, but he was proud of his social standing and of the variety of trades he plied for a living, among them the immolation of the goats. Thanks to the tax, I was able to get meat from him all through the year, whereas formerly, he told me, I should have had to get along with having it very rarely. He was also caretaker for several property owners who did not live in the village, he kept an eye on the peasants, served as auctioneer, arranged marriages, and knew everyone in the neighborhood. Rarely did he fail to put in a silent appearance at any event, great or small, with his lame leg, his black suit, and a foxy expression on his face. He was intensely curious, but sparing of words; his sentences stopped short as if to imply that he knew a great deal more than he could say, and he brought them out in a solemn and dignified manner that belied the gay meaning of his name, Carnovale.

When he heard that I was searching for lodgings, possibly large and light enough for painting, he thought hard for a moment and then said I might take the house of his cousins, with whose names I was perhaps acquainted because they were well known physicians in Naples. I might rent part of the house, two or three rooms. He would write to them at once and I should consider myself lucky, because no other house in the village could possibly suit me so well. The place was empty, but he could let me have a bed and other necessary furnishings. Meanwhile, if I wanted to see the house, he would send his nephew to unlock it and show it to me. I went with the boy, who was serious, melancholy, and clothed in black just like his uncle.

The road sloped down beyond the square as far as to where the ravines on either side left no room for any houses between them; here it ran along a narrow ridge between two low walls with a sheer drop below them. This stretch of a hundred yards or so between Upper and Lower Gagliano was exposed to a continual violent wind. Halfway across, where the ridge widened slightly, was one of Gagliano's two fountains, the second being at the higher end of the village near the church, where I had been in the morning. This fountain, which provided water for all of Lower Gagliano and a good part of the upper village, was surrounded, as I was to see it at every hour of the day, by a crowd of women. They were grouped around the fountain, old and young, some standing and others sitting, all of them with small wooden barrels balanced on their heads and carrying terra cotta jars of the Ferrandina make.

One by one they approached the fountain and waited patiently for the slender stream of water to fill the receptacles. Their wait was a long one; the wind stirred the white veils that fell over their backs, which were straight and taut as they balanced the jars on their heads with easy grace. They stood motionless in the sunlight like a flock of animals at pasture and even smelled like them. I heard a vague, continuous sound of voices, an uninterrupted murmur. Not one of them moved as I went by, but I felt the impact of dozens of black eyes following me with a fixed, intense stare until I had passed the narrow ridge and started the short ascent to the built-up section of Lower Gagliano, before the road went down again toward the caved-in church and the landslide.

We soon came to the house we were looking for, by far the most impressive structure in the whole village. From the outside it looked decidedly gloomy with its blackened walls, narrow barred windows, and all the marks of long neglect. It had been the home of a titled family which had gone away long ago; then it had served as a barracks for the *carabinieri* until they had moved to their newly-built modern headquarters, and the filth and squalor of the walls inside still bore witness to its military occupation. The drawing room had been cut up into dark prison cells, with high grated windows and heavy chains on the doors. The doors, swollen by rain and ice, could no longer be closed and the windowpanes were all broken; a thick layer of dust blown in by the wind covered everything in sight. Strips of plaster and cobwebs hung down from the gilded and painted ceiling; the black and white tiles of the floor, originally laid in a pattern, were loose, and stalks of gray grass had pushed up through the cracks.

As we went from room to room, we were greeted by a quick, furtive sound like that of frightened animals running to shelter. I threw open a French window and went out on a balcony that had a crumpled eighteenth-century iron railing. When I stepped out of the darkness I was almost blinded by the sudden dazzling light. Below me lay a ravine; straight ahead, with nothing to block my view, infinite wastes of white clay, with no sign of human life upon them, shimmering in the sunlight as far as the eye could see until they seemed to melt away into the white sky. Not a single shadow broke the monotony of this sea on which the sun beat down from directly overhead. It was high noon, time to go home.

How could I manage to live in this noble ruin? But there was a melancholy enchantment about the place; I could pace up and down on the loose tiles; and as nighttime companions

I preferred bats to the tax collectors and bedbugs of the widow's abode. Perhaps, I thought, I could have new glass put in the windows, have a mosquito net sent from Turin to protect me from malaria, and give back some life to the rough and crumbling walls. I told the lame man, who was waiting in the square with his quartered goat, to write to Naples, and I walked back up to my temporary lodgings.

When I came to the Fossa del Bersagliere I saw a tall, fair-haired, well-built young man, wearing a short-sleeved city shirt, come out of the narrow door of a run-down house with a plate of steaming spaghetti in his hand. He crossed the square, put the plate down on the wall that bordered this side of it, whistled loudly, and finally returned whence he had come. Out of curiosity I stopped to look from a distance at the abandoned spaghetti. Suddenly from a house across the way appeared another young man, tall, dark, and very handsome, with a pale, melancholy face, and dressed in a well-tailored gray suit. He went to the wall, picked up the plate of spaghetti and retraced his steps. Just before going into his house, he cast a wary eye about the deserted square, then turned toward me, smiled, and waved his hand in a friendly way before he stooped to enter the low door and disappear from view. Don Cosimino, the hunchback postmaster, was just closing his office for lunch and from his hidden corner he, too, had witnessed this scene. Aware of my astonishment, he gave me an understanding nod, and I perceived a certain sympathy in his keen, sorrowful eyes.

"This performance takes place every day at the same time," he told me. "They're two political prisoners like you. The fair-haired one is a Communist mason from Ancona, a very fine fellow. The other is a student of political science from Pisa; he was an officer in the Fascist Militia and he's a Communist, too. He comes from a humble family, but they don't give him any subsistence money because his mother and sister are schoolteachers and they are supposed to make enough to support him. Originally those who were here in compulsory residence could make friends among themselves, but a few months ago Don Luigi Magalone gave orders that they were not even to see one another. These two used to cook their meals together in order to save money, but now they take turns at cooking, and every day one of them leaves the other's meals on the wall to be called for as soon as he is out of sight. If they were by chance to meet, think what a danger there would be to the State!"

We walked toward the upper part of the village together. Don Cosimino lived with his wife and several children not far from the widow's house.

"Don Luigi has an eye out for these things; he's a great one for discipline. He and the sergeant think them up together. With you I hope it will be different. Don't take things too hard, anyhow, Doctor." Don Cosimino looked up at me consolingly:

"They can't help playing up to the part of policemen, and they stick their noses into everything. The mason got himself in trouble. He was talking to some peasants, and he tried to tell them about Darwin's theory that men are descended from monkeys. I'm no follower of Darwin, myself," and Don Cosimino smiled maliciously, "but I don't see anything wrong with such things if you believe them. Well, of course, Don Luigi came to know about it. He made a dreadful scene; you should have heard him shout! He told the mason that Darwin's ideas were contrary to the Catholic religion, that Catholicism and Fascism were one and the same, and that to talk about Darwin amounted to anti-Fascism. He even wrote

51

to the police at Matera that the mason was carrying on sub-versive propaganda. But the peasants like the fellow; he's obliging and can turn his hand to almost anything." We had reached Don Cosimino's house. "Cheer up," he said. "You've just come and you'll have to get used to it. But it will all be over one day." Then, almost as if he were afraid that he had said too much, the kindly hunchback abruptly murmured goodbye and left me.

Chapter Seven

THAT AFTERNOON THE MAYOR was waiting in the square to take me to meet his sister. Donna Caterina Magalone Cuscianna was expecting us; she had prepared coffee and homemade cakes for our benefit. She welcomed me very cordially at the door and led me into the drawing room, simply furnished, with gewgaws strewn around: cushions with a clown design and stuffed dolls. She asked after my family, expressed pity for my loneliness, assured me that she would do all she could to render my stay less unpleasant; in short she was the soul of amiability. She was a woman some thirty years old, small and stout, with a certain facial resemblance to her brother, but with a stronger-willed and more intense look about her. Her hair and eyes were jet black, while her yellowish and shiny skin and neglected teeth gave her an unhealthy appearance. She was dressed like a busy

housewife, with her clothes somewhat disarrayed from working in the heat. She spoke with a high, rasping voice, in an
affected manner:

"You'll be happy enough here, Doctor. I shall look out for
a house for you. There's nothing free at the moment but there
will be soon. You need a comfortable place with a room to
receive your patients. And I'll find you a servant, too. Try one
of these cakes. Of course you're used to greater delicacies.
Your mother can probably do better. These cakes are country
style. And how did you ever come to be sent here? It must
have been a mistake. Mussolini can't know everything that's
going on and there must be men around him who get things
wrong no matter how conscientious they may be. And in a big
city a man makes enemies. In these parts we even have some
Fascists in compulsory residence. Arpinati, the Party Secretary
of Bologna, is in a village not far from here, but he's free to
come and go as he chooses. Now there's a war on. My husband went as a volunteer; with his position, of course, he had
to set a good example. Well, ideas are not so important; it's
our country that matters. You, too, are for *Italy*, aren't you?
It must have been all a mistake to send you here. But we're
very lucky to have you."

Don Luigi, with a noncommittal air about him, was silent,
and a little later, saying that he had business to attend to, he
went away. After we were left alone Donna Caterina filled my
Japanese cup with coffee and asked me to taste her homemade
quince jam, plying me the while with exaggerated compliments and promising me her help in obtaining whatever I
might need. I wondered what her motive was: natural cordiality, a womanly and maternal protective instinct, or a desire
to display her social prominence and her culinary ability to
a gentleman from the North. There was something of all
these: cordiality, maternal instinct, social ambition and

54

culinary ability, indeed Donna Caterina made excellent jams, preserves, cakes, baked olives, dried figs stuffed with almonds, and sausages with Spanish peppers. But there was something else besides: a definite personal ambition into which my unexpected arrival somehow fitted, a passion which my arrival revived as a sudden wind fans a dying fire.

"Yes, it's luck for us that you've come. You're to stay three years? Of course you'd rather leave sooner and for your sake I hope that you do, but as far as we're concerned I should like you to stay. This isn't such a bad place; all of us are good Italians and good Fascists. Luigi is mayor and my husband was the local Party leader. I'm taking his place while he's away; there's really not much work to do. You can feel quite at home here. And we shall at last have a decent doctor, instead of having to take a trip every time we're ill. By the way, I'd like you to look at my father-in-law, who lives with me. Uncle Giuseppe, that is, Dr. Milillo, is old and it's time for him to retire. And the other man, who's poisoning the countryside with the drugs dispensed by his two nieces, will poison us no longer. He and those vile women, those . . . sluts!"

Donna Caterina's voice had suddenly risen to a high pitch of exasperation; there was no doubt about it, the concealed passion which she could not disguise was hate, single-minded hate in the form of a fixation. Because she was a woman and there was nothing else in her mind, this hate was down-to-earth, resourceful and creative. Donna Caterina hated the "vile women" who kept the pharmacy, she hated their uncle, Dr. Concetto Gibilisco, she hated the whole clan of relatives and cronies around him, and the officials in Matera who protected him.

I had been sent by Divine Providence; little did it matter what was the political pretext for my arrival since my real use

55

was to serve as an instrument of her hate. I was to turn Gibilisco into the street, to close the pharmacy or at least to take it away from his nieces.

Donna Caterina was an active and imaginative woman, and she, in reality, ran the village. She was more intelligent and stronger-willed than her brother and she knew that she could do with him what she wanted as long as she left him an appearance of authority. She neither knew nor cared about Fascism; in her mind, to be the local Party leader was simply a means of holding the reins of power. As soon as she had heard of my arrival she had laid a plan, imposed it upon her brother and, with greater difficulty, upon her uncle as well. She thought that I was keen on practicing medicine and earning all I could out of it; it was up to her to encourage me and to persuade me that with their backing I should not run into trouble; that, in fact, my success depended on their support. She had to show me every courtesy and at the same time to make me aware of her power, in order that I should not by any mischance fall in with their enemies. Don Luigi, whose custom it was to treat his political prisoners severely, was afraid to compromise himself by dealing with me too kindly; he had been unwilling to ask me to his house lest his enemies report him to those higher up, and for this reason she had intervened and tried to win me over to their side.

Donna Caterina's grudge was but one facet of the typical feud existing between the two groups of leading families, and perhaps here, as at Grassano, it could be traced back to a previous epoch. Perhaps, although I never found out for certain, a century earlier the Gibiliscos, who came of a medical family, were liberals and the Magalones, who were of more recent and humbler vintage, had connections with the partisans of the Bourbons and the brigands. Aside from this traditional enmity, however, Donna Caterina had reasons all her own for hating the Gibiliscos. Through indiscretions on her part and the gossip of the village women it did not take me long to find out why. Donna Caterina's husband, Nicola Cuscianna, schoolteacher, Party leader and right-hand man of his sister and brother-in-law in running the village, was a big fellow with an arrogant and stupid military type of face. His photograph in the uniform of a captain dominated the drawing room. He had been bewitched by the beautiful black eyes, the peaches-and-cream complexion, and the tall, sinuous body of the druggist's daughter, in spite of the fact that she belonged to the hostile camp. Whether they were actually lovers or whether this story was exaggerated by loose talk I never knew, but Donna Caterina was convinced that they were. Donna Caterina was no longer young, and her rival's youth and beauty could not but cause her to tremble. The supposed lovers were never able to see one another in so small a village, where a thousand eyes watched them, including the ever vigilant eyes of Donna Caterina, who never for a moment let them out of her sight. In the jealous imagination of the betrayed wife there was only one way they could satisfy their overwhelming passion: she, Donna Caterina, must die and then they would be free to marry. The dark-haired siren and her insignificant blonde sister were the undisputed and incompetent proprietors of the pharmacy, although they had no right to run it, and the whole neighborhood grumbled and stood in fear of their careless measurement of prescriptions. The means for getting rid of Donna Caterina, then, were right at hand: poison. Poison would take effect without danger of discovery, because, of the two local doctors, one was their uncle and probably their accomplice, while the other, because he was in his dotage, could not possibly notice anything wrong. Donna Caterina would die and the lovers, unpunished and happy, would laugh together over her grave.

How much truth, I wondered, lay behind this picture of crime in Donna Caterina's imagination? What secret clues, what discovered love letters, what veiled references in the course of their everyday life had aroused in her violent and jealous spirit first a doubt and then a certainty which came to be an obsession? I did not know, but Donna Caterina believed in the product of her fancy and she laid the blame for the future crime not so much upon her husband, who had been bewitched, as upon her rival and all those who had anything to do with her. The long-standing feud and the struggle for power over the village, with the addition of this personal grudge, became fierce and violent. The poisoner and her family must pay dearly for their crime.

As to her husband, Donna Caterina knew how to handle him. There was to be no scandal, no one must have the slightest suspicion. In the privacy of their own four walls Donna Caterina accused him every day of adultery and murder, and forbade him access to her bed. The powerful and feared Party leader of Gagliano lost every bit of his arrogance as soon as he entered his own house, where in the darting black eyes of his wife he was a hopeless reprobate and unforgivable sinner, and he had to settle down to a solitary sleep on a couch in the drawing room. This sad life went on for six months until there appeared a last chance for redemption: the war with Abyssinia.

The humiliated sinner enrolled as a volunteer with the idea that in this way he might expiate his sins, reconcile himself with his wife when he came back, and meanwhile obtain the pay of a captain, which was considerably higher than his salary as a schoolteacher. His example, unfortunately, was not followed. Captain Cuscianna and Lieutenant Decunto of Grassano, of whom I have spoken, were the only volunteers from their respective villages. But few as are the beneficiaries, even war has its uses. Captain Cuscianna was considered a hero and Donna Caterina a hero's wife, a distinction of which none of the opposing faction could brag to the authorities at Matera. Now I had appeared upon the scene, obviously sent by Divine Providence in order to help Donna Caterina wreak vengeance upon her enemies.

"Luigino wanted to enlist, too, along with my husband. They're just like brothers, always together, always standing up for one another. But Luigino's health is poor; half the time he's ill. It's a good thing that we have you here. Then if he were gone who would be left here to keep order and carry on propaganda?"

While Donna Caterina was speaking, her father-in-law, Don Pasquale Cuscianna, attracted by the smell of the fresh cakes, came into the room with short, slow, awkward steps. He was wrapped in a cloak, with a quilted skull-cap on his head and a pipe in his toothless mouth. He was an obese, heavy, deaf old man, greedy and grasping like an enormous silk-worm. He, too, had been a schoolmaster before his retirement. Indeed, Gagliano, like all of Italy, was in the hands of schoolmasters. Don Pasquale was generally respected. He spent the day sleeping and eating, or else sitting on the wall at one side of the square to smoke. His daughter-in-law had told me that he was ailing: he had an affliction of the prostate gland and possibly a touch of diabetes, which did not prevent him, however, from falling promptly upon the left-over cakes and wolfing them voraciously. Then he hoisted himself with grunts of satisfaction into a chaise longue, pretended with an occasional mutter to join our conversation, of which on account of his deafness he could hear not a word, and soon, mumbling and puffing in turn, he fell asleep.

I was about to go when two girls of about twenty-five, a fairly advanced age in these parts for the marriageable, rushed into the room, shrieking, jumping, gesticulating, making exclamations of astonishment, raising their arms to heaven, and embracing Donna Caterina. They were stocky and plump, as dark-skinned as coal sacks, with short, curly, flying black hair, fiery black eyes, and black hairs above their full lips and on their continually moving arms and legs. These were Margherita and Maria, the daughters of Dr. Milillo, whom Donna Caterina had sent for in order to introduce them to me. The girls had painted their lips with a thick coat of garish lipstick for the occasion, covered their faces with white powder, put on high-heeled shoes, and lost no time in coming. They were good girls at heart, incredibly ingenuous and ignorant, without a thought in their heads. Everything astonished them; they exclaimed shrilly over my dog, my suit, and my paintings with the nervous motions of two black grasshoppers. Then they began to talk about cakes and cooking in general and Donna Caterina praised their housekeeping abilities to the skies. Probably in her mind Margherita and Maria were to serve the double purpose of persuading their uncle, Dr. Milillo, to look upon me with benevolence and of allying me definitely with her family. What worthier object of a man's desires could there be, in these surroundings, than a doctor's daughter? Donna Caterina had asked me whether or not I was engaged to be married, and she could easily check the truth of my negative reply through the private censorship which her brother exercised over the mail.

The two hapless girls, who, like me, were the unconscious instruments of a higher power, had with them a boy of about eighteen. He was badly dressed, with a yellowish stupid face and a pendulous lower lip, and he stood, silent and dull, in a corner. This was their brother, the only male of the Milillo line. The old doctor, who meanwhile had put in an appearance, confided in me that although he was a good boy he was a source of considerable worry because he had been left mentally retarded after a brain fever and there was no way of getting him to study. He had sent him to a high school, an agricultural school, and other institutions, without success. Now the boy was about to go away to start a course of training for noncommissioned officers of the *carabinieri* and he could think of nothing but the uniform. This was not the future that his father had dreamed of for him, but none the less it meant a good position. On this point I could not take issue with the doctor; the poor defective would make a harmless sergeant.

Donna Caterina changed the subject, for her uncle's benefit, to my medical skill. To my efforts to convey to her that I was interested only in painting, she paid not the slightest attention. The doctor, with his usual embarrassed stammer, advised me strongly, if I attended the sick, not to deprive myself of my due by a generosity which was sure to be taken for weakness. Everyone tried to get out of paying the doctor, but the fees were obligatory and set by the government; a doctor must see to it that they were kept up, out of a sense of duty toward his colleagues and a respect for general standards, and so on. The old man belonged only passively to the political faction led by his nephew and niece and he shared their ambition only because they were his relatives; as Donna Caterina and Don Luigi said, he was "too kind." He was a former follower of Nitti and in private he occasionally deplored the mayor's Fascist tenets and criticized his love of display, his air of authority, and his tendency to play the policeman. But in the long run, for the sake of peace and quiet, he had reconciled himself to these things and even turned them to his own advantage.

Under the spur of his niece and nephew and perhaps with a look to the best interests of his daughters, he would consent not to block my way, but he had no intention of being taken for an old man of no account who could be maneuvered to suit their whims; no, he had his honor and his self-respect. I had, therefore, to listen to a number of complicated explanations of the lay of the land and to his paternal and personal advice. I was to make sure that I was paid, to respect the established fees and not to believe the tales of the peasants, because they were ignorant liars and the more you did for them the more ungrateful they were. He had lived in the place for more than forty years, looking after them all and showing them every kindness, only to be repaid by their saying that he was senile and incompetent. Whereas he was anything but senile. It was sad to see the peasants' ingratitude. And their superstitions. And their stubbornness. And so on, and so on.

It was dusk when at last I managed to escape from the vacuous stammering of the doctor, the enthusiastic squeals of his daughters, the grunts of Don Pasquale, and Donna Caterina's hinting smiles. The peasants were coming up the road with their animals and surging into their houses, as they did every evening, with the monotony of a ceaseless tide, in a dark, mysterious world of their own where there was no hope. As for the others, the gentry, I already knew them too well and I had a feeling of disgust for the clinging contact of the ridiculous spiderweb of their daily life, a dust-covered and uninteresting skein of self-interest, low-grade passion, boredom, greedy impotence, and poverty. Today and tomorrow and always, as I trod the only street of the village, I should have to see them gather in the square and to listen indefinitely to their envious complaints. What in the world was I doing in this spot?

The sky was a mixture of rose, green, and violet, the enchanting colors of malaria country, and it seemed far, far away.

Chapter Eight

I STAYED THREE WEEKS IN the widow's house, waiting to find other quarters. The summer was at its dreary pinnacle; the sun seemed to have come to a stop straight overhead and the clayey land was split by the burning heat. In its thirsty crevices nested the deadly poisonous, stubby snakes which the peasants call *cortopassi*, "short-steps": *Cortopassi, cortopassi, ove te trova là te lassi.* Snake in the grass; let lie and pass. A continual wind dried up men's bodies, and the days went by monotonously under the pitiless light until sunset and the cool of the evening. I sat in the kitchen gazing at the random flight of the flies, the only token of life in the motionless silence of the dog days. My eyes focused lazily on the thousands of stationary, buzzing black dots which covered the greenish-blue wooden shutters. Every now and then, one of the back dots suddenly disappeared in the whir of an abrupt and invisible flight, and its place was taken by a very bright white point, ringed with gold, like a tiny star, whose light gradually died away. Then another fly took off into the air and another star came out on the blue of the shutters. At last Barone, who lay asleep at my feet, was awakened by a dream; he jumped to his feet and caught a fly on the wing, breaking the silence with the violent snapping of his jaws.

Strings of figs hung from the balcony railing, black with flies that were busy sucking the last moisture from them before the blazing sun dried them out altogether. Out on the street, on wide-rimmed tables below the black pennants decorating the front doors, blood-red liquid masses of tomato conserve lay drying. Swarms of flies walked without wetting their feet over the portions already solidified, in numbers as vast as those of the children of Israel, while other swarms plunged into the watery Red Sea, where they were caught and drowned like Pharaoh's armies as they hotly pursued their prey. The pervading silence of the countryside hung heavily over the kitchen, and the monotonous buzzing of the flies marked the passing hours with an endless refrain.

All of a sudden the bell began to ring out from the church near by, in honor of some unknown saint or as a summons to some unattended function, and its lament filled the whole room. The bell-ringer, a ragged, barefoot boy of about eighteen, with a hypocritical, thieving smile, rang the bell according to an interminable, mournful fancy all his own, in the rhythm of a funeral march. My dog, who was sensitive to the presence of spirits, could not bear this lugubrious sound and at the first note he began to howl in pain, as if death were brushing our shoulders. Or was there something of the devil in him that was ruffled by this sacred music? Anyhow I had to get up and take him outside in order to quiet him. Big, hungry fleas in search of a refuge jumped on the white paving-stones; ticks hung in ambush from blades of grass. The village seemed empty of men; the peasants were in the fields and the women were hidden behind half-closed doors. The street sloped down between the houses that bordered it and the ravines behind them all the way to the landslide without a fragment of shade. I climbed slowly in the opposite direction, toward the cemetery, in search of the slender olive trees and the cypresses.

An animal-like enchantment lay over the deserted village. In the midday silence a sudden noise revealed a sow rolling in a pile of garbage; then the echoes were awakened by the shattering outburst of a donkey's braying, more resonant than the church bell in its weird, phallic anguish. Roosters were crowing; their afternoon song had none of the glorious shrill-ness of their early morning call, but reflected rather the bottomless sadness of the desolate countryside. The sky was filled with black crows and, above them, circling hawks; their still, round eyes seemed to follow me. Invisible animal presences continued to make themselves felt in the air until finally a goat, the queen of the region, jumped with its bow legs from behind a house and stared at me with blank yellow eyes. Some half-naked, ragged children were chasing it; among them a four-year-old girl wearing the habit, wimple, and veil of a nun, and a five-year-old boy in the cowl and cord of a monk. It is a local custom for parents, in fulfilment of a vow, to dress them thus, in a miniature of religious garb or like the princelings painted by Velasquez. The children wanted to ride the goat; the little monk seized its beard and put his arms around its face, the nun tried to get up on its back, while the others held its horns and tail. For a moment they all managed to straddle it until the beast jumped abruptly, shook itself, tossed them into the dust, and stopped to look at them with an evil smile. The children picked themselves up, recaptured the goat, and mounted it again; the goat ran away, jumping wildly, until the whole lot of them disappeared around a curve.

The peasants say that there is something satanic about goats. This is true of all the animal world, and of the goat in particular. Not that it is wicked or has anything to do with the devils of the Christian religion, in spite of the fact that they often show themselves in its guise. It is demoniacal like every living thing, and even more so than the rest, because some strange power lurks behind its animal exterior. To the peasants the goat represents the ancient satyr, indeed a living satyr, lean and hungry, with curling horns, a crooked nose, and pendulous teats or male organ; a poor, hairy, brotherly, wild satyr, looking for grass on the edge of a precipice.

Under the gaze of these eyes, neither human nor divine, and accompanied by these mysterious powers, I climbed slowly toward the cemetery. But the olive trees gave no shade; the sun pierced their delicate foliage as if it were lacework. I decided to go through the broken-down gate into the enclosure of the cemetery proper; here was the only cool and private spot in the village, and perhaps the least melancholy as well. As I sat on the ground, the dazzling reflection of light from the clay disappeared behind the wall; the two cypresses swayed in the breeze and clusters of roses bloomed among the graves, a strange sight in this flowerless land. In the middle of the cemetery there was a ditch, a yard or two deep, neatly cut out of the dry earth in readiness for the next dead body. A ladder made it easy to get in and out of this open grave, and I had made it my custom on these hot days when I came up here to lower myself into it and lie down. The earth was smooth and dry, and the sun had not burned it. I could see

66

nothing but a rectangle of clear sky, crossed occasionally by a wandering white cloud; not a single sound reached my ears. In this freedom and solitude I spent many hours. When my dog tired of chasing lizards on the sunny wall he peered questioningly into the ditch, then lowered himself down the ladder, curled up at my feet and soon fell asleep. I, too, listening to the cadence of his breathing, eventually let my book fall from my hand, and closed my eyes.

We were awakened by a strange voice, without sex, or tone, or age, mumbling incomprehensible words. An old man was leaning over the edge of the grave and talking to me through his toothless gums; I could see him against the sky, tall and a little bent, with long, thin arms like the vanes of a windmill. He was almost ninety, but his face gave an effect of timelessness; it was shapeless and wrinkled like a dried-up apple; two magnetic bright blue eyes shone out from among the folds of flesh. Not a single strand of beard grew or had ever grown on his chin, and this gave an odd effect to the texture of his skin. He spoke a dialect other than that of Gagliano, a mixture of tongues; he had lived in a number of places, with the idiom of Pisticci predominant, because there, in faraway times, he was born. This mixture, the toothlessness that garbled his words, and the terse and proverbial form of his speech at first made it hard for me to understand him, but as I gradually caught on, we held long conversations together.

I never knew whether he really listened to me or whether he simply followed the mysterious skein of his own thoughts, which seemed to issue forth from the shadowy, remote reaches of a primitive world. This indefinable being wore a torn, dirty shirt open over his hairless chest, which had a prominent breastbone like that of a bird. On his head he wore a reddish cap with a visor, perhaps the badge of one of his many public functions; he was now both grave-digger and

67

town crier. At all hours of the day he went through the village street, blowing a trumpet, beating a drum which he wore hung about his neck and calling out in his unhuman voice the news of the day: the arrival of a peddler, the slaughter of a goat, an edict of the mayor, the hour set for a funeral. And it was he who carried the dead to the cemetery, dug their graves and buried them.

These were his normal activities, but behind them lay another existence, filled with a dark, impenetrable power. The women teased him when he went by, because he had no beard, and rumor had it that he had never made love all his life long. "Coming to bed with me tonight?" they called from the doorways, laughing and hiding their faces in their hands. "Why do you leave me to sleep alone?" They teased him, but at the same time he inspired them with respect and something like fear. The old man had a secret talent: he was in touch with forces below the earth, he could call up spirits, and he had a power over animals. His original trade, before old age and vicissitude had brought him to Gagliano, was that of wolf-tamer. He could either make the wolves come down into the villages, or keep them away, as he wished; they simply could not resist him, but had to bend to his will.

People said that when he was young he wandered over the mountains followed by savage wolf-packs. This talent caused him to be held in high esteem, and when the winter was severe, various villages called upon him to keep away the woodland beasts that cold and hunger drove to invade them. Every kind of animal was susceptible to his power, although he could not wield it over women; and not only animals but the elements and the spirits that dwell in the air as well. In his youth he could mow as much wheat in a day as fifty men because an invisible presence worked for him. At the end of the day when the other peasants were covered with dirt and

68

sweat, their backs aching from fatigue and their heads buzzing from exposure to the sun, the wolf-tamer was as fresh as he had been in the morning.

I climbed out of my ditch to speak to him and offered him a cigar, which he put into a blackened holder made from the right hindleg of a buck rabbit. As he leaned on his shovel—for he was always digging new graves—he bent over to pick up a human shoulder blade, which he held for a while in his hand while he talked and then tossed aside. The ground was full of calcified bleached bones which flowered out of graves worn away by rain and sun. To the old man these bones, the dead, animals, and spirits were all familiar things, bound up, as indeed they were to everyone in these parts, with simple everyday life. "The village is built of the bones of the dead," he said to me in his thick jargon, gurgling like a subterranean rivulet suddenly emerging among the stones, and twisting the toothless hole that served him for a mouth into what might have been meant for a smile. Whenever I tried to make him explain what he meant he paid no attention, but laughed and repeated exactly what he had said before, with not a word added to it: "That's it; the village is built of the bones of the dead." The old man was quite right, whether he meant these words literally or symbolically, as a figure of speech.

A short time later, when the mayor ordered an excavation made not far from the widow's house for the foundations of a small building to house the Fascist Scout organization, thousands of bones were turned up instead of dirt, and for days wagons carried these ancestral remains through the village and dumped them down the Fossa del Bersagliere. The bones from the tombs which had lain under the pavement of the fallen church, the Madonna of the Angels, were of more recent vintage. Some of them still had vestiges of flesh or parchment-like skin attached to them, and the dogs fought over them whenever they dug them up; they ran up the village street barking madly in the pursuit of one of their number with a tibia in his mouth. Here where time has come to a stop, it seemed quite natural that bones of all ages, recent, less recent, and very ancient, should turn up all together at the traveler's feet. The dead of the Madonna of the Angels, in their ruined tombs, were the most unfortunate. Not only did birds and dogs disperse their remains, but other and more terrifying presences visited the dreadful, slimy hole under the ruins where they had come to rest.

One night some few months or few years before (he could not tell me exactly when, because his notions of time were vague) the wolf-tamer, on his way back from Gaglianello, had just reached a slight rise of ground across from the church, known as the Mound of the Madonna of the Angels, when he felt a strange weariness in his body and had to sit down on the steps of a small side-chapel. He could not get up again and go on his way; someone was holding him back. The night was black and the old man could not see through the darkness, but from the ravine a bestial voice called him by name. A devil, who had settled down there among the dead, forbade him to go farther. The old man made the sign of the cross and the devil began to gnash his teeth and to cry out in pain. Among the shadows the old man made out for a second the form of a goat, which leaped with terror over the ruins and disappeared. The devil fled howling down the ravine. "Uuuuuhhhh!" he bayed as he vanished. All at once the old man felt free and strong again, and a few steps brought him into the village. He had had endless adventures of the sort and when I drew him out he told them to me without ascribing to them the least importance. He had lived so long that it was inevitable such meetings should have been numerous.

He was so old that in the days of the brigands he was

already a full-grown young man. I could never find out for certain whether, as was most likely, he had been one of them, but he had known the famous Ninco Nanco and he described to me as if he had seen her only the day before this brigand's consort, Maria 'a Pastora, who was, like himself, from Pisticci. Maria 'a Pastora was a beautiful peasant woman who lived with her lover in the wooded mountains, fighting and robbing at his side, clad like a man, and always on horseback. Ninco Nanco's band was the cruelest and most daring of the region, and Maria 'a Pastora took part in the raids on farms and villages, the highway robberies, the division of spoils, and the murders for revenge. When Ninco Nanco tore out with his bare hands the heart of the *bersagliere* who had captured him, Maria 'a Pastora handed him his knife. The grave-digger remembered her distinctly, and there was pleasure in his strange voice when he told me how beautiful she was, with the pink and white coloring of a flower and black braids that hung down to her feet, as she sat straight, astride her horse. Ninco Nanco was killed, but the old man did not know what had been the end of Maria 'a Pastora, goddess of the peasant war. She neither died nor was captured, he told me; she was seen at Pisticci, swathed in black, then she disappeared on horseback into the woods and was never heard of again.

Chapter Nine

I DID NOT GO TO THE cemetery only to seek rest and solitude and to listen to stories. This was the one place, within bounds, that was not built up and where a few trees broke the geometrical outline of the peasants' huts. For this reason it was the first subject I chose for a picture. I went out with my canvas and brushes when the sun started to go down, set up my easel in the shade of an olive tree or behind the cemetery wall and started to paint.

The first time I did this, a few days after my arrival, my occupation appeared suspect to the sergeant, who immediately informed the mayor and meanwhile, in order to be on the safe side, sent one of his men to watch me. The *carabiniere* stood stiffly a few steps behind me and looked at my work from the first to the last stroke of the brush. It is tiresome to paint with someone looking over your shoulder, even if you're not afraid of evil influences (as they say was the case with

Cézanne), but in spite of all I could do he was not to be budged; he had his orders. Gradually the expression of his stupid face shifted from inquiry to interest and finally he asked me whether I would be able to make an enlargement in oils of a photograph of his dead mother, this being to a *carabiniere* the apex of art. The hours went by, the sun set, and objects took on the enchantment of twilight, seeming to shine with a light of their own, from within rather than from without. An enormous, transparent, unreal moon hung in the rose-tinted sky over the gray olive trees and the houses lower down, like a cuttlefish bone corroded by the salt of the ocean. At this time I had a particular feeling for the moon, because for many months I had been shut up in a cell where I could not see it, and to find it again was a pleasure. As a greeting and a token of regard I painted it, round and light in the center of the sky, to the astonishment of the *carabiniere*.

At this point the twin masters of the village came to inspect my work, the decorous sergeant in his impeccable uniform with a sword at his side, and the mayor, all compliments and smiles and affected benevolence. Don Luigi, of course, was a connoisseur and wanted me to know it; he was unsparing in his praise of my technique. Besides, it was flattering to his local pride that I should find his native place worthy of painting. I took advantage of his satisfaction to suggest that if I were to do justice to its beauties I should have to go a little farther away from the village limits. The mayor and the sergeant were unwilling to commit themselves to breaking the rules, but little by little in the course of the following weeks we reached a sort of tacit agreement which enabled me, for the purpose of painting, to go two or three hundred yards out of bounds. I owed this privilege less to respect for art than to Donna Caterina's intrigues and her desire to please me and to her brother's panicky fear of falling ill. Don Luigi was perfectly well. Aside from a glandular disturbance which showed itself in his sadistic and infantile disposition but had no physical effects except a high-pitched voice and a tendency to obesity, he was bursting with health. However, to my good fortune, he was continually prey to the fear of illness: today it was tuberculosis, tomorrow heart trouble, the next day stomach ulcers; he counted his pulse, took his temperature, examined his tongue in the mirror, and every time we met I had to reassure him. At last the hypochondriac had a doctor at his beck and call. And so I could go a little afield to paint from time to time, not too often and not so far that I should be out of sight. The whole thing was to be at my own suggestion and my own risk since he had many enemies who might write anonymous letters to Matera, putting him in a bad light because he had made me this concession.

I gained very little breathing-space. The place was hemmed in by ravines, and apart from the walk leading out of the cemetery, beyond which I could not venture without going downhill and out of sight, only two paths led away from the village. One led up and down along the crest of the ravine from Gagliano to Gaglianello, and in this direction I could go as far as the Mound of the Madonna of the Angels, where the devil had appeared to the old grave-digger, not far from the last village houses. A narrower path, only a few feet wide, branched off from this to the right and went down in a series of steep zigzags to the bottom of the chasm two hundred yards below. This was the dangerous passageway that most of the peasants took every day with their donkeys and goats, when they went to their fields down by the Agri Valley, and again at night when they came back, bent over like the damned under their loads of wood or fodder. The other path was at the higher end of the village; it ran off to the right of the church, near the widow's house, to a little spring, which until a few years before was Gagliano's only supply of water. A thin stream came out of a rusty pipe and fell into a wooden trough in which the women still came at times to wash; after it spilled over from this there was nothing to drain it off and it made a marshy spot where mosquitoes bred. The path continued through fields of stubble dotted with occasional olive trees and lost itself in a labyrinth of mounds and holes in the white clay, which ended abruptly at a precipice not far from the Sauro River. Here I used to walk and paint and here one day I met a poisonous snake, but the loud barking of my dog warned me of its approach.

The strange and broken outline of this terrain made Gagliano into a sort of natural fortress, with a limited number of entrances and exits. The mayor took advantage of this lay of the land during days of what was supposed to be patriotic frenzy. He then called public meetings in order, he said, to brace up the morale of the people, herding them into the square to listen to radio broadcasts by the leaders who were then laying plans for the war with Abyssinia. When Don Luigi decided to call one of these gatherings he sent the old town crier and grave-digger through the street the evening before with his trumpet and drum, and the ancient voice was heard to shout a hundred times over, in front of every house, on one high, impersonal note: "Tomorrow morning at ten o'clock, everyone come to the square in front of the town hall to hear the radio! Nobody stay away!"

"We'll have to get up two hours before sunrise," muttered the peasants, unwilling to lose a working day, although they knew that Don Luigi would station *carabinieri* and Fascist Scouts at every exit from the village with orders not to let anyone by. Most of them managed to leave for the fields while it was still dark and the watchers had not yet arrived, but the late risers had to take their stand in the square with the women and school children, just below the balcony, from which cascaded the rapt and visceral eloquence of the mayor. They stood there with their hats on, sober and mistrustful, and his speechmaking poured over them without leaving a trace.

The gentry were all Party members, even the few like Dr. Milillo who were dissenters. The Party stood for Power, as vested in the Government and the State, and they felt entitled to a share of it. For exactly the opposite reason none of the peasants were members; indeed, it was unlikely that they should belong to any political party whatever, should, by chance, another exist. They were not Fascists, just as they would never have been Conservatives or Socialists, or anything else. Such matters had nothing to do with them; they belonged to another world and they saw no sense in them. What had the peasants to do with Power, Government, and the State? The State, whatever form it might take, meant "the fellows in Rome." "Everyone knows," they said, "that the fellows in Rome don't want us to live like human beings. There are hailstorms, landslides, droughts, malaria and . . . the State. These are inescapable evils; such there always have been and there always will be. They make us kill off our goats, they carry away our furniture, and now they're going to send us to the wars. Such is life!"

To the peasants the State is more distant than heaven and far more of a scourge, because it is always against them. Its political tags and platforms and, indeed, the whole structure of it do not matter. The peasants do not understand them because they are couched in a different language from their own, and there is no reason why they should ever care to understand them. Their only defense against the State and the propaganda of the State is resignation, the same gloomy resignation that bows their shoulders under the scourges of nature.

76

For this reason, quite naturally, they have no conception of a political struggle; they think of it as a personal quarrel among the "fellows in Rome." They were not concerned with the views of the political prisoners who were in compulsory residence among them, or with the motives for their coming. They looked at them kindly and treated them like brothers because they too, for some inexplicable reason, were victims of fate. During the first days of my stay whenever I happened to meet along one of the paths outside the village an old peasant who did not know me, he would stop his donkey to greet me and ask in dialect: "Who are you? Where are you going?" "Just for a walk; I'm a political prisoner," I would answer. "An exile? (They always said exile instead of prisoner.) Too bad! Someone in Rome must have had it in for you." And he would say no more, but smile at me in a brotherly fashion as he prodded his mount into motion.

This passive brotherliness, this sympathy in the original sense of the word, this fatalistic, comradely, age-old patience, is the deepest feeling the peasants have in common, a bond made by nature rather than by religion. They do not and can not have what is called political awareness, because they are literally *pagani*, "pagans," or countrymen, as distinguished from city-dwellers. The deities of the State and the city can find no worshipers here on the land, where the wolf and the ancient black boar reign supreme, where there is no wall between the world of men and the world of animals and spirits, between the leaves of the trees above and the roots below. They can not have even an awareness of themselves as individuals, here where all things are held together by acting upon one another and each one is a power unto itself, working imperceptibly, where there is no barrier that can not be broken down by magic. They live submerged in a world that rolls on independent of their will, where man is in no way

77

separate from his sun, his beast, his malaria, where there can be neither happiness, as literary devotees of the land conceive it, nor hope, because these two are adjuncts of personality and here there is only the grim passivity of a sorrowful Nature. But they have a lively human feeling for the common fate of mankind and its common acceptance. This is strictly a feeling rather than an act of will; they do not express it in words but they carry it with them at every moment and in every motion of their lives, through all the unbroken days that pass over these wastes.

"Too bad! Someone had it in for you." You, too, are subject to fate. You, too, are here because of the power of ill will, because of an evil star; you are tossed hither and yon by the hostile workings of magic. And you, too, are a man; you are one of us. Never mind what motives impelled you, politics, legalities, or the illusion of reason. Such things as reason or cause and effect, do not exist; there is only an adverse fate, a will for evil, which is the magic power of *things*. The State is one shape of this fate, like the wind that devours the harvest and the fever that feeds on our blood. There can be no attitude toward fate except patience and silence. Of what use are words? And what can a man do? Nothing.

Armed, then, with silence and patience, taciturn and impenetrable, the few peasants who had not escaped to the fields attended the gathering in the square. They seemed not to hear the blithe trumpeting of the radio, which came from too far away, from a land of ease and progress, which had forgotten the existence of death and now called it up as a joke, with the frivolity of an unbeliever.

CHAPTER TEN

B Y THIS TIME I KNEW A good many of the peasants of Gagliano. At first sight they all seemed alike, short, sunburned, with dull expressionless black eyes like the empty windows of a dark room. Some I met in the course of my brief walks, others nodded to me from their doorways in the evening, but most of them came to me for medical treatment. I had to resign myself to carrying out the functions of a doctor, but at first I worried like a novice about the welfare of my patients and I was disturbed by a consciousness of my own inadequacy. Their ingenuous, blind confidence in me called for some return, and, against my will, I took their sufferings upon myself and felt responsible for them. Luckily I had a medical education behind me, but I had never practiced, and here I had neither books nor instruments at hand. My attitude was neither impersonal nor scientific; in fact, I must confess that I was in a state of continual anxiety.

Hence a brief visit from my sister who is a very able doctor, as well as a kind and intelligent woman, was particularly precious to me. I learned of her unexpected coming through a telegram which arrived just in time for me to send a car to pick her up where the bus stopped at the crossroads by the Sauro River. The car was Gagliano's only motor vehicle, a rattling old Fiat, the property of a mechanic, an "American," a big light-haired fellow with a motorcylist's cap on his head. He was notorious in the village for an enormous detail of his anatomy, similar to that which gossip in France attributes to Herriot; it made him desirable, perhaps, but in any case dangerous, to women. In spite of or on account of this peculiarity he had the reputation of a peasant Don Juan, and it was difficult for his unfortunate sweethearts to conceal their illicit passion from his wife's jealousy and the curiosity and amusement of the village. He had purchased the car with the last of the savings he had brought back from New York, hoping that public demand for his services would enable him to turn it to profit. But he made no more than a trip or two every week, usually to take the mayor to the prefecture in Matera, or to accommodate the tax collector or the *carabinieri*; occasionally to transport a sick person to Stigliano or to call for freight there.

The village authorities were seriously considering at the time the advisability of using this car instead of a mule to call every day for the mail; by so doing they would set up a regular service for travelers coming or going by bus. But because a man's time and labor were unimportant in these parts and cost practically nothing, there was quite a difference in the expense, and perhaps, also, various family and social relationships had to be taken into account; in any case the question was postponed from day to day, and when I left it was still unsettled. From time to time, when he went to pick up someone at the bus stop the mechanic brought the mail back with him and it was distributed several hours earlier than usual. People knew when this was going to happen and a small crowd waited in front of the church for the return of the car. When its loud rattle could be heard coming around the curve they all surged forward to enjoy the novelty of the sight.

Thus it was in the midst of this expectant public that the familiar figure of my sister, who seemed to come from very far because I had not seen her for so long, stepped out of the car. Her precise gestures, simple dress, frank tone of voice, and open smile were just as I had always known them, but after long months in prison and the days I had spent in Grassano and Gagliano they seemed like the sudden living apparition of a world existent only in memory. Those purposeful gestures and that ease of motion belonged to a place infinitely re-moved from this one, and they were quite incredible here. I had not yet appreciated this elementary physical difference; her arrival was that of an ambassadress from one country to another one, a country this side of the mountains.

After we had embraced and she had given me messages from my mother, father, and brothers and we were alone, away from public staring, in the widow's kitchen, I questioned my sister, Luisa, impatiently. She gave me news of my family and friends and of what had gone on in the world at large during my absence; we talked of books and paintings and what people we knew and people in general were thinking and saying and doing in Italy. These were the things I cared most for, the things that occupied my thoughts every day, just as if they were close at hand. But now when they were brought before me in words they seemed to belong to another period of time, to have a different rhythm, and to obey laws that here would be considered foreign, as if they were of a land farther away than China or India. All at once I understood how it was that these two periods were hermetically shut off from one another, that these two civilizations could have no communication except by a miracle. I realized why the peasants looked on strangers from the North as visitors from another world, almost as if they were foreign gods.

My sister had come from Turin and she could stay for only four or five days.

"I wasted entirely too much time getting here," she said, "because I had to come by way of Matera in order to have the police there stamp my permit to visit you. Instead of coming directly through Naples and Potenza, which would have taken me only two days I had to take the roundabout route via Bari to Matera, and at Matera I lost a whole day waiting for the bus. What a place that is! From the glimpse I had of Gagliano just now I'd say it wasn't so bad; it couldn't be worse than Matera, anyhow."

She was horrified and frightened by what she had seen. I told her that the violence of her reaction must be due to the fact that she had never before been in these parts and that Matera had been the scene of her first meeting with this landscape and the desolate race of men that lived in it.

"I didn't know this part of the country, to be sure," she answered, "but I did somehow picture it in my mind. Only Matera. . . . Well, it was beyond anything I could possibly have imagined. I got there at about eleven in the morning. I had read in the guidebook that it was a picturesque town, quite worth a visit, that it had a museum of ancient art and some curious cave dwellings. But when I came out of the railway station, a modern and rather sumptuous affair, and looked around me, I couldn't for the life of me see the town; it simply wasn't there. I was on a sort of deserted plateau, surrounded by bare, low hills of a grayish earth covered with stones. In the middle of this desert there rose here and there eight or ten big marble buildings built in the style made fashionable in Rome by Piacentini, with massive doors, ornate architraves, solemn Latin inscriptions, and pillars gleaming in the sun. Some of them were unfinished and seemed to be quite empty, monstrosities entirely out of keeping with the desolate landscape around them. A jerry-built housing project, for the benefit, no doubt, of government employees, which had already fallen into a state of filth and disrepair, filled up the empty space around the buildings and shut off my view on one side. The whole thing looked like an ambitious bit of city planning, begun in haste and interrupted by the plague, or else like a stage set, in execrable taste, for a tragedy by d'Annunzio. These enormous twentieth-century imperial palaces housed the prefecture, the police station, the post office, the town hall, the barracks of the *carabinieri*, the Fascist Party headquarters, the Fascist Scouts, the Corporations, and so on. But where was the town? Matera was nowhere to be seen.

"I decided to attend at once to my business. I went to the police station, of resplendent marble without but dirty and bug-ridden within, its ill-kept rooms piled up with dust and sweepings. I was received, for the purpose of getting a stamp on my permit, by the assistant chief, who was also the head of the local political police. I was worried about the danger of malaria and so I asked him whether there was any chance of your being transferred to a healthier climate. Another officer who was in the room burst into the conversation abruptly: 'Malaria? There isn't any such thing. It's all imagination. One case a year, perhaps. Your brother is quite well off where he is.' But when he realized that I was a doctor he was silent, and his superior answered me in an entirely different tone: 'There's malaria everywhere,' he said. 'We can transfer your brother, if you like, but he'll find conditions just the same as at Gagliano. There's only one place in the whole province that's free of malaria, and that's Stigliano, because it's almost three thousand feet above sea level. Perhaps later we can send him there, but for the time being it's impossible.' (I caught on to the fact that only dissident Fascists were sent to Stigliano.) 'No, your brother had better stay put. Look at us; we live here in Matera, and we're not political prisoners. And it's no better here, as far as malaria is concerned, than at Gagliano. If we can stick it, then he can stick it too.'

"To this argument there was really no answer, so I pursued the matter no further, and went out. I wanted to buy you a stethoscope as I had forgotten to bring one from Turin and I knew that you needed one for your medical practice. Since there were no dealers in medical instruments I decided to look for one in a pharmacy. Among the government buildings and the cheap new houses I found two pharmacies, the only ones, I was told, in the town. Neither had what I was looking for and what's more their proprietors disclaimed all knowledge of what it might be. 'A stethoscope? What's that?' After I had explained that it was a simple instrument for listening to the heart, made like an ear trumpet, usually out of wood, they told me that I might find such a thing in Bari, but that here in Matera no one had ever heard of it.

"By now it was noon and I repaired to the restaurant that was pointed out to me as the best in town. There, all at one table with a soiled cloth on it and napkin rings that showed they came there every day, sat the assistant chief of police with several of his subordinates, looking bored to tears. You know that I'm not hard to please, but I swear that when I got up to leave I was just as hungry as when I came.

"I set out at last to find the town. A little beyond the station I found a street with a row of houses on one side and on the other a deep gully. In the gully lay Matera. From where I was, higher up, it could hardly be seen because the drop was so sheer. All I could distinguish as I looked down were alleys and terraces, which concealed the houses from view. Straight across from me there was a barren hill of an ugly gray color, without a single tree or sign of cultivation upon it, nothing but sun-baked earth and stones. At the bottom of the gully a sickly, swampy stream, the Bradano, trickled among the rocks. The hill and the stream had a gloomy, evil appearance that caught at my heart. The gully had a strange shape: it was formed by two half-funnels, side by side, separated by a narrow spur and meeting at the bottom, where I could see a white church, Santa Maria de Idris, which looked half-sunk in the ground. The two funnels, I learned, were called Sasso Caveoso and Sasso Barisano. They were like a schoolboy's idea of Dante's Inferno. And, like Dante, I too began to go down from circle to circle, by a sort of mule path leading to the bottom. The narrow path wound its way down and around, passing over the roofs of the houses, if houses they could be called They were caves, dug into the hardened clay walls of the gully, each with its own façade, some of which were quite handsome, with eighteenth-century ornamentation. These false fronts, because of the slope of the gully, were flat against its side at the bottom, but at the top they protruded, and the alleys in the narrow space between them and the hillside did double service: they were a roadway for those who came out of their houses from above and a roof for those who lived beneath. The houses were open on account of the heat, and as I went by I could see into the caves, whose only light came in through the front doors. Some of them had no entrance but a trapdoor and ladder. In these dark holes with walls cut out of the earth I saw a few pieces of miserable furniture, beds, and some ragged clothes hanging up to dry. On the floor lay dogs, sheep, goats, and pigs. Most families have just one cave to live in and there they sleep all together; men, women, children, and animals. This is how twenty thousand people live.

"Of children I saw an infinite number. They appeared from everywhere, in the dust and heat, amid the flies, stark naked or clothed in rags; I have never in all my life seen such a picture of poverty. My profession has brought me in daily contact with dozens of poor, sick, ill-kempt children, but I never even dreamed of seeing a sight like this. I saw children sitting on the doorsteps, in the dirt, while the sun beat down on them, with their eyes half-closed and their eyelids red and swollen; flies crawled across the lids, but the children stayed quite still, without raising a hand to brush them away. Yes, flies crawled across their eyelids, and they seemed not even to feel them. They had trachoma. I knew that it existed in the South, but to see it against this background of poverty and dirt was something else again. I saw other children with the wizened faces of old men, their bodies reduced by starvation almost to skeletons, their heads crawling with lice and covered with scabs. Most of them had enormous, dilated stomachs and faces yellow and worn with malaria.

"The women, when they saw me look in the doors, asked me to come in, and in the dark, smelly caves where they lived I saw children lying on the floor under torn blankets, with their teeth chattering from fever. Others, reduced to skin and bones by dysentery, could hardly drag themselves about. I saw children with waxen faces who seemed to me to have something worse than malaria, perhaps some tropical disease such as Kala Azar, or black fever. The thin women, with dirty, undernourished babies hanging at their flaccid breasts, spoke to me mildly and with despair. I felt, under the blinding sun, as if I were in a city stricken by the plague. I went on down toward the church at the bottom of the gully; a constantly

86

swelling crowd of children followed a few steps behind me.
They were shouting something, but I could not understand
their incomprehensible dialect. I kept on going; still they followed and called after me. I thought they must want pennies,
and I stopped for a minute. Only then did I make out the
words they were all shouting together: '*Signorina, dammi 'u
chinì!* Signorina, give me some quinine!' I gave them what
coins I had with me to buy candy, but that was not what
they wanted; they kept on asking, with sorrowful insistence,
for quinine. Meanwhile we had reached Santa Maria de Idris,
a handsome baroque church. When I lifted my eyes to see the
way I had come, I at last saw the whole of Matera, in the
form of a slanting wall. From here it seemed almost like a real
town. The façades of the caves were like a row of white
houses; the holes of the doorways stared at me like black
eyes. The town is indeed a beautiful one, picturesque and
striking. I reached the museum with its Greek vases, statuettes, and coins found in the vicinity. While I was looking at
them the children still stood out in the sun, waiting for me
to bring them quinine."

Where should my sister put up? The lame goat-killer had
received an answer from Naples. They weren't anxious to rent
the house, but they might let me have a room or two at the
very high price, for which they apologized, of fifty lire a
month. Lodgings in the back country, they said, were at a
premium, because people were expecting war to be declared
and they feared a bombardment from the British fleet. The
owners, or their friends, might take refuge in Gagliano. Meanwhile I had lost my enthusiasm for this crumbling and
romantic dwelling, which I began to think was really not fit
to live in. The student from Pisa, the political prisoner whom
I had seen fetching his dinner from the wall, sent word to me

through a peasant that in a few days the rooms would be free that he had taken for his mother and sister, the schoolteachers. They had come to pay him a visit, but because they stayed in the house most of the time I had not seen them about. He could not afford to keep the rooms for himself, and as soon as they were gone I could move in. The lame man and Donna Caterina both approved. Meanwhile my sister was obliged to share the widow's spare room with me and to make acquaintance there with the insect life of Lucania. After what she had seen of the caves of Matera she swore that this melancholy room was a palace, and fortunately neither the tax collector nor any other visitor came during the nights she was there.

My sister's visit was quite an event; the gentry turned out to welcome her and Donna Caterina confided to her the details of her liver complaint and her cooking secrets, and treated her with extreme kindness. A lady from the North, so simple in her ways and a doctor to boot; they had never seen the like of her, and they were anxious to make a favorable impression. The peasants accepted her more naturally. Many of them had been in America; they were not surprised to see a woman doctor and of course they took full advantage of her professional status.

Hitherto they had thought of me as a sort of man from Mars, the only one of my species, and the discovery that I had blood connections here on earth seemed somehow to fill in their picture of me in a manner that pleased them. The sight of me with my sister tapped one of their deepest feelings: that of blood relationship, which was all the more intense since they had so little attachment to either religion or the State. It was not that they venerated family relationship as a social, legal, or sentimental tie, but rather that they cherished an occult and sacred sense of communality. A unifying web, not only of family ties (a first cousin was often as close as a brother), but of the acquired and symbolic kinship called *comparaggio*, ran throughout the village. Those who pledged friendship to each other on the midsummer night of June 23 and thus became *compari di San Giovanni* were even closer than brothers; their choosing and the ritual initiation they went through made them members of the same blood group and within the group there was a sacred tie which forbade intermarriage. This fraternal tie, then, was the strongest there was among them.

Toward evening, when my sister and I walked arm in arm along the main street, the peasants beamed at us from their houses; the women greeted us and covered us with benedictions: "Blessed is the womb that bore you!" they called out to us from the doorways; "Blessed the breasts that suckled you!" Toothless old creatures looked up from their knitting to mumble proverbs: "A wife is one thing, but a sister's something more!" "Sister and brother, all to one another." Luisa, with her rational, city-bred way of looking at things, never got over their strange enthusiasm for the simple fact that I had a sister.

But what surprised and shocked her most was that no one had any wish to improve the village. She had a constructive temperament, sanguine, as the ancients would have it, "solar," the astrologists would call it, and because her vigorous kindness would brook no delay she spent her time talking to me of what might be done and setting forth practical plans for helping the peasants of Gagliano and the children of Matera: hospitals, homes, a campaign against malaria, schools, public works, government doctors, and perhaps volunteers, a nation-wide drive for the benefit of these villages, and so on. She herself would gladly devote her time to a cause that seemed to her so worthy; there was no time to be lost; something must be done. She was quite right and what she suggested was reasonable and fair, but things in this part of the world are a good deal more complex than they appear to the clear-thinking mind of a good man or woman.

The four days of my sister's visit were soon over. When the mechanic's small car bore her away in a cloud of dust, around the curve behind the cemetery, the world of creative activity and cultural values, of which I too had once been a part and which, while she was with me, had put in a momentary reappearance, seemed to melt away, as if it were sucked back into time, in the faraway cloud of memory.

Chapter Eleven

I WAS LEFT WITH BOOKS, medicines, and good advice, and all of them proved useful almost immediately. Quite apart from those that are contagious a number of the most dissimilar diseases seem to travel in cycles. For weeks there may be no illness at all or only very light cases; then, when something serious arrives it is certain to be followed by more of the same kind.

One such period, the first since I had been in Gagliano, came soon after my sister had gone away; there was a whole series of difficult and dangerous cases which frightened me considerably. Every illness, indeed, as I met with it here, had an acute and fatal aspect, quite different from what I had been accustomed to see in the orderly rows of beds at the University Medical Clinic of Turin. Perhaps it was the chronic anemia of those long afflicted with malaria, or undernourishment, or the lack of stamina and the passive resignation characteristic of the peasants, but, whatever the reason may have been, from the very first days of a given illness the most varied symptoms piled up, while the patient's face had the drawn expression of final agony. I was perpetually astonished to see cases that any good doctor would have branded as hopeless improve and recover with the simplest kind of care. It seemed as if some strange sort of luck were with me.

At this time I went to see the priest. He was subject to intestinal hemorrhages, but, misanthropic as he was, he said nothing and continued to walk about the village without paying them the least attention. Don Cosimino, the kindly postmaster, the only friend of the old man, who spent hours in the post office reciting his epigrams, begged me to pay him a friendly visit and at the same time see if there was anything I could do for him.

Don Trajella lived with his mother in one large room, a sort of cavern, in a dark alley not far from the church. When I went in I found them both at dinner; between them they had but one plate and one glass. The plate was full of badly cooked beans, the staple of their meal; sitting at one corner of the uncovered table, mother and son took turns dipping into them with old tin spoons. At the back of the room two cots, separated by a tattered green curtain, were still unmade. Piles of books were stacked up in disorder against the walls, with chickens perched on top of them. Other chickens flew and ran about the room, which had not been dusted for who knows how long and had the suffocating smell of a chicken-house. The priest showed a liking for me and seemed to consider me, along with Don Cosimino, one of the few people he could talk to because we were not among his enemies. He greeted me cordially, and with a smile on his keen, sorrowful face. He introduced me to his mother, begging me to excuse her lack of response, because she was somewhat old and weak, *vetula et infirma*. Then he hastened to offer me wine, which I had to accept in order not to hurt his feelings, in spite of the fact that it was in the glass that his mother and he must have used for years without washing, at least to judge from the black, greasy crust around the rim. Don Trajella had no servant and by now he was so accustomed to the filth that he no longer noticed it. After we had spoken of his affliction he noticed that I was looking curiously at his books and said:

"What do you expect? In a place like this there's no point in reading. I had some fine books. Can you see? There are some rare editions among them. When I came here the swine that carried my books smeared them with tar, just to annoy me. I lost all desire to open them and I left them just like that on the floor; they've lain there for years."

I went closer. The books were covered with a layer of dust and chicken dirt; here and there on the parchment bindings there were spots of tar, left from the old outrage. I picked up some of them at random; they were old seventeenth-century volumes of theology, casuistry, lives of the saints and fathers of the Church, and the Latin poets. Before the chickens had roosted on it he must have had the library of a cultivated and enlightened priest. Among the books were some crushed and tarred pamphlets written by Don Trajella himself: historical and apologetical studies of San Calogero of Avila.

"He is a little known Spanish saint," said the priest. "I made a series of paintings at that time, *temporibus illis*, of the various episodes of his life."

I insisted that he show them to me and finally he hauled them out from under his bed, where, he said, he had left them untouched since the day of his arrival. They were done in tempera in a popular style, but they were effective, well-composed pictures with a multitude of tiny, carefully drawn figures, representing the birth, life, miracles, death, and glory of the saint. He also brought out from under the bed some painted baroque wood and terra cotta statuettes of angels and saints which he had modeled with considerable facility after the style of the seventeenth-century Neapolitan crèche. I congratulated him as a fellow artist.

"I've done nothing ever since I've been here among the heathen, *in partibus infidelium*, bringing the sacraments of Mother Church, as they say, to these heretics who will have none of them. Once upon a time such things amused me. But here they're quite impossible. There's no point in doing anything in this place. Have another glass of wine, Don Carlo."

While I looked for a pretext to stave off another glassful, bitterer than any conceivable philter, the old mother, who had sat in her chair as quietly as if she were not there, suddenly stood up, shouting and waving her arms. The chickens took fright and began to flutter about the room, on the beds, the books, and the table. Don Trajella tried to chase them off the sheets, railing the while at "this Godforsaken country!" The chickens cackled louder than ever in stupid terror, raising clouds of dust which shone in the beam of sunlight coming in through the narrow aperture of the half-raised window. I took advantage of the confusion to make my way out, amid flapping wings and billowing black skirts.

Don Trajella's predecessor (to my good luck, as it turned out) had been quite a different sort, a fat, rich, gay priest, somewhat of a rake, known for his excellent table and the number of children he had begotten. He died, so rumor had it, of overeating. The house where I took up my abode a few days later, after the family of the student prisoner from Pisa had gone, had been built by him and it was, in a manner of speaking, the only civilized house in the village. He had built it close by the old church, the Madonna of the Angels, and after this had collapsed in the landslide, it was left close to the edge of the precipice. There were three rooms, one after the other. One entered the house, from an alley to the right of the main street, through the kitchen, next came a room where I put my bed, and then a larger room, with five windows, which I used for a living room and studio. From a door leading out of the studio four stone steps went down to a small garden, with a fig tree in the center, closed at the other end by a small iron gate. There was a little balcony off the bedroom and a stair up the side of the house to a terrace covering the whole roof, with a view that swept the horizon. The house was a modest one, economically built and far from beautiful; it had no character, neither the aristocracy of a noble ruin nor the poverty of a peasant hut, but abounded in the stuffy mediocrity of ecclesiastical taste. The studio and the terrace had the colored tile floors to be found in many a country sacristy, whose geometrical design was distasteful to me because it constantly drew my eyes away from my painting. The colors of the cheap tiles ran whenever they were wet and Barone, who loved to roll on the floor, would turn from a white dog into a rose-colored one. But the plaster of the walls was in good condition, the doors were varnished in blue, and there were green shutters.

Most important of all, in compensation for even the worst defect, the late priest's comfort-loving spirit had endowed the house with one priceless treasure: a toilet, without running water, of course, but none the less a real toilet, equipped with a porcelain seat. It was the only toilet in the village, and probably there was not another one within a radius of fifty miles. In the houses of the well-to-do there were still ancient seats of monumental proportions in carved wood, miniature thrones with an air of authority about them. I was told, although I never saw them with my own eyes, that there existed pairs of matrimonial seats, side by side, for couples so devoted that they could not endure even the briefest separation. The poor, of course, had nothing, and this lack made for strange customs. In Grassano, at almost regular hours, in the early morning and again in the evening, windows were surreptitiously opened and the wrinkled hands of old women were to be seen emptying the contents of chamber pots into the street. These were "black magic" or bad luck hours. In Gagliano the ceremony was neither as widespread nor as regular; so precious a fertilizer for the fields could not be wasted.

The complete absence of this simple apparatus in the region created almost ineradicable habits, which, entwined with other familiar ways of doing things, came to possess an almost poetic and sentimental character. Lasala, the carpenter, an alert "American," who had been mayor of Grassano many years before and who kept in the depths of the enormous radio-gramophone he had brought back with him from New York along with recordings of Caruso and of the arrival of the transatlantic flier, De Pinedo, in America, some speeches commemorating the murdered Matteotti, told me this story. A group of immigrants from Grassano used to meet every Sunday for an outing to the country after their hard week's work in New York . . .

"There were eight or ten of us: a doctor, a druggist, some tradesmen, a hotel waiter, and a few workers, all of us from the same town and acquainted with each other since we were children. Life is depressing there among the skyscrapers, where there's every possible convenience, elevators, revolving doors, subways, endless streets and buildings, but never a bit of green earth. Homesickness used to get the better of us. On Sundays we took a train for miles and miles in search of some open country. When finally we reached a deserted spot, we were all as happy as if a great weight had been lifted from our shoulders. And beneath a tree, all of us together would let down our trousers . . . What joy! We could feel the fresh air and all of nature around us. It wasn't like those American toilets, shiny and all alike. We felt like boys again, as if we were back in Grassano; we were happy, we laughed and we breathed for a moment the air of home. And when we had finished we shouted together: '*Viva l'Italia!*' The words came straight from our hearts."

My new house had the advantage of being at the lower end of the village, out of sight of the mayor and his acolytes; at last I should be able to take a walk without running at every step into the same people and the same conversation. The gentry hereabouts, when they meet someone on the street, do not say: "How are you?" Instead they greet him with the question: "What did you have to eat today?" If their interlocutor is a peasant he answers silently with a gesture of one hand brought up to the level of his face, turning slowly on its own axis, the thumb and little finger spread out and the other fingers closed, which means: "Little or nothing." If he is a man of position he lists in detail the sorry dishes of his dinner and asks after the fare of his friend. Then, if no local feud or intrigue engages their passions, the conversation continues for some time with this exchange of gastronomic confidences.

Now I should be able to stick my head out without ramming my nose into the enormous stomach (so enormous as to take up the whole street) of Don Gennaro, the local constable and dog-catcher, the factotum and spy of the mayor, who kept an eagle eye on the whereabouts of political prisoners and an ear cocked to hear what the peasants were saying. Perhaps he was not a bad fellow at heart, but he was obsequious toward the authorities and particularly Don Luigi; he stubbornly enforced strange edicts aimed at regulating pig and dog traffic, and pinned fines, for no good reason, on women who had no money to pay them.

Above all, the house was a place where I could be alone and work. I hastened, then, to take leave of the widow and to begin a new life in my permanent home. The house belonged to the priest's heir, Don Rocco Macioppi, an unpretentious, middle-aged landlord, agreeable, ceremonious, somewhat of a church-mouse in glasses, and to his niece, Donna Maria Maddalena, an old maid of twenty-five, who had been educated in a convent at Potenza, and was pale, anemic, and given to sighing. It was agreed that they should keep the use of the garden for growing lettuce, and would enter it by the outside gate, but that I should be free to walk there at will. The house was nearly empty, but the owner and the lame man, who was his friend, supplied me with the necessary furniture. I brought with me several things I had just sent for: a large easel and the armchair that went with it, the one for painting and the other for looking at my pictures while they were in progress. I was attached to both of these to the point of not being able to get on without them; both had followed me on my wanderings about the world.

There was also a box of recently arrived books, which necessitated a special visit from the mayor and the sergeant. Don Luigi sent word to me that he must be present when I opened the box in order to make sure there were no forbidden items and, with the assistance of his right-hand man, he examined my volumes one by one. He did this, of course, with the air of a man of learning, who cannot be surprised by anything, wreathed in understanding smiles and content with both his wisdom and his authority. Of forbidden books there were none. But there was, for instance, an ordinary edition of Montaigne.

"This is French, isn't it?" exclaimed the mayor, with a wink intended to warn me against trying to pull the wool over his eyes.

"Yes, Don Luigi, but the writer is an old-style Frenchman!"

"Of course, Montaigne, the French Revolution, and all that. . . ."

I tried very hard to convince him that there was nothing subversive in these essays, but the schoolmaster knew what he was talking about and smiled smugly in order to make it quite clear that if he let me keep this book, which it was his duty to confiscate, it was out of sheer benevolence and sympathy for a fellow-savant.

The house was in order and my belongings in place. Now I had to tackle the problem of finding a woman to do my cleaning, fetch water from the fountain, and cook my meals. My landlord, the goat-killer, Donna Caterina, and her nieces were all in agreement: "There's only one woman that will do for you. You mustn't take anyone else!" And Donna Caterina said:

"I'll talk to her and get her to come. She respects me and she'll not say no."

The problem was more difficult than I had imagined. Not because there weren't plenty of women at Gagliano, and dozens of them eager for light work and good pay. But I lived alone, without a wife or mother or sister, and it was not fitting that a woman should enter my house unaccompanied. A very old and severe custom, which formed the basis of the relationship between the sexes, forbade it. The peasants consider love, or sexual attraction, so powerful a force of nature that no amount of will-power can resist it. If a man and a woman are alone in a sheltered spot, no power on earth can prevent their embrace; good intentions and chastity are of no avail. If, by chance, nothing comes of their propinquity, it is just the same as if something had come of it, because the mere fact of their being together implies love-making. So great is the power of the god of love and so simple the impulse to obey him that there is no question of a code of sexual morals or even of social disapproval for an illicit affair. There were many unmarried mothers, and they were neither snubbed nor pointed at with scorn; at worst they might have difficulty finding a husband within the village and have to look elsewhere or be content with a fellow with a limp or some other physical shortcoming. But since there is no moral curb on unbridled desire, custom intervenes and staves off the occasion of sin. No woman can talk to a man except in the presence of others, particularly if the man is unmarried. This taboo is extremely rigid; the most innocent violation is tantamount to sin. The rule applies to all women, because love is no respecter of age.

I once attended a grandmother, a seventy-five-year-old peasant woman, Maria Rosano, with clear blue eyes in a kindly face. She had a heart disease whose symptoms were very serious indeed and she felt extremely weak.

"I'll not get up from this bed again, Doctor. My time has come," she said. Because I felt that luck was with me I assured her of the contrary. One day, to cheer her up, I said:

"You'll get well; never fear. You'll get up from this bed without any assistance. A month from now you'll be well, and you'll come, quite alone, to my house at the other end of the village, to pay me a visit."

The old woman did recover and a month later I heard a knock at my door. Maria had remembered my words and had come to thank and bless me, with her arms full of presents, dried figs, sausages, and homemade cakes. She was a pleasant soul, full of common sense and motherliness; there was wisdom in her words and a patient and understanding optimism

100

in her wrinkled old face. I thanked her for the presents and tried to engage her in conversation, but I soon saw that the old woman was ill at ease; she stood first on one foot and then on the other and glanced at the door as if she were screwing up her courage to move toward it.

At first I did not understand, then I realized that she had come alone. The other women who came to see me professionally or to call me to the house had always a friend with them or at least a child, the company of the latter signifying a bow in the direction of custom, while in reality reducing it to nothing more than symbol. I suspected, then, that here lay the reason for Maria's discomfort, and she admitted to the truth of my suspicion. She considered me her benefactor and savior and she would gladly have died for me, because I had saved not only herself, an old woman with one foot in the grave, but her favorite granddaughter too, from a bad attack of pneumonia. And I had said that she should come, quite alone, to pay me a visit when she was well. I meant, of course, that she would not need a helping hand, but she had taken my words literally and had not dared to disobey. She had made a real sacrifice for my sake in letting no one come with her, and now she was upset because, in spite of her obviously innocent intentions, she had violated custom. I couldn't help laughing, and she laughed with me, but she said that custom was older than either of us, and went away content.

The rule does not exist that can stand up against necessity or overwhelming passion. Hence custom, in this instance, was reduced to a mere formality, but the formality was none the less respected. Still the countryside was wide, life was fraught with unexpected turns, and intriguing chaperones and accommodating friends were not hard to come by. Behind their veils the women were like wild beasts. They thought of nothing but love-making, in the most natural way in the world, and they spoke of it with a license and simplicity of language that were astonishing. When you went by them on the street their black eyes stared at you, with a slanting downward glance as if to measure your virility, and behind your back you could hear them pass whispered judgments on your hidden charms. If you turned around they buried their faces in their hands and peered at you between their fingers. No real feeling went with this atmosphere of desire that oozed out of their eyes and seemed to permeate the village, except for one of enslavement to fate, to an inescapable higher power. Their love was blended, not with hope or enthusiasm, but with resignation. The occasion was fleeting and it should not be passed by; understanding was swift and wordless.

All that people say about the people of the South, things I once believed myself: the savage rigidity of their morals, their Oriental jealousy, the fierce sense of honor leading to crimes of passion and revenge, all these are but myths. Perhaps they existed a long time ago and something of them is left in the way of a stiff conventionality. But emigration has changed the picture. The men have gone and the women have taken over. Many a woman's husband is in America. For a year, or even two, he writes to her, then he drops out of her ken, perhaps he forms other family ties; in any case he disappears and never comes back. The wife waits for him a year, or even two; then some opportunity arises and a baby is the result. A great part of the children are illegitimate, and the mother holds absolute sway. Gagliano has twelve hundred inhabitants, and there are two thousand men from Gagliano in America. Grassano has five thousand inhabitants and almost the same number have emigrated. In the villages the women outnumber the men, and the father's identity is no longer so strictly important; honor is dissociated from paternity, because a matriarchal regime prevails.

During the day, when the peasants are far away in the fields, the villages are left to the women, queen bees reigning over a teeming mass of children. Babies are adored and spoiled by their mothers, who tremble for them at the slightest thing wrong, nurse them for years, and never leave them, carrying them wrapped in black shawls on their backs or in their arms when they come with jars balanced on their heads from the fountain. Many of the babies die; the others age prematurely, turn yellow and melancholy with malaria; then they grow up to be men, go to war or to America, or else stay in their native village, where they bear the yoke like dumb animals, every day of the year.

If illegitimate children are no real disgrace to a woman, they are, of course, even less of one to a man. Almost all the priests have children, and no one sees in this fact any dishonor reflected upon their calling. If God does not take them to Himself when they are little, they are sent to school at Potenza or Melfi. The letter-carrier at Grassano, a spry old man with a slight limp, and a fine handle-bar moustache, was renowned and revered in the village because, like Priam, he was said to have fifty children. Twenty-two or twenty-three of them belonged to his two or three wives; the rest, scattered about the village and its surroundings, many of them perhaps legendary, were attributed to him, but he paid no attention to them and in many cases appeared to ignore their existence. He was called "King," on account of either his surpassing virility or his regal moustache, and his children, of course, were known as "princes."

The matriarchal structure of society, the primitive and direct approach to love, and the want of balance between the sexes following upon emigration had none the less to combat a residue of family feeling, the strong consciousness of blood relationship, and age-old customs tending to separate men and women. The only women who could come to work in my house were those in some way exempt from the general rule, who had many children of unidentified fathers, who, although they had not embraced prostitution (no such trade existed in the village), displayed a tendency to be free and easy, and who were concerned with all that pertained to love, above all the means of obtaining it. In a word, witches.

There were at least twenty such women at Gagliano, but, Donna Caterina told me, they were too dirty and disorderly, or they were unable to keep house decently, or they had land to attend to, or they were already employed by one of the leading families . . .

"There's only one who will do for you; she's clean and honest and knows how to cook, and then the house where you live is one where she feels at home. She lived there for years with the priest, until he died, God bless him!"

I decided to go to see her, and she accepted my offer and entered my service. Giulia Venere, called Giulia of Sant' Arcangelo, because she was born in that white village beyond the Agri River, was forty-one years old, and she had had, between normal births and abortions, seventeen pregnancies, brought about by fifteen different men. Her first child was born of her husband during the last war; then he had gone to America, taking the child with him and somewhere in that vast continent he dropped out of sight and was never heard from again. The other children had come later; she had had twins, stillborn, by the priest. Almost all her brood died young; I never saw but two of them. One was a twelve-year-old girl, who lived with a family of shepherds in a near-by village and came occasionally to see her mother, a sort of wild little goat with black eyes, dark skin, and unruly black hair falling over her forehead, who maintained a shy and resentful silence, not answering when she was spoken to and looking as if she would run away any minute. The other, her youngest, was a two-year-old boy called Nino, a fat, healthy baby whom Giulia always carried with her under her shawl; and who his father was I never knew.

Giulia was a tall and shapely woman with a waist as slender as that of an amphora between her well-developed chest and hips. In her youth she must have had a solemn and barbaric beauty. Her face was wrinkled with age and yellowed by malaria, but there were traces of former charm in its sharp, straight lines, like those of a classical temple which has lost the marbles that adorned it but kept its shape and proportions. A small head, in the shape of a lengthened oval, covered with a veil, rose above her impressively large and erect body. Her forehead was straight and high, half hidden by a lock of smooth black hair; her almond-shaped, opaque, black eyes had whites with blue and brown veins in them like those of dogs. Her nose was thin and long, slightly hooked; her wide mouth with thin, pale lips, somewhat turned down at the corners in bitterness, opened when she laughed, over powerful, sparkling, wolflike teeth. Her face as a whole had a strongly archaic character, not classical in the Greek or Roman sense, but stemming from an antiquity more mysterious and more cruel which had sprung always from the same ground, and which was unrelated to man, but linked with the soil and its everlasting animal deities. There were mingled in it cold sensuality, hidden irony, natural cruelty, impenetrable ill-humor and an immense passive power, all these bound together in a stern, intelligent and malicious expression. In billowing veils and a wide, short skirt, firmly planted on legs as long and sturdy as the trunks of trees, her large body moved slowly and with harmony and balance, bearing proudly and erectly on its monumental and maternal base the small, black head of a serpent.

Giulia came to my house gladly, as if she were a queen returning, after an absence, to visit one of her favorite provinces. She had lived so many years and borne so many children there; she had reigned over the priest's kitchen and his bed, and he had given her the long gold earrings she was wearing. She knew all the secrets of the house: the chimney with a bad draught, the window that wouldn't open, the position of every nail driven into the walls. In the old days the house had been full of furniture, stocks of food, wine, preserves, and every kind of abundance. Now it was empty; there were only a bed, a few chairs and a kitchen table. There was no stove, and food had to be cooked over the open fire. But Giulia knew how to obtain whatever was necessary, where to find coal and wood and the loan of a barrel to hold water until a peddler should come through the village.

Giulia knew everyone and everything that went on; from her nothing in Gagliano was hidden; she was acquainted with the most intimate affairs of every man and woman in the village, and the hidden springs of all their actions. She seemed to be hundreds of years old and nothing escaped her. Hers was not the proverbial kindly wisdom of an old woman, linked to an impersonal tradition, nor the gossip of a busybody; it was a cold, passive awareness, where life was reflected pitilessly and without any moral judgment; there was neither blame nor compassion in her ambiguous smile. She was, like the beasts, a spirit of the earth; she had no fear of time, or work, or man. Like all the women in these parts, who do the work of men, she could carry the heaviest weights. She took a barrel that held over seven gallons to the fountain and brought it back full on her head, without even steadying it with her hands which were busy holding her child, clambering over the stones of the steep street with the nimble agility of a goat. She built a fire peasant-fashion with great economy of wood, lighting the logs at one end and pulling them closer together as they burned. On this fire, with the meager resources of the village, she made the tastiest dishes. She cooked goats' heads in a covered earthenware pot, over the embers, after she had dipped the brains in a raw egg and marjoram. With the tripe she made a dish called in dialect *gnemurielli* rolling it like a skein of thread around a piece of liver or fat and a laurel leaf and roasting it on a spit directly over the flames. The smell of burning meat and the gray smoke spread through the house and onto the street, heralding a barbaric treat. Giulia was a mistress of the art of making philters, and young girls came to her for advice on how to prepare their love potions. She could cure illness with the repetition of spells and she could even bring about the death of anyone she chose by uttering terrible incantations.

Giulia had a house of her own, not far from mine, lower down, near the Mound of the Madonna of the Angels. There she slept at night with the most recent of her lovers, the local barber, a young albino with the pink eyes of a rabbit. Early in the morning with her baby she knocked at my door; she went to fetch water, lit the fire, and cooked my dinner. She left in the afternoon and I had to prepare my own supper. Giulia came and went at will, but she had none of the airs of a mistress of the house. She understood that times had changed and that I was quite a different sort from the old priest; perhaps I was even more mysterious to her than she could be to me. She thought that I was endowed with great powers and, in her passive way, she was satisfied. Cold, impassable, and earthy creature that she was, this peasant witch was an excellent servant.

Thus came to an end the first period of my stay at Gagliano, which I spent in the higher part of the village, in the widow's house. Now, content with my new solitude, I stretched out on my terrace and watched the shadow of the clouds drift over the wastes of clay, like a ship on the sea. From the room below I could hear Giulia's steps and the dog's barking. These two strange beings, the witch and Barone, were from now on to be my everyday companions.

Chapter Twelve

IT WAS SEPTEMBER AND THE heat was giving way to promises of autumn. The wind came from a different direction; it no longer brought with it the burning breath of the desert, but had a vague smell of the sea. The fiery streaks of the sunset lingered for hours over the mountains of Calabria and the air was filled with bats and crows. From my terrace the sky seemed immense, covered with constantly changing clouds; I felt as if I were on the roof of the world or on the deck of a ship anchored in a petrified ocean. Toward the east the piled-up huts of Lower Gagliano cut off the rest of the village from view, because it was built along the crest of an irregular ridge and the whole of it could never be seen at one time; behind their yellowish roofs appeared the edge of a mountain above the cemetery, and beyond this one could feel, without seeing, the dip of a valley beneath the sky. At my left, toward the south, there was the same view as from the palace I had looked at when I first started my house-hunting: endless stretches of clay, with scattered villages standing out as white spots, as far as the invisible sea. At my left, toward the north, the landslide tumbled into the ravine; the hills on the opposite side were bare of vegetation and at the bottom wound the path where I could see the peasants, no bigger than ants, going to and from their fields. Giulia was surprised that at such a distance I could tell the men of Gagliano from those of other villages and peasants from peddlers. For all my good eyesight I did, just as she thought, have recourse to magic. The secret lay simply in my observation of their ways of walking. The peasants walked quite stiffly, without moving their arms. Whenever I saw one of the black dots in the valley advance with a swinging or rocking motion, almost that of a dance, I knew that it was someone from the city. Soon the trumpet of the grave-digger and town crier would announce his arrival and call the women to buy his wares.

In front of me, toward the west, behind the big green and gray leaves of the fig tree in the garden and the roofs of the last peasants' huts on the slope of the ravine, rose the Mound of the Madonna of the Angels. It was an elevation all hollows and bulges, with a little stubby grass on its most gently rising side, like a human bone, the knob of a giant femur, which still had clinging to it shreds of desiccated flesh. To the left of the Mound, for a long way, until far below, toward the Agri Valley, where the terrain flattened out in a place called the Bog, there was a succession of hillocks, holes, eroded cones marked with stripes, natural caves, ditches, and pieces of rising ground, all of the same white clay, as if the whole earth had died and all that was left under the sun was a whitened skeleton washed by many waters. Behind this desolate collection of bones, above the malaria-ridden river, was Gaglianello and beyond this lay the banks of the Agri. On the first line of gray hills beyond the river rose Giulia's village, Sant' Arcangelo, and behind it were other tiers of hills, bluer in color, with barely perceived villages on their slopes, and still farther away the Albanian settlements on the foothills of Mount Pollino, and the Calabrian Mountains which filled in the horizon.

A little above and to the left of Sant' Arcangelo, halfway up a hill, was a white church. Here the people of the valley came in pilgrimage; it was the center of much devotion, possessing a miraculous Madonna. In this church were preserved the horns of a dragon which in ancient times had infested the region. Everyone in Gagliano had been to see these horns, but unfortunately I could not fulfil my wish to do so. The dragon, they told me, once lived in a cave near the river; it devoured the peasants, carried off their daughters, filled the land with its pestiferous breath, and destroyed the crops, until life in Sant' Arcangelo became impossible. The peasants tried to defend themselves but they were helpless before the beast's monstrous power. Brought to despair and obliged to scatter among the hills like animals, they finally decided to seek aid from the strongest lord of the land, Prince Colonna of Stigliano.

The prince came, armed to the teeth, on horseback; he went to the dragon's cave and challenged him to come out and fight. But the monster's resources were great, from the flames pouring out of his jaws to his widespread batlike wings, and the prince's sword was of no avail. At a certain moment the hero felt his courage weaken and he was about to flee or fall into the clutches of the dragon, when the Madonna appeared to him, clad in blue, and said with a smile: "Take heart, Prince Colonna!" Then she drew to one side and stayed leaning against one wall of the cave to watch the struggle. The prince's ardor was increased a hundredfold and he fought so well that the dragon fell dead at his feet. He cut off the head, detached the horns and built this church to house them forever.

When the terror was gone and the countryside was free, the people of Sant' Arcangelo went back to their homes, and so did those of Noepoli and Senise, who had likewise taken refuge in the hills. The prince had then to be rewarded for the service he had done them. In those days the nobles, for all their chivalry and love of glory and the protection given them by the Madonna, did not put themselves out for nothing. And so the people of all the villages made safe by the death of the dragon took counsel together. Those of Noepoli and Senise proposed giving the prince feudal rights over some of their land, but those of Sant' Arcangelo, who are even today reputed to be astute to the point of avarice, made another suggestion: "The dragon," they said, "came out of the river. Let the prince take the river, then, and be the lord of the waters." Their suggestion prevailed; the Agri was offered to Colonna and he accepted it. The peasants of Sant' Arcangelo thought they had made a profitable deal and defrauded their savior, but in this they were mistaken. The waters of the Agri served to irrigate the fields, and from that day on they had to pay the prince and his heirs for ever and ever for their use. This was the origin of a feudal privilege which lasted until the second half of the last century. I do not know whether there are still direct heirs of the medieval knight and whether they still claim a right to the waters of the Agri. A friend of mine, Colonna the orchestra leader, who is descended from a collateral line of the princes of Stigliano and has a right to bear their title, when I told him this story years later, did not even know where Stigliano was, much less anything about the dragon, one of his family glories. But the peasants, who have paid tribute for centuries and who still make pilgrimages to gaze at the monster's horns, remember the dragon, and the prince, and the Madonna.

There is nothing strange in the fact that there were dragons in these parts during the Middle Ages. (The peasants and Giulia used to say: "A long time ago, more than a hundred years, long before the brigands . . .") Nor would it be strange if dragons were to appear again today before the startled eyes of the country people. Anything is possible, where the ancient deities of the shepherds, the ram and the lamb, run every day over the familiar paths, and there is no definite boundary line between the world of human beings and that of animals or even monsters. There are many strange creatures at Gagliano who have a dual nature. A middle-aged peasant woman, married and having children, with nothing out of the ordinary about her appearance, was the daughter of a cow. So the village said, and she herself confirmed it. The older people clearly remembered her cow mother, who followed her everywhere when she was a child, mooing to her and licking her with a rough tongue. This did not alter the fact that she had also had a human mother, who had been dead for many years. No one saw any contradiction in this dual birth, and the woman herself, whom I knew personally, lived quietly and happily, like both her mothers, for all her animal heredity.

Some people take on this mixture of human and bestial natures only on particular occasions. Sleepwalkers become wolves, or werewolves, and their identity is completely lost in that of the animal. There were some of these at Gagliano and they went out on winter nights to join the real wolves, their brothers. "They go out by night," Giulia told me, "while they are still men; then they turn into wolves and they gather with their fellows around the fountain. You have to be very careful when they come home. When one knocks at the door the first time his wife mustn't open. If she did she would see her husband while he was still a wolf and he would eat her up and run off to the woods, never to be seen again. When he knocks for the second time she still mustn't open, for she would see him with a man's body and a wolf's head. Only at the third knock can she let him in; by that time the change is complete, the wolf has disappeared and he is the same man he was before. Never, never open the door before they have knocked three times. They must have time to change their shape and also to lose the fierce wolflike look in their eyes and the memory of their visit to the animal world. Later they remember nothing at all."

At times the dual nature is horrible and terrifying, as in the case of these werewolves. Yet it carries with it a mysterious attraction and creates a kind of respect, as if it had something divine about it. Everyone in the village instinctively had a feeling of this kind for my dog. They looked on him not as an ordinary canine, but as an unusual being, different from the rest of his species, and worthy of particular regard. Indeed, I myself always thought that there was something childishly angelic or diabolical about him and that the peasants were not altogether wrong to see in him a duality which called for worship. Even his origin was mysterious. He was found on a train going from Naples to Taranto, with a sign hung around his neck saying: "My name is Barone. Whoever finds me, take good care of me." No one ever knew where he came from; perhaps from a big city; he might even be the son of a king. Railway employees took him and kept him for some time at the station at Tricarico, and the men there handed him on to the station employees at Grassano. The mayor of Grassano saw the dog, had the railway men turn it over to him, and took it into his household of children. But the dog made too much noise so he gave him to his brother, the secretary of the Fascist peasants' union, who took him everywhere he went in the surrounding country. Everyone at Grassano knew Barone and considered him quite out of the ordinary.

One day, while I was living there all alone, I happened to say to some of my peasant and tradesmen friends that I should like to have a dog to keep me company. The next morning they brought me a puppy, one of the usual yellow hunting dogs. I kept him for a while, but I didn't care for him; I couldn't seem to housebreak him and he dirtied my room. Finally I came to the conclusion that he didn't have much sense and I gave him back, resolving to drop my fancy for a dog. But when I received sudden orders to go to Gagliano, these good people, who showed considerable fondness for me and were as afflicted as if some undeserved misfortune had overtaken them, wanted to give me something that would be a constant reminder that there were good Christian souls at Grassano who wished me well. They remembered the desire that I had by then forgotten and decided to give me another dog. No dog was good enough but the famous Barone, and Barone should be mine. They made such a to-do that they persuaded his master to give him up; then they washed and brushed him and got him a collar, muzzle, and leash. Antonino Roselli, the young barber and flute-player, whose dream it was to follow me to the ends of the earth in the capacity of a private secretary, clipped him like a young lion, leaving his hair long in front and shaving him behind, with a thick clump left at the tip of his tail. The wild Barone, thus civilized, immaculate, perfumed, and completely disguised, was given to me the day before I left as a remembrance of the fair town of Grassano.

In this beautified rig I myself could not tell what breed of dog he was; he looked like a cross between a poodle and a sheep dog. Perhaps he actually was a sheep dog, but of an uncommon strain or mixture, for I never saw another like him. He was of middling size, all white except for black spots at the ends of his ears, which were very long and hung down the side of his face. His face was handsome, like that of a Chinese dragon, terrifying in his moments of anger or when he bared his teeth, but with round almost human hazel eyes that followed my movements without his even turning his head. His expression ranged from tenderness to independence to a certain childish malice. His hair hung down almost to the ground, soft, curly and shiny as silk; his tail which he carried curved and waving in the air like the plume of an Oriental warrior, was as thick as that of a wolf. He was a gay, free, wild creature, affectionate without servility and obedient without forfeiting his liberty, a sort of hobgoblin or familiar spirit, good-natured but elusive. He jumped rather than walked, leaping from one point to another, his ears and skin twitching. He chased butterflies and birds, frightened the goats, picked fights with cats and dogs, and ran all alone through the fields looking up at the clouds, always on the alert, sniffing the air as if he were following the fluttering thread of some innocent supernatural thought, the bounding incarnation of some woodland sprite.

As soon as we arrived in Gagliano everyone stared at my strange companion, and the peasants, who live immersed in animal magic, were immediately aware of his mysterious nature. They had never seen such a beast. In the village there were only wretched, beaten, mongrel hunting dogs and occasionally, following a shepherd and his flock, a fierce sheep dog from the Maremma, his collar bristling with nails to protect him from the wolves. And then my dog was called Barone. In these parts names have a meaning and a magic power; they are not mere empty, conventional syllables, but have a reality all their own and a potential influence. My dog was to the peasants a real "baron," a gentleman, a personage worthy of respect. I owed in no small measure to my dog the cordial and almost admiring attitude I met among the common people. When he went by, jumping madly and barking wildly, the peasants pointed at him and boys shouted: "Look, look! He's half baron and half lion!" They thought of Barone as an heraldic animal, the rampant lion on a nobleman's coat of arms. He was, of course, only a dog, an animal like all the rest, but at the same time he had a dual and mysterious nature. I too loved him for his combination of simplicity and variety. Now he is dead, like my father to whom I gave him, and he lies buried under an almond tree overlooking the sea, in Liguria, that land of mine where I can no longer set foot, because those in power, in their fear of all that is sacred, seem to have discovered that I too have a dual nature and am, like my dog, half baron and half lion.

To the peasants everything has a double meaning. The cow-woman, the werewolf, the lion-baron, and the goat-devil are only notorious and striking examples. People, trees, animals, even objects and words have a double life. Only reason, religion, and history have clear-cut meanings. But our feeling for life itself, for art, language, and love is complex, infinitely so. And in the peasants' world there is no room for reason, religion, and history. There is no room for religion, because to them everything participates in divinity, everything is actually, not merely symbolically, divine: Christ and the goat; the heavens above, and the beasts of the field below; everything is bound up in natural magic. Even the ceremonies of the church become pagan rites, celebrating the existence of inanimate things, which the peasants endow with a soul, and the innumerable earthy divinities of the village.

It was mid-September and a local feast of the Virgin Mary. Since early morning the streets had been crowded with peasants in black suits; there were strangers also, the band from Stigliano and men from Sant' Arcangelo to set off fireworks, with their Roman candles and mortars. The sky was clear, the air light, and every now and then there was a volley of gunfire, as melancholy as the sound of church bells. The peasants, with their gleaming-barreled rifles, were starting the festivities.

In the afternoon, when the heat of the day had subsided, there was a procession, beginning at the church and winding its way through the village. First it went up to the cemetery, then down to the main square and on to the lesser square and the Madonna of the Angels in Lower Gagliano, then back by the same route to the church where it had begun. First in line were boys carrying poles with white sheets and cloths attached to them for banners which they waved in the breeze, then the band-players from Stigliano with their loud and shiny brasses. After them, on a throne supported by two long shafts, which a dozen men at a time took turns in carrying, came the Madonna. She was a paltry papier mâché affair, a copy of the powerful and famous Madonna of Viggiano, with the same black face, and decked out with sumptuous black robes, necklaces, and bracelets. Just behind the Madonna walked Don Trajella with a white surplice over his greasy cassock and his usual weary and bored expression; then the mayor and the sergeant, the gentry, and, bringing up the rear, the women with their fluttering veils, the children, and the peasants. A strong cool breeze had come up, raising clouds of dust and blowing skirts, veils, and banners indiscriminately; perhaps it was bringing the rain so vainly desired and prayed for during months of drought. As the procession went by, two rows of miniature mortars lined up along both sides of the street went off noisily. The powder train was lighted and then the sound of the explosion joined the rifle-fire of the peasants who stood in their doorways to see the procession go by. The popping and crackling were continuous, interrupted only by the sudden detonation of some bigger firing-piece, which swelled in intensity and echoed among the surrounding ravines.

Amid this warlike thundering there was no religious happiness or ecstasy in the people's eyes; instead they seemed prey to a sort of madness, a pagan throwing off of restraint, and a stunned or hypnotized condition; all of them were highly wrought up. The animals ran about wildly, goats leaped, donkeys brayed, dogs barked, children shouted, and women sang. Peasants with baskets of wheat in their hands threw fistfuls of it at the Madonna, so that she might take thought for the harvest and bring them good luck. The grains curved through the air, fell on the paving-stones and bounced up off them with a light noise like that of hail. The black-faced Madonna, in the shower of wheat, among the animals, the gunfire, and the trumpets, was no sorrowful Mother of God, but rather a subterranean deity, black with the shadows of the bowels of the earth, a peasant Persephone or lower-world goddess of the harvest.

Before the doors of some of the houses, where the width of the street permitted, were tables covered with white cloths, like small rustic altars. Here the procession came to a halt, Don Trajella mumbled a blessing or two, and the peasants and their women came forward with offerings. They pinned to the Madonna's robes five and ten lire notes and even dollar bills jealously saved from their labors in America.

Most of them, however, hung garlands of dried figs around her neck or put fruit and eggs at her feet; they ran after her with other gifts when the procession had already moved on and mingled with the throng amid the noise of the trumpets and the shooting and shouting. As the procession advanced, it became more and more crowded and uproarious, until, after it had gone through the entire village, it went back into the church. A few heavy drops of rain fell, but soon the wind swept away the clouds, the storm blew over and calm returned along with the first evening stars. This guaranteed the success of the fireworks. Everyone ate a quick supper and as soon as it was dark the entire village turned out along the edge of the ravine. This was the occasion on which I saw groups of young fellows climb up on the roof of the monumental public toilet in order to get a better view. In honor of the Madonna even we political prisoners were allowed to stay out an hour later than usual.

This was a great feast day, the celebration of the harvest, and the one occasion of the year for fireworks. Three thousand lire were spent on them, and this was a lean year; often it came to five or six thousand, and larger villages, on their feast days, went to even greater expense. Three thousand lire, in Gagliano, was an enormous sum, the total savings of six months, but the people threw it away gladly on fireworks and no one had the slightest regret. Expert pyrotechnicians all over the province had competed for the job; could the villagers have afforded it they would have engaged those of Montemurro or Ferrandina, but they had to content themselves with the men from Sant' Arcangelo, who carried it off very well indeed. Amidst applause and shouts of terror and admiration from the women and children the first Roman candle shot straight up into the star-studded sky, then another and another. There followed pinwheels, Bengal lights, showers of gold and the rest, a splendid show.

It was ten o'clock, time for me to go home. From my terrace, with Barone, who sniffed the air excitedly and barked at every burst of fire, I looked for a long time at the lights, as they rose and fell sputtering on the Mound, and listened to the booming of the explosions. At last twenty giant firecrackers went off in quick succession and there was a final crash ending. I heard footsteps on the street and doors opening and shutting as the crowd scattered. The peasant holiday was over, with its fiery and frenzied excitement. The animals slept, and silence and the empty blackness of the sky hung once more over the darkened village.

Chapter Thirteen

THE RAIN DID NOT COME, EVEN in the following days, in spite of the procession, Don Trajella's prayers, and the high hopes of the peasants. The earth was too hard to be worked and the olives began to dry up on the parched trees, but the black-faced Madonna remained impassive, pitiless and deaf to all appeals, like indifferent Nature. Homage was paid to her in abundance, but it was rather the homage due to power than that offered to charity. The Black Madonna was like the earth; it was in her power to raise up and destroy, but she was no respecter of persons, and appointed the seasons according to an inscrutable plan of her own. To the peasants the Black Madonna was beyond good and evil. She dried up the crops and let them wither away, but at the same time she dispensed food and protection and demanded worship. In every household, tacked up on the wall above the bed, the image of the Black Madonna of Viggiano looked on with expressionless eyes at all the acts of daily life.

The peasants' houses were all alike, consisting of only one room that served as a kitchen, bedroom, and usually as quarters for the barnyard animals as well, unless there happened to be an outhouse, which they described with a dialect word of Greek derivation, *catoico*. On one side of the room was the stove; sticks brought in every day from the fields served as fuel, and the walls and ceiling were blackened with smoke. The only light was that from the door. The room was almost entirely filled by an enormous bed, much larger than an ordinary double bed; in it slept the whole family, father, mother, and children. The smallest children, before they were weaned, that is until they were three or four years old, were kept in little reed cradles or baskets hung from the ceiling just above the bed. When the mother wanted to nurse them she did not have to get out of bed; she simply reached out and pulled the baby down to her breast, then put him back and with one motion of her hand made the basket rock like a pendulum until he had ceased to cry.

Under the bed slept the animals, and so the room was divided into three layers: animals on the floor, people in the bed, and infants in the air. When I bent over a bed to listen to a patient's heart or to give an injection to a woman whose teeth were chattering with fever or who was burning up with malaria, my head touched the hanging cradles, while frightened pigs and chickens darted between my legs.

But what never failed to strike me most of all—and by now I had been in almost every house—were the eyes of the two inseparable guardian angels that looked at me from the wall over the bed. On one side was the black, scowling face, with its large, inhuman eyes, of the Madonna of Viggiano; on the other a colored print of the sparkling eyes, behind gleaming glasses, and the hearty grin of President Roosevelt. I never saw other pictures or images than these: not the King nor the Duce, nor even Garibaldi; no famous Italian of any kind, nor any one of the appropriate saints; only Roosevelt and the Madonna of Viggiano never failed to be present. To see them there, one facing the other, in cheap prints, they seemed the two faces of the power that has divided the universe between them. But here their roles were, quite rightly, reversed. The Madonna appeared to be a fierce, pitiless, mysterious, ancient earth goddess, the Saturnian mistress of this world; the President a sort of all-powerful Zeus, the benevolent and smiling master of a higher sphere. Sometimes a third image formed, along with these two, a trinity: a dollar bill, the last of those brought back from across the sea, or one that had come in the letter of a husband or relative, was tacked up under the Madonna or the President, or else between them, like the Holy Ghost or an ambassador from heaven to the world of the dead.

To the peasants of Lucania Rome means very little; it is the capital of the gentry, the center of a foreign and hostile world. Naples has more right to be their capital, and in some ways it is; it is the capital of poverty. Those who live there have pale faces and feverish eyes; on sweltering summer days you can see half-dressed women asleep at tables, through the open doors of the one-story houses of the poor along the steep alleys off the Toledo. But at Naples, for a long time, there has been no king, and the peasants go there only to embark for other shores. The Kingdom of Naples has perished, and the kingdom of the hopelessly poor is not of this world. Their other world is America. Even America, to the peasants, has a dual nature. It is a land where a man goes to work, where he toils and sweats for his daily bread, where he lays aside a little money only at the cost of endless hardship and privation, where he can die and no one will remember him.

At the same time, and with no contradiction in terms, it is an earthly paradise and the promised land.

Yes, New York, rather than Rome or Naples, would be the real capital of the peasants of Lucania, if these men without a country could have a capital at all. And it *is* their capital, in the only way it can be for them, that is as a myth. As a place to work, it is indifferent to them; they live there as they would live anywhere else, like animals harnessed to a wagon, heedless of the street where they must pull it. But as an earthly paradise, Jerusalem the golden, it is so sacred as to be untouchable; a man can only gaze at it, even when he is there on the spot, with no hope of attainment. The peasants who emigrate to America remain just what they always were; many stay there and their children become Americans, but the rest, those who come back twenty years later, are just the same as when they went away. In three months they forget the few words of English they ever learned, slough off the few superficial new habits and are the same peasants they were before, like stones which a rushing stream has long coursed over but which dry out under the first warm rays of the sun. In America they live apart, among themselves; for years they eat nothing but bread, just as they did in Gagliano, saving all their meager earnings. They live next door to the earthly paradise, but they dare not enter.

Then one day they come back to Italy, with the intention of staying only long enough to visit their family and friends. But someone offers to sell them a parcel of land, and they run into a girl whom they knew when they were children and decide to marry her. Before they are aware of it, six months have gone by, their re-entry permit has expired, and they have to stay home. The land was sold to them at an exorbitant price, and the savings of years of hard work in America go to pay for it; it is a mass of clay and rocks, they must pay taxes on it, and the harvest never makes up for their expenses; they have children and their wife falls ill. Soon they sink back into poverty, the same everlasting poverty they lived in so many years ago, before they went away. Along with poverty they regain their agelong patience and resignation and all their former peasant habits; in short these "Americans" can in no way be distinguished from the rest, unless it be by deeper bitterness, and the regret that from time to time haunts them for their lost riches. Gagliano is full of these returned emigrants who look on the day of their return as the unluckiest of their lives.

1929 was the fateful year; they speak of it as of a cataclysm. This was the year of the "crash," when the dollar tottered and banks closed their doors. The emigrants, however, were little hurt by these events because they had put their savings in Italian banks and changed them into lire. But New York was in a panic, and Fascist propaganda agents went around saying, God knows why, that in Italy there was work and money and security for all and that the emigrants should return. So it was that in this fateful year many were persuaded to give up their work and sail for their native village, where they were trapped like flies in a spider web. Soon they were peasants again, setting off every morning with their donkeys and goats for the lowlands ridden with malaria. Others tried to keep up the trade they had practiced in America, but there was not enough work for them to make a living.

"Damn 1929 and the bastards who got me back here!" Giovanni Pizzilli, the tailor, would say, while he measured me in inches with a new and complicated American system for lowering the shoulders and added finishing touches to a hunting suit he was making for me. He was a clever craftsman, better at his trade than many a fashionable, big-city tailor, and for fifty lire he made me the handsomest corduroy suit I have ever had. In America he had earned good money, now he was living in poverty with four or five children on his hands. He had no hope of bettering his lot, and every bit of energy and confidence had left his still youthful face, leaving only a lasting expression of despair.

"Over there I had a shop of my own and four assistants," my barber told me. "In 1929 I came here for six months, but I got married and didn't go back. Now I've only this miserable hole in the wall, and I'm up against it." His hair was already gray at the temples and there was a mournful and solemn look about him. There were three barber shops in Gagliano, and the "American's," at the upper end of the village, near the church and just below the widow's house, was the only one open all the time; it was patronized by the gentry. The barber of Lower Gagliano was Giulia's albino lover; he took care of the peasants. His shop was almost always closed because he had land to look after, and he rarely wielded the razor except on Sunday mornings.

The third shop was in the middle of the village, near the main square, and it too was usually closed, because the barber was out on other business. People crept mysteriously into his parlor and asked for him in a low voice. He was fair-haired, with the keen face of a wolf and bright eyes, quick in his movements and possessed of an active and clever mind. During the war he had been a corporal in a medical unit and this had given him some skill at doctoring. Although his official trade was that of a barber, Christian beards and hair were the least of his occupations. He clipped goats, purged donkeys, and tended sick animals in general, but his real specialty was tooth-pulling. For two lire he would extract a molar without too much pain. The village was lucky to have him, for I had no notion of dentistry and the other two doctors knew even less than I. He was able to make injections, even intravenous ones, set dislocated or fractured bones, take blood specimens, and puncture abscesses. He was versed, moreover, in herbs, pomades, and plasters; in short, he was invaluable. The two doctors hated him, largely because he took no pains to hide his opinion of their ignorance and because he was sought after by the peasants; every time either of them passed the shop, he threatened to report him for fraudulent medical practice.

It was not a matter of idle threats; from time to time an anonymous letter went off to a prefecture, or the sergeant issued a solemn warning. The barber had to call on all his resources in order to cover up his tracks and keep out of trouble. At first he distrusted me too, but he soon realized that I would not give him away and he became my friend. He had real skill and I called on him for help in minor operations and asked him to make injections. Little did it matter that he had no license. He did a good job, but he had to work under cover, because Italy is a land of degrees and diplomas, where so-called culture is often reduced to the chase after a profitable position and spasmodic feeble efforts to hold onto it. Many a peasant of Gagliano, who might have limped all his life long if the official practitioners had handled him, is walking today, thanks to this barber and stealthy jack-of-all-trades, this quick-witted and swift-footed witch-doctor, at odds with the forces of the law.

The barber shop of the "American," patronized by the gentry, was the only one that looked like the real thing. There was a mirror clouded with fly-tracks, some straight chairs, and, on the walls, clippings from American newspapers with photographs of Roosevelt and other political leaders and screen actresses and advertisements for cosmetics. These were

128

the remains of his sumptuous establishment in New York. When the barber thought of old times his face grew dark and sad. What was left to him of the life of ease he had led on the other side? A little house at the upper end of the village, with an elaborately carved door and geranium pots on the balcony, a sickly wife, and poverty. "If only I hadn't come back!" You can tell these Americans of 1929 by their whipped-dog expression and their gold teeth.

Gold teeth were a luxury and a paradox in the wide peasant mouth of Faccialorda (Dirty Face), a big strong man, astute and stubborn in appearance. Faccialorda must have owed this nickname to his complexion, but in reality he was one of those who had come out on top in the fierce struggles of the emigrants and he was now living on his laurels. He had returned from America with a sizable bankroll, and although he had wasted most of it on the purchase of a piece of barren land, he was still able to live fairly comfortably. The real feature of his fortune was that he had made it not by hard work but by wile. In the evening when he had come up from the fields, standing in the doorway of his house or walking around the square, Faccialorda enjoyed telling me of his American adventure and the pride he took in his achievement. He was born into a family of peasants but in America he was a mason.

"One day they gave me an iron pipe to empty, the sort they use in mines, that was packed with dirt. I drove a nail into it, but instead of dirt there was dynamite and the pipe shattered in my hands. One arm was scratched, and I was left stone-deaf with one eardrum broken. Over there in America a fellow's insured and they were supposed to pay up. They had a doctor look me over and he told me to come back in three months. After three months I felt quite all right, but since I'd had an accident they owed me the money. Three thousand dollars I was supposed to get. I pretended I was still deaf;

they yelled at me and fired guns, but I couldn't hear them. They made me shut my eyes; I staggered and fell flat on the ground. The doctors said there was nothing wrong with me and they didn't want to give me my compensation. They examined me over and over again. I never heard a word they said and I kept on falling down. By God, they were going to give me my money! Two years went by, and I stayed away from work; in spite of what the doctors said I stuck to my story that I was no good any more, that I was done in. Finally these doctors, the best doctors in America, came to believe me and when the two years were up they gave me my three thousand dollars. Well, I had it coming to me. That's when I came back to Gagliano, and here I am today, fit as a fiddle."

Faccialorda was proud of the fact that he had fought single-handed against American science, and that he, a mere peasant from Gagliano, armed only with obstinacy and patience, had won out over the American doctors. He was convinced, what's more, that he was in the right, that his malingering was legitimate. If anyone had told him that he had come by his three thousand dollars dishonestly he would have been sincerely astonished. I never taxed him with anything of the sort; to tell the truth, I thought there were points in his favor. He told me his story over and over again; at bottom he felt that he was a defender of the poor, whom God had rewarded for his struggle against their enemy, the State. Faccialorda reminded me of other Italians I had seen the world over, proud of having made war on the organized forces of civilized society and of having saved themselves from the ridiculous clutches of bureaucracy.

At Stratford-on-Avon I once met an old man who had an ice cream wagon pulled by a pony with a fancy harness and bells. His name was Saracino (anglicized as Saracine on the side of the wagon) and he was from Frosinone; he still had rings in his ears and mumbled in Roman dialect. As soon as he saw that I was Italian he told me that he had fled from Italy fifty years before in order to evade military service for the King of Italy, and that he had never returned. His ice cream trade had flourished until all the wagons in the neighborhood were his, and his sons were highly educated; one of them was a doctor and the other a lawyer. When war came in 1914 he packed them off to Italy so that they should not have to serve the King of England and when, a year later, the King of Italy called them to the colors. . . . "Never fear, we saw to it that they didn't serve him either . . ." To old Saracino as to Faccialorda there was nothing shameful about this; on the contrary, he was proud of it. When he had gleefully told me his story he whipped his pony and drove away.

Faccialorda had won out, to be sure, but then he had come back home and soon, in spite of his gold teeth, he would be just another peasant again. The narration of his story refreshed his memories, one-sided and limited as they were, of America. His fellows forgot more quickly; soon America came to mean to them the same thing as long ago, before they ever went away: an earthly paradise. I saw a few in Grassano who were slightly more alert and Americanized, more like those who had stayed on the other side, but then they weren't peasants and they took pains not to let themselves be reabsorbed into peasant life. One of them used to sit in front of his house on the square every day, looking at the passing throng. He was a middle-aged man, tall, thin, and strong, with a keen face and aquiline nose, always dressed in black and wearing a wide-brimmed panama hat. He had not only gold teeth, but a gold tie pin, watch chain, cigarette case and gold cuff links, rings, and good-luck charms as well. He had made a fortune in America as a businessman and broker; I imagine he exploited his more ignorant countrymen; in any case he seemed accustomed to giving orders and he looked down on the people of Grassano. Nevertheless he came back to his house there every three or four years and delighted in showing off his dollars, his uncouth English and even worse Italian. But he took good care not to be sucked in.

"I could perfectly well stay here," he said to me; "I've plenty of money. They might make me mayor and there's plenty of work to be done here, building the place up, American style. But it would be a colossal failure, a complete waste. Besides, I have business interests to look after in the States. . . ."

Every day he scanned the paper and listened to the radio; when he felt sure that soon there would be a war with Abyssinia he packed his bags and left on the first boat, in order not to be caught in Italy.

After the fateful year of 1929 few came back from New York and few went over. The villages of Lucania, with half their people on one side of the ocean and half on the other, were split in two. Families were broken up and many women were left alone. To those who were left behind America seemed farther away than ever, and their every hope of salvation gone. Only the mail faithfully brought remembrances from overseas, gifts to their families from those blessed by fortune. Don Cosimino was kept busy with these packages; they sent a stream of scissors, knives, razors, farm tools, scythes, hammers, pincers—in short, all the gadgets of everyday use. Life at Gagliano was entirely American in regard to mechanical equipment as well as weights and measures, for the peasants spoke of pounds and inches rather than of kilograms and centimeters. The women wove on ancient looms, but they cut their thread with shiny scissors from Pittsburgh; the barber's razor was the best I ever saw anywhere in Italy, and the blue steel blades of the peasants' axes were American. The peasants had no prejudice against these modern instruments, nor did they see any contradiction between them and their ancient customs. They simply took gladly whatever came to them from New York, just as they would take gladly whatever might come from Rome. But from Rome came nothing. Nothing had ever come but the tax collector and speeches over the radio.

Chapter Fourteen

THERE WERE A GREAT NUMber of speeches at this time and Don Luigi was zealous in calling public meetings. It was October and our troops had crossed the Mareb; the war with Abyssinia had begun. Italians, arise! America receded ever more into the distance, lost in the mists of the Atlantic like an island in the sky. God alone knew when it would be visible again, perhaps never.

The peasants were not interested in the war. The radio thundered and Don Luigi spent all the hours of the school day, when he was not smoking on the balcony, haranguing the children so loudly that he could be heard all over the village and teaching them to sing "Little Black Face." Holding forth in the square he announced that Marconi had invented a secret weapon, a death ray that would cause the entire British Navy to explode. He and his chief assistant at the school and radio collaborator went around saying that the war was made to order for the benefit of the peasants of Gagliano, who soon would have all the land they wanted, and such good land that all you had to do was put seeds in it and the crops would shoot up without further aid.

Unfortunately the two schoolteachers talked so much of the grandeur of Rome that the peasants had no confidence in anything they said; they simply shook their heads in silent and mistrustful resignation. So the "fellows in Rome" wanted war and had chosen to wage it against the Abyssinians? All well and good. It couldn't be much worse to die in an Abyssinian desert than to perish from malaria in a pasture by the Sauro River. It seemed that school children and their teachers, Fascist Scouts, Red Cross ladies, the widows and mothers of Milanese veterans, women of fashion in Florence, grocers, shopkeepers, pensioners, journalists, policemen, and government employees in Rome, in short, all those generally grouped together under the name of "Italian people," were swept off their feet by a wave of glory and enthusiasm. Here in Gagliano I could see nothing. The peasants were quieter, sadder, and more dour than usual. They had no faith in a promised land which had first to be taken away from those to whom it belonged; instinct told them that this was wrong and could only bring ill luck. The "fellows in Rome" didn't usually put themselves out on their behalf and this latest undertaking, in spite of all the fuss made over it, must have a remote purpose in which they had no part.

"If they have money enough for a war, why don't they repair the bridge across the Agri which has been down for four years without anyone moving a finger to fix it? They might make a dam or provide us with more fountains, or plant young trees instead of cutting down the few that are left. We've plenty of land right here, but nothing to go with it."

War they considered just another inevitable misfortune,

like the tax on goats. They were not afraid to go: "To live like dogs here or to die like dogs there is just the same," they said. But no one, except Donna Caterina's husband, enlisted. It soon became clear that not only the purpose of the war but the way it was being conducted as well was the business of that other Italy beyond the mountains, and had little to do with the peasants. Only a few men were called up, two or three in the whole village, besides those who had reached the age for military service, and one other boy, Don Nicola, a priest's son, brought up by the monks of Melfi and a regular noncommissioned officer, who was one of the first to go. A few of the very poorest peasants, who had neither land of their own nor food to eat, were attracted by Don Luigi's speeches and the promise of large salaries. They applied for manual labor as civilians but never received an answer. "They don't know what to do with us," these wretched fellows said to me. "They don't even want us to work. The war is for the benefit of those in the North. We're to stay home until we starve. And now there's no chance of going to America."

October 3, which marked the official opening of the war, was a miserable sort of day. Twenty or twenty-five peasants, roped in by the *carabinieri* and the Fascist Scouts, stood in the square to listen to the historical pronouncements that came over the radio. Don Luigi had ordered flags displayed over the town hall, the school, and the houses of the well-to-do; their bright colors waving in the breeze made a strange contrast to the black death pennants on the doors of the peasants' huts. The bell-ringer rang out the usual funereal strains, and the war so lightheartedly set in motion from Rome was greeted in Gagliano with stony indifference. Don Luigi spoke from the balcony of the town hall. He enlarged upon the eternal grandeur of Rome, the seven hills, the wolf that suckled Romulus and Remus, Caesar's legions,

Roman civilization, and the Roman Empire which was about to be revived. He said that the world hated us for our greatness, but that the enemies of Rome would bite the dust and then we would once more triumphantly tread the Roman roads, because Rome was everlasting and invincible. In his falsetto voice he said a great many more things about Rome which I no longer remember, then he opened his mouth and started to sing *Giovinezza,* motioning imperiously with his hands to the school children in the square below to accompany him in chorus. Around him on the balcony were the sergeant and everyone of importance; all of them sang except Dr. Milillo, who did not share their enthusiasm. Huddled against the wall below, the peasants listened in silence, shielding their eyes with their hands from the sun and looking as dark and gloomy as bats in their black suits.

On the wall of the town hall, next to the balcony, was a white marble stone with the names of all those who had died in the World War. There were many of them for such a small village—almost fifty—all of the familiar names of Gagliano: Rubilotto, Carbone, Guarini, Bonelli, Carnovale, Racioppi, Guerrini—none was missing. Directly or through the ties of cousinship or *comparaggio* not a single house had been spared; besides there were the sick and wounded and those who came back safe and sound. How did it happen, then, that in my talks with the peasants no one ever mentioned the war, even to speak of his own accomplishments, the places he had seen, and the sufferings he had undergone? The only one who ever referred to it was the barber who pulled teeth, and then only to tell me how he had acquired some notions of surgery when he was a stretcher-bearer on the Carso. This tremendous and bloody conflict in the so recent past did not interest the peasants at all; they had endured it and now it was as though they had forgotten it. No one boasted of his prowess, told his children about mighty battles, displayed his wounds, or complained of what he had gone through. When I questioned them on this subject they answered briefly and with indifference. The whole thing had been a great misfortune, and they had borne it like the rest.

That war, too, was waged from Rome; then, too, they were called to follow the flag whose bright colors, the heraldic symbol of another Italy, seemed so crude and out of place—the red shameless and the green absurd—against this background of gray trees and grassless clay. These and all other colors are appendages of aristocracy; they belong on the coat of arms of a nobleman or the banners of a city. But what have the peasants to do with them? They have only one color, the color of their sad, sorrowful eyes and their clothes, and it is not a color at all, but rather the darkness of earth and death. Their pennants are black, like the face of the Madonna. All other flags have the motley hues of another civilization, which does not belong to them as it moves along the main road of History, toward progress and conquest. This other world is stronger and better organized and they must submit to it; they must march out to die for it, today in Abyssinia, as yesterday on the Isonzo and the Piave and for centuries past in every corner of the globe, behind one bright flag or another.

At this time I was reading an old history of the town of Melfi by Del Zio, which I had found among a heap of dusty tomes in the house of Dr. Milillo, where I went almost every day for a cup of coffee and a chat with the two ingenuous, playful, and moustached girls, Margherita and Maria. The history was written during the second half of the last century and it mentions as an object of local pride an old peasant with a wooden leg who had been conscripted into Napoleon's army and had lost his leg at the crossing of the Beresina in the Russian campaign. For more than half a century this peasant limped through the streets of Melfi bearing before the eyes of his fellow-citizens the absurd sign of a civilization which had marked him forever, but of which he knew nothing. What could Russia or the Emperor of France mean to a peasant from Melfi? History, as Victor Hugo might have said, baroque fashion, took his leg and left him none the wiser.

This same History, to which these villages had always been forced to bow, had left other and deeper marks on the townsmen of the limping peasant. Melfi, once a populous and prosperous town, owed its ruin to the fact that a French captain, warring in the mountains against the Spaniards of Charles V, happened to shut himself up there with his followers. The Spanish troops of Pietro Navarro, under orders from Lautrec, laid siege to Melfi, took it, and killed all the citizens they could lay their hands on, folk who knew little of France and Spain, or Francis I and Charles V. They razed most of the houses and gave what was left of the town to Philbert of Orange and later, as a reward for his maritime victories, to Andrea Doria of Genoa, with whom the citizens were even less acquainted. Doria never troubled to visit his vassals, nor did his successors. They simply sent agents to collect as much tribute as they could. Thus, by the inscrutable will of History, with which they had no real connection, the peasants of Melfi lived for centuries after in dire poverty. How many conquerors, with motives the conquered could not know, have, like the French and the Spanish, passed over this land? After thousands of years of this same experience it was only natural that the peasants had little enthusiasm for war, that they looked with misgivings on all flags, and listened in silence while Don Luigi sang from the balcony of the grandeur of Rome.

Governments, Theocracies and Armies are, of course, stronger than the scattered peasants. So the peasants have to resign themselves to being dominated, but they cannot feel as their own the glories and undertakings of a civilization that is radically their enemy. The only wars that touch their hearts are those in which they have fought to defend themselves against that civilization, against History and Government, Theocracy and the Army. These wars they fought under their own black pennants, without military leadership or training and without hope, ill-fated wars that they were bound to lose, fierce and desperate wars, incomprehensible to historians.

The peasants of Gagliano were indifferent to the conquest of Abyssinia and they neither remembered the World War nor spoke of its dead, but one war was close to their hearts and constantly on their tongues; it was already a fable, a legend, a myth, an epic story. This was the war of the brigands. Brigandage came to an end in 1865, seventy years before, and only a very few of them were old enough to remember it, either as participants or eyewitnesses. But all of them, old and young, men and women, spoke of it with as much passion as if it were only yesterday. When I talked to the peasants I could be sure that, whatever was the subject of our conversation, we should in one way or another slip into mention of the brigands. Their traces are everywhere; there is not a mountain, gully, wood, fountain, cave, or stone that is not linked with one of their adventures or that did not serve them as a refuge or hideout; not a dark corner that was not their meeting-place; not a country chapel where they did not leave threatening letters or wait for ransom money. Many places, like the Fossa del Bersagliere, were named for their deeds. Every family was at one time for or against them: one of its members was an outlaw, or they took in and hid a brigand, or a wandering band killed some relative, or set fire to their crops. Then it was that the feuds arose which were to be handed down from generation to generation and which rage even today. The peasants, with a few exceptions, were all on the side of the brigands and, with the passing of time, the deeds which so struck their fancy became bound up with the familiar sites of the village, entered into their everyday speech with the same ease as animals and spirits, grew into legends and took on the absolute truth of a myth.

I do not mean to extol the brigands, as is the fashion among certain aesthetes and two-faced politicians. From an historical point of view, studied against the background of the Italian Risorgimento, there is no defense for brigandage. From a liberal and progressive standpoint this phenomenon seems a last gasp of the past, which has to be ruthlessly uprooted, a wild and baneful movement set up against Italian unity, a threat to liberty and civilized institutions. Such it was, indeed, in its character of a war fomented by the Bourbons, Spain, and the Pope, for their own particular motives. If we look at it from a strictly historical point of view we shall not only find it indefensible, but we shall fail to understand it at all.

But to the peasants brigandage is something quite different. They neither judge nor defend it and, when they dwell on it with such passion, they are not boasting. Of the historical motives, the interests of the Bourbons, the Pope, and the feudal barons, they are not conscious, although they dimly perceive that these are sorry and unpleasant affairs. But the myth of the brigands is close to their hearts and a part of their lives, the only poetry in their existence, their dark, desperate epic. Even the appearance of the peasants today recalls that of the brigands: they are silent, lonely, gloomy and frowning in their black suits and hats and, in winter, black top coats, armed whenever they set out for the fields with gun and axe. They have gentle hearts and patient souls; centuries of resignation weigh on their shoulders, together with a feeling of the vanity of all things and of the overbearing power of fate. But when, after infinite endurance, they are shaken to the depths of their beings and are driven by an instinct of self-defense or justice, their revolt knows no bounds and no measure. It is an unhuman revolt whose point of departure and final end alike are death, in which ferocity is born of despair. The brigands unreasonably and hopelessly stood up for the life and liberty of the peasants against the encroachments of the State. By ill luck they were unwitting instruments of History, and History, quite outside their ken, was working against them; they were on the wrong side and they came to destruction. But through the brigands the peasants defended themselves against the hostile civilization that never understands but everlastingly enslaves them; instinctively they looked on the brigands as heroes. The peasant world has neither government nor army; its wars are only sporadic outbursts of revolt, doomed to repression. Still it survives, yielding up the fruits of the earth to the conquerors, but imposing upon them its measurements, its earthly divinities, and its language.

I was struck by the peasants' build: they are short and swarthy with round heads, large eyes, and thin lips; their archaic faces do not stem from the Romans, Greeks, Etruscans, Normans, or any of the other invaders who have passed through their land, but recall the most ancient Italic types. They have led exactly the same life since the beginning of time, and History has swept over them without effect. Of the two Italys that share the land between them, the peasant Italy is by far the older; so old that no one knows whence it came, and it may have been here forever. *Humilemque videmus Italiam*; this was the low-lying, humble Italy that first met the eyes of the Asiatic conquerors as the ships of Aeneas rounded the promontory of Calabria.

There should be a history of this Italy, a history outside the framework of time, confining itself to that which is changeless and eternal, in other words, a mythology. This Italy has gone its way in darkness and silence, like the earth, in a sequence of recurrent seasons and recurrent misadventures. Every outside influence has broken over it like a wave, without leaving a trace. Rarely has it risen to defend itself from mortal danger and only on those few occasions has it fought, in vain, a truly national war. The first of these was the resistance to Aeneas. A mythological history must have its root in myth and for this reason Vergil is a great historian. The Phoenician invaders from Troy brought with them a set of values diametrically opposed to those of the ancient peasant civilization. They brought religion and the State, and the religion of the State. The religious tradition or *pietas* of Aeneas could not be understood by the ancient Italians, who lived beside the beasts of the field. The invaders brought also arms and an army, escutcheons, heraldry, and war. Their religion was a violent one, demanding human sacrifice; on the funeral pyre of Pallas the pious Aeneas made a burnt offering of prisoners to the gods of the State. The ancient Italians, meanwhile, lived on the land, knowing neither sacrifice nor religion. The Trojans met with insuperable hostility among the natives, and the two civilizations clashed. Aeneas found his only allies among the Etruscans, city people, like him from the Orient, perhaps of the same Semitic origin, and similarly ruled by a military oligarchy. With these allies, then, he waged war. On one side there was an army in shining armor forged by the gods; on the other, as Vergil describes them, were peasant bands, risen in self-defense, with no god-given weapons but only axes, knives, and scythes, the tools of their daily work in the fields. These, too, were valorous brigands, doomed to defeat. Italy, the humble Italy, was conquered:

> Per cui morì la vergine Cammilla
> Eurialo e Turno e Niso di ferute.

> On whose account the maid Camilla died,
> Euryalus, Turnus, Nisus of their wounds.

Then came Rome and perfected the governmental and military theocracy of its Trojan founders, who had to accept, however, the customs and language of the people they had conquered. Rome, too, met with opposition among the peasants, and the series of Italic Wars were the most stubborn obstacles in its path. Here again the Italians suffered a military defeat, but they kept their individuality and did not mingle with their conquerors. After this second national war the peasant world, hemmed in by Roman order, lay in waiting, dormant, as it were. The feudal civilization that came after, with the passing of time and peoples, was not a creation of the peasants, but it was close to the earth, limited by the boundaries of great estates, and less in opposition to the rural way of life. This is why the Swabians are popular even today with the peasants; they speak of Conradin as a national hero and mourn for his death. After him, indeed, this flourishing land fell into ruin.

The fourth national war of the peasants was brigandage and here, too, the humble Italy was historically on the wrong side and bound to lose. The brigands had neither the arms forged by Vulcan nor the heavy artillery of the government troops. Even their gods were powerless: of what avail was a poor Madonna with a black face against the Ethical State of the Neapolitan followers of Hegel? Brigandage was an access of heroic folly and desperate savagery, a desire for wreaking death and ruin, with no hope of final victory. "If the world had only one enormous heart, I'd tear it out," said Caruso, one of the most fearful brigand chiefs.

This blind urge to destruction, this bloody and suicidal will to annihilation, has lurked for centuries beneath the patient endurance of daily toil. Every revolt on the part of the peasants springs out of an elementary desire for justice deep at the dark bottom of their hearts. After the end of brigandage this land sank into an uneasy peace. But every now and then in some village or other, when the peasants have no representation in the government and no defense in the law, they rise up with death in their hearts, burn the town hall or the barracks of the *carabinieri*, kill the gentry, and then go off in silent resignation to prison.

Of the real brigands, those of 1860, hardly any are left. One still lived, Giulia told me, in nearby Missanello. He was ninety years old, with a long white beard, and he was considered a saint. Once he was the leader of a band that spread terror throughout the countryside. Now he lived in the village, revered by the peasants as if he were a patriarch; they came to ask his counsel whenever they were in trouble. I met another brigand one day at Grassano. I was getting a shave from Antonino Roselli, barber, flute-player, and at odd moments my secretary, when a robust old codger with pink cheeks, a thick white moustache, keen blue eyes, and proud bearing came into the shop, clad in the corduroy suit of a hunter. I had never seen him before. While he was waiting for his turn he lit a pipe and asked me who I was.

"An exile?" he said, using the common word hereabouts

for a political prisoner. "Someone in Rome has it in for you!" I asked him his age.

"I was a boy at the time of the brigands," he answered. "When I was fifteen my brother and I killed a *carabiniere*. Have you seen the old oak tree two hundred yards or so outside the village? We met him there and he wanted to stop us; that's why we had to kill him. We hid his body in a ditch but they soon found it. They arrested my brother and he died in prison a few years later in Naples. I hid here in the village. For seven months I lived in a room just above this barber shop, disguised as a woman. Finally they discovered me, but because I was young I got off with a four-year sentence." The old brigand was happy and at peace with himself; this ancient murder did not weigh on his conscience in the least and he talked about it as if it were the most natural thing in the world. To him this was a war story.

"Do you see that gentleman who is just passing?" the barber asked me, pointing through the open door. "He is Don Pasquale, a landowner. His grandfather had a big farm and when the brigands came he refused to give up either feed or livestock. The brigands burned his house to the ground and he was so ill-advised as to lie in ambush for them with the *carabinieri*. The brigands captured him and sent word to his wife that if she wanted to see him again alive she must pay five thousand lire ransom within two days. The family did not want to pay the money and hoped that the soldiers would free him. On the third day the wife received an envelope; in it was one of her husband's ears."

If the brigands cut off the ears, nose, and tongue of the gentry in order to obtain a ransom, the soldiers, in their turn, cut off the heads of the brigands they caught and mounted them on poles in the village as an example. Thus the war of destruction went on. These clay mountains are studded with holes and natural caves. Here the brigands lay low, hiding in the trunks of hollow trees the money obtained from robbery and ransom. When the brigand bands were at last dispersed, their loot remained in the woods. At this point the history of the brigands passes into legend and is bound up with age-old superstitions. For the brigands hid their spoils in the places where the peasants had always imagined there was hidden treasure. In this way the brigands came to be looked upon as beings with the dark powers of the nether regions.

Chapter Fifteen

So many peoples have passed through this land that traces of them are constantly being dug up by the plow. Classical vases, statuettes, and coins from some ancient tomb are brought to light by the turn of a shovel. Don Luigi had some of these from one of his fields down by the Sauro. There were worn pieces of money, whether Greek or Roman I could not tell, and plain black vases of very handsome lines. I also saw with my own eyes a brigand's hidden treasure, of modest size; it was shown to me by the man who had found it, Lasala the carpenter. One evening when he had put a big log on the fire he saw something shining in the flames. It was a handful of Bourbon silver crowns, which had been stored away in a tree trunk.

To the peasants such things are only crumbs of the immense treasure sealed up in the bowels of the earth. They believe that mountainsides, caverns, and deep woods are teeming with bright gold, which only awaits discovery. But the hunt for buried treasure is fraught with danger; it is a work of the devil and involves contact with the powers of darkness. It is no use to dig at random in the ground; treasures appear only to the man who is fated to find them. There are only two ways of going about treasure hunting: one is to look for inspiration in dreams, the other, and more favorable, to obtain the guidance of one of the sprites or gnomes that watch over them.

Treasure is wont to appear to a sleeping peasant in all its glory. He sees a pile of gold and the exact place where it is hidden in the woods, near a certain oak tree with a mark on it, beneath a great stone. He has only to go and get it. He must go by night; by day the treasure might disappear. He must go alone and tell no one of his going; if a single word escapes him the treasure is lost. The danger is immense, for dead men's ghosts wander in the woods; few men are brave enough to run the gauntlet without fear or failing.

A peasant of Gagliano, who lived not far from me, once dreamed of treasure buried in the Accettura Forest, just below Stigliano. He screwed up his courage and set out by night, but when he found himself surrounded by ghosts in the black shadows he began to shake in his boots. Through the trees he saw a distant light; the lantern of a coal miner from Calabria, fearless as all those of his calling are, who was spending the night near his mine. The temptation was too strong for the frightened peasant; he could not help telling the miner his dream and asking for help in the search. They started out together to look for the stone, the peasant emboldened by the company and the dauntless Calabrian armed with a strong knife. They found the stone, exactly as it had appeared in the dream. Luckily there were two of them, for the stone was very heavy and they were barely able to budge it. When they finally managed to move it and the peasant leaned over to look underneath he saw an enormous mass of gold gleaming at the bottom of a deep hole. Pebbles displaced by the shifting of the stone were falling onto the money with a metallic sound that warmed the cockles of his heart. All that was left to do was to go down into the hole and take hold of the treasure, but at this point the peasant once more lost his nerve. He begged his companion to climb down and hand him up the money which he would put in his sack until they should divide it between them. The miner, who feared neither ghosts nor devils, got down in the hole, when, all of a sudden, the shimmering gold became opaque and black; before his eyes the treasure turned into coal.

The difficulties and disappointments involved in following a dream are done away with when a man is told the hiding-place of a treasure and led to it by one of the tiny gnomes that know all the secrets of the earth. These gnomes are the spirits or ghosts of children who have died without being baptized; they are numerous in these parts because the peasants often put off the baptism of their offspring for years. When I was called to the bedside of a ten- or twelve-year-old, the mother's first question was: "Is there any danger of his dying? If so, I must call the priest to come baptize him. We've not had it done, but if he were to die . . . God forbid . . ."

The gnomes are tiny, airy creatures that run hither and yon; their greatest delight is to tease good Christian souls. They tickle the feet of those who are sleeping, pull sheets off the beds, throw sand into people's eyes, upset wine glasses, hide in draughts of air so as to blow papers about, and make wet clothes fall off the line into the dirt, pull chairs out from under women, hide things in out-of-the-way places, curdle milk, pinch, pull hair, buzz and sting like mosquitoes. But they are innocent sprites, their mischief is never serious but always in the guise of a joke; however annoying they may be, they never cause serious harm. Their character is capricious and playful and it is almost impossible to lay hands on them. On their heads they wear a red hood that is bigger than they are and woe unto them if it is lost; they weep and are quite disconsolate until they have found it. The only way to ward off the tricks is to seize them by the hood and if you can take it away from them, they will throw themselves at your feet in tears and implore you to give it back. Beneath their whimsicality and childish playfulness the gnomes are very wise; they know everything below the surface of the earth and, of course, the location of buried treasure. In order to recover his red hood, without which he cannot live, a gnome will promise to tell you where a treasure is hidden. But you must not give him back his hood until he has led you to it; as long as the hood is yours the gnome will serve you, but if he can lay hands on it he will leap away, mocking and jumping for joy, and he will not keep his promise.

These gnomes or sprites are often seen, but it is very hard indeed to lay hold of them. Giulia had seen them, and her friend La Parroccola, and many other peasants of Gagliano, but not one of them had ever laid hands on a gnome's hood and obliged him to lead the way to a buried treasure.

At Grassano there was a young workman, about twenty years old, Carmelo Coiro, a husky fellow with a square sunburned face, who came often in the evening to drink a glass of wine at Prisco's inn. He was a day laborer in the fields or on the roads, but his dream was to be a bicycle racer. He had read about the two Italian cyclists, Binda and Guerra, and they appealed to his fancy. He spent all his free time on his old broken-down bicycle and every Sunday he practiced on the curves and hills around Grassano; sometimes he rode in the dust and heat all the way to Matera and even to Potenza. He lacked neither strength nor patience nor breath, and he wanted to go north on his bicycle and become a racer. When I told him that if he carried out this plan I could recommend him to an acquaintance, a sports writer, who was a personal friend and biographer of Binda, Carmelo was overcome with joy and whenever I saw him in Prisco's kitchen his face beamed with delight.

At this time Carmelo was one of a group of road-menders who were repairing the road to Irsina along the Bilioso, a malaria-ridden stream that flows past Grottole into the Basento River. During the hottest hours of the day, when work was impossible, the road-menders used to go to sleep in a natural cave, one of many dotting the whole of the valley, and formerly a brigand hideout. In the cave there was a gnome, which began to play tricks on Carmelo and his companions. As soon as they fell asleep, half-dead with weariness and heat, he tweaked their noses, tickled them with straws, threw pebbles at them, sprinkled them with cold water, hid their coats and shoes, whistled, stamped about and would not leave them in peace. They could see him dart from one part of the cave to another under his red hood and they tried their best to catch him, but he was quicker than a cat and cleverer than a fox and they soon decided that there was no chance of snatching the hood. In order that they might escape his teasing and enjoy their rest, one after another took his turn at mounting guard, hoping to stave off the gnome even if he could not capture him. This, too, was useless. The sly gnome played the same tricks as before, with a mocking laugh at their impotence.

In despair they took counsel with the engineer who was supervising the repairs; he was an educated man and perhaps he could succeed better than they in taming the rampant gnome. The engineer came, with his assistant, the foreman, both of them armed with double-barreled shotguns. When they arrived the gnome began to make faces, laugh, and leap about like a goat at the far end of the cave where they could all see him. The engineer raised his loaded gun and fired a shot. The bullet struck the gnome and bounced back at the engineer, grazing his head with a terrifying whistle, while the gnome leaped higher and higher, in mad joy. The engineer did not fire again; he dropped his gun and, together with the foreman, Carmelo, and the rest of the workers, he fled in terror from the cave. After that the road-menders lay down in the open air with their hats over their faces. The other caves in the neighborhood, where the brigands had taken refuge, were also full of gnomes, and they never set foot in any of them again.

The persistent and athletic Carmelo had considerable experience of such strange encounters. A few months before, he told me, he was going home after nightfall from the direction of the Bilioso. He was with his uncle, a customs guard whom I had met while he was taking a vacation at Grassano. The two of them were climbing up the steep path through the valley, where I often went in those days to walk and paint. It was a cold winter evening, the sky was cloudy, and it was pitch black. They had been fishing some distance away, below Irsina, and night had overtaken them before they were aware of the time. The uncle had with him a Mauser automatic pistol loaded with twenty-four rounds, and so their minds were at ease in regard to the chance of any untoward meeting. When they were halfway up, at a point where there were two oak trees near a small farmhouse, they saw a big dog coming toward them in the center of the path. They recognized him as belonging to the peasant friend who lived there. The dog was barking fiercely and was unwilling to let them go by.

They called him by name and tried first to coax and then to threaten him, all to no avail. The animal seemed stricken with madness and set upon them with bared teeth. The two men were frightened, and seeing no other way to save their skins, the uncle whipped out his pistol and fired all twenty-four rounds in succession. At every shot the dog opened wide his huge red mouth and swallowed the cartridges one by one, as if they were rolls, all the time growing bigger and bigger as he bore down on them wildly. The men thought their last hour had come, but just in time they remembered San Rocco and the Madonna of Viggiano; they implored their aid and made the sign of the cross. The dog, which had by this time assumed gigantic proportions and was as big as a house, stopped short; the twenty-four cartridges in his stomach exploded with a terrible noise one after the other, and finally the animal burst like a soap bubble and disappeared into thin air. The path was open and soon they came to the house of Carmelo's mother. This old woman was a witch and she often conversed with the souls of the dead, met gnomes, and talked to real devils in the cemetery. She was a thin, clean, good-natured peasant.

The air over this desolate land and among the peasant huts is filled with spirits. Not all of them are mischievous and capricious gnomes or evil demons. There are also good spirits in the guise of guardian angels.

One day at the end of October toward dusk a peasant came to ask me to change the bandage on an abscess. I threw the dirty bandage and cotton on my studio floor and called Giulia to sweep them up. Giulia had the regular Gagliano habit of throwing sweepings out of the door and onto the street. Everyone does it, and the pigs have a way of cleaning the streets. But on this particular evening I saw that Giulia swept the bandages into a little heap just inside the door and left them there. I asked her why, since I was sure that hygiene was not the motive.

"Evening has come," Giulia answered. "I can't throw them out. The angel, God forbid, might take offense." Then, surprised at my ignorance, she explained further: "At dusk three angels come down from the sky to every house. One stands at the door, another sits at the table, and the third watches over the bed. They look after the house and protect it. Neither wolves nor evil spirits can enter the whole night long. If I threw the sweepings outside the door they might land on the face of the angel, whom we can't see; the angel might take offense and never come back. I'll throw them out tomorrow, after the angel has gone, at sunrise."

Chapter Sixteen

IN THIS LIGHT AND AIRY AT-
mosphere the time passed, as the angels watched over me by
night and Giulia's witchcraft by day. I attended to the sick,
painted, read, and wrote, in a solitude that was pervaded by
animals and spirits. I managed to keep out of the quarrels and
intrigues of the gentry by staying almost all day in the house.
But I did meet them every morning when I had to go to sign
the register at the town hall and walked under the balcony of
the schoolhouse, where Don Luigi sat smoking, cane in hand,
then again after lunch when I went to Dr. Milillo's house for a
cup of coffee and above all in the evening, when everyone
waited in the square for the arrival of the mail and the newspapers.

October, with its even temperature, had slipped away; the
weather was colder and the rains had come, but they made
the landscape no greener; it remained a dingy yellowish-white

color. On fine days I painted outside, but most of the time I worked either in my studio or on the terrace. I did a great many still lifes, and I often used the boys for models, as they had fallen into the habit of coming to see me and hung about the house most of the day. I should like to have painted the peasants, but the men were away in the fields and the women, although they were flattered by my requests, were unwilling. Even Giulia claimed that she had no time to pose for me, and I realized that there was some mysterious reason for her reluctance.

Giulia considered me her master and she never said no to anything I asked; in fact, she went out of her way, with all the ease in the world, to do me services which I should never have dreamed of demanding. I had procured from Bari an enameled tub for bathing and in the morning I took it into my bedroom to wash, closing the door into the kitchen where she was at work with her child. These doings seemed very strange to Giulia and one morning she opened the door and, without the slightest display of embarrassment at finding me stark naked, she asked how I managed to take a bath with no one to soap my back and help me to dry. I never knew whether the priest had broken her in to this duty, or whether it came straight down to her from the Homeric tradition whereby women washed the warriors and anointed them with oil. But from this day on she never failed to soap and rub my back with her rough, strong hands. Giulia was surprised that I showed no desire to make love to her.

"You're well built," she used to say, "and there's nothing missing." But that was as far as she went; she never said more. She was accustomed, in this, to an animal-like submissiveness, and she respected my coldness as if there must be some mysterious reason for it. So she confined herself to praising my good looks. "What a fine fellow you are!" she would say.

"How fine and fat!" In these parts, as in the Orient, fatness is a mark of beauty; perhaps because the underfed peasants can never hope to attain it and it remains the prerogative of the well-to-do.

Giulia, then, although she was ready to render me any service, absolutely refused to pose for her portrait. I realized that magic lay behind her refusal and this she one day corroborated. A portrait takes something away from the sitter—to be exact, an image of herself. By this means the painter acquires complete power over anyone who poses for him. For the same reason many people unconsciously avoid being photographed. Giulia, who lived in a world ruled by magic, was afraid of my painting her, not so much because I might use the portrait as a waxen image and cast an evil spell upon her, but rather on account of the tangible sway I should exercise over her just as, to her mind, I undoubtedly exercised it over the people and things and trees and villages that were the subjects of my painting. I further realized that in order to overcome her scruples I should have to make use of a magic even stronger than fear, an irresistible power, namely violence. I threatened, therefore, to beat her and made as if to do so; in fact I actually started, without too much difficulty, as her arms were no stronger than mine. As soon as she saw my raised hand and felt the first blow, Giulia's face filled with joy and she smiled beatifically, showing the full array of her wolflike teeth. Just as I had imagined, she knew no greater happiness than that of being dominated by an absolute power. All of a sudden she became as gentle as a lamb and sat willingly for her portrait. Face to face with the unanswerable argument of brute force, she forgot all her natural and justifiable fears. I painted her with a black shawl framing her old yellow serpent face.

Again I painted her on a larger scale, lying down with her

baby in her arms. Hers was a motherliness devoid of sentimentality, a physical and earthly attachment made up of bitterness, pity, and resignation; she was like a wind-beaten flood-swept mountain out of which had grown a rolling green hill. Giulia's baby was round, fat, and good-natured; he hardly knew how to talk and I understood little of what he said as he trotted about my rooms after Barone, dividing with the dog the dried figs, bits of bread, and candy that I gave him. Nino would stand on the tip of his toes and raise as high as possible the little hand that clasped his treasure, but Barone was bigger than he was and with a frisky leap, taking care not to hurt him, he would snatch it away. When Barone stretched out on the floor, Nino lay down on top of him and they played together. Then, when the baby was tired, he fell asleep and the dog remained motionless beneath him, like a cushion, hardly daring to breathe lest he be awakened. They lay this way for hours in the kitchen.

In spite of my work and all that I had to do about the house, the days went by with the most dismal monotony, in this deathlike existence, where there was neither time, nor love, nor liberty. One living presence would have been more real to me than the company of infinite numbers of bodiless spirits, constantly staring at me and followng me about: the continual magic of animals and things weighed upon me with a funereal enchantment, but the only way to be free of them was to possess a magic even stronger. Giulia taught me her philters and love spells. But what is more diametrically opposed to love, which is a release, than magic, which is a power of repression? There were spells for winning the hearts of those nearby, others for binding those of the absent. One, which Giulia swore was particularly effective, reached loved ones over land and sea, and impelled them to drop everything, heeding the call of love, and to return to the abandoned lover. This was a verse in which lines that made sense alternated with absurd repetitions of witchcraft:

> *Stella, da lontano te vuardo e da vicino te saluto*
> *'N faccia te vado e 'n vocca te sputo.*
> *Stella, non face che ha da murì*
> *Face che ha da turnà*
> *E con me ha da restà.*

> Star, that I see in the distance, I greet you;
> I swagger up to you and spit in your mouth.
> Star, let him not die;
> Let him come back,
> Come back and stay with me.

The verse must be recited at night, standing in the doorway and gazing up at the star to which it is addressed. I tried it from time to time, but it never worked. I stood leaning against the door, with Barone at my feet, and looked at the sky. October was gone, and in the black heavens shone the stars that watched over my birth, the cold, brilliant stars of Sagittarius.

Chapter Seventeen

IN THE MIDST OF THIS PAUSE from emotion, this tedious and lonely round of the seasons, charged with words that met no answer, came a letter out of the blue from Matera. I was to be allowed to spend several days in Grassano to finish some paintings that I had begun there, on condition that I pay out of my own pocket for my trip and for that of the *carabinieri* who would have to escort me. This permission was in answer to a request that I had made long ago and already forgotten. When I was transferred to Gagliano with only a day's notice, I had sent a telegram to the authorities in Matera asking for a respite of ten days because I had started some paintings which I very much wanted to complete. In reality this had been only a pretext, under cover of which I hoped to linger on indefinitely. There was no reply and I had had to pack my bags and go. But artistic motives had a tardy influence on the police, and after three months of their meditation I was rewarded with a holiday as welcome as it was unexpected.

I never knew the officials at Matera who had charge of political prisoners, but they were apparently not a bad lot. Because the post was so undesirable it must have been filled by old war horses, heirs to Bourbon skepticism and hide-bound by paperwork and routine. Into these bureaucratic old heads there had not yet, thank God, penetrated the new schoolmasters' culture, the idealism of the night schools which animated the hysterical zeal of the young and led them to imagine that the State had an ethical quality, that it was a person like themselves with a similar personal morality, and that it should impinge upon the individual as an extension of his own petty ambitions and paltry sadism and exhibitionism, while at the same time it should appear to the profane as inscrutable, sacred, and enormous. The young Fascist zealots derived from this identification of themselves with their idol the same physical pleasure that they got from love-making. Don Luigi was, in some ways, one of them. But the officials at Matera seemed to be of the old school; they observed the safe custom of letting all papers lie idle in the files for at least three months before they even looked at them.

Don Luigi gave me the great news with the kindly smile of a king bestowing a favor upon one of his subjects. Because he represented the State he felt that he had a share in the tardy generosity of the police and he was happy that the State he represented was a paternalistic one. But there was a touch of wounded civic pride in his happiness and a vague resentment that marred its completeness. Why was I so happy at the prospect of going away for a few days? Did I like Grassano better than Gagliano? As a representative of the State, Don Luigi held that political prisoners deserved harsh treatment and should not enjoy being under his jurisdiction, but as a citizen of Gagliano, indeed its first citizen, he claimed that they should be, or at least pretend to be, better off there than in any other village of the province. This contradictory and jealous frame of mind allowed him to indulge in the first and oldest virtue of his land, hospitality. In the name of hospitality the peasants are wont to open the door to a perfect stranger and ask him to share their humble fare, without even inquiring his name; every village strives for the reputation of being the friendliest and most welcoming to the passer-by, who may, after all, be a god in disguise. To Don Luigi's way of thinking I had no right to rejoice over my departure. I might speak ill of him to the gentry over at Grassano, who were so much nearer to Matera, the provincial capital. And if I got myself transferred again and never came back to Gagliano, who would look after his imaginary ailments? Who would take patients away from his enemy Gibilisco until the old doctor died of sheer rage?

Don Luigi, in his own way, and within the limitations of his arid and infantile character, had grown attached to me and was sorry to see me go. I had to set his mind at rest by telling him that I was excited chiefly over the idea of taking a trip, a simple pleasure to which I was no longer accustomed, that work was the only reason for my wanting to go to Grassano and that I should be very happy indeed to return to his territory as soon as my pictures were finished.

And so early the next morning I set out, with a bundle of canvases, my portable easel, my paint-box, Barone, and two *carabinieri*. I knew the road well, as Grassano was as familiar to me as my own bedroom. Usually I do not care to return to a place where I have lived before, but my feelings about Grassano were pleasant ones. I had arrived there after months of solitary confinement and, I had there laid eyes again on the sun and the stars, on growing things and animals and human faces, so that I connected it with a sort of liberation. Prolonged solitude leads to a detachment from the senses that sometimes is similar to a kind of saintliness; the return to normal life is acute and painful, like a convalescence. The poverty and desolation of Grassano, set in a monotonously sad landscape empty of softness and sensuousness, made it as inoffensive as possible under the circumstances and well suited to my gradual recovery. I had been happy there and I loved it.

What a joy it was, that morning, in the "American's" little car, to glimpse the forbidden land beyond the cemetery, the road down to the Sauro, and the heights of Stigliano! How gaily Barone frisked about while we waited at the crossroads by the river for the mail bus, full of new faces. One by one, as in a film turning backwards, we passed through the places I had first met going in the opposite direction: Stigliano, Accettura, San Mauro Forte, the bus stops with the bustling in and out of peasants and their women, the woods, and the houses peopled with creatures of my imagination. And finally, in the distance, appeared the wide, white river bed of the Basento and the railway station for Grassano. Here the bus veered off toward Grottole and Matera, while we waited for some vehicle to carry us the winding, steep, dusty ten miles up to the village. We had a long wait until a car came down to meet the train from Taranto. I spent the time looking at the river bed where the first arch of the bridge, swept away by a flood, for years had waited in vain to be repaired. Before me, like a great wave on the surface of the earth, rose the solid bare mountain of Grassano, and, poised upon its peak like a mirage, was the village. It seemed even more airy and unreal than when I had last seen it, because during my absence all the houses had been whitewashed and now they looked like a herd of timorous sheep huddled together on the yellowish-gray crest of the mountain.

164

At last we heard from afar the honking of a horn and we saw first a cloud of dust coming down the road and then the car itself teetering over the boardway laid down alongside the broken bridge and pulling up at the station. The driver, who had taken me to Gagliano three months before, recognized Barone and myself and gave us our first welcome. The train whistled into the station and went on its way again without the arrival or departure of a single passenger. Now we had to wait for the train going the other way, from Naples and Potenza, which was due to arrive soon after but was very late. I was in no hurry and I did not mind waiting in the valley where I might never again return, walking in the noonday silence and sitting down on the white stones of the wide, dry river bed, which disappeared on either side into the mountains. I ate the lunch I had brought with me and bided my time. An hour later the train from Naples came in, as empty as was its predecessor; we got into the car and began the ascent.

There are hundreds of curves along the ten miles of road, which passes among caves and hillocks and fields of stubble where the wind raises flurries of dust and there is not a single tree to be seen. We climbed up gradually until we were a quarter of a mile from the village, turning first one way and then the other, with the view shut off by the raised and rounded outlines of the parched fields. Then we came to a great cleft, almost like a wound in the earth, around which the road swung in a wide circle. This is called the ditch of the carcasses, because in it are thrown the dead bodies of diseased and inedible animals, whose white bones now cover its bottom. We were close upon the village; there was the sloping, open cemetery, looking like a white handkerchief spread out to dry on the hillside; there the beginning of the path running between two high hedges of rosemary where in the early days I used to sit for hours to read until a goat would suddenly come out and gaze at me with mysterious eyes; and there was the tree where, seventy years ago, the old brigand had killed his *carabiniere*. One last curve and we saw the life-size Christ on a wooden cross raised above the road, then one more short climb and the road was closed in between the village houses. With a loud honk of the horn, which caused pedestrians to flatten themselves against the walls, we drew up at the door of Prisco's inn. I was greeted by the booming voice of the landlord, who called his wife and children: "Capità! Guagliò! Here's Don Carlo!" Shouting excitedly, they trooped around me.

They were a fine family. Prisco was a lean, strong man of about fifty, vociferous and enterprising, with a round head, close-cropped hair and astute, darting eyes. He was active and cheery, always making deals with traveling salesmen and doing business with neighboring villages. His wife was as gentle and quiet as her husband was quick and noisy; a tall, shapely woman, dressed in black, imperturbable and motherly in the midst of continual bustle. She was already cooking some bread in oil for me and I could not hear her voice among the others. The oldest son was called "Capitano" because he was the recognized ringleader of the village boys, lording it over them by virtue of his precocious intelligence and acumen. He was thirteen or fourteen years old, and was short and lame. He had sparkling, alert, and sensual eyes set in a pale, thin face, where a few whiskers were starting to sprout. He was quick-witted and talked very fast, leaving half his sentences unfinished. I never saw a boy his age do sums with such speed or grasp an idea so rapidly, especially where business matters were concerned. He played slap-jack at such lightning speed that the cards hardly hit the table before he covered them. All the other boys were under his sway and everywhere in the village you could hear the call of "Capitano" and see his thin, agile frame and limping gait. His younger brother was completely different, tall and slender with enormous eyes and a mild expression on his face; he took after his mother, as did the little girls.

I had not yet finished greeting the Prisco family when Antonino Roselli, the barber, and Riccardo, his brother-in-law, arrived on the scene; they had already sent word around to my other friends, who soon put in an appearance. Antonino was the dark young fellow with a black moustache, who played the flute. He was anxious, like everyone else in Grassano, to get away, and he still cherished the hope of following me around Europe as my private secretary. He planned to shave me, set up my easel, prepare my paints and brushes, find models, sell my pictures, play the flute to me when I was bored, care for me when I was ill, and, in general, attend to my needs even better than the faithful Elia who trailed after Vittorio Alfieri, the poet, over the plateaus of ancient Castile. Perhaps I should have fallen in with his wishes, but alas, this was one of the thousand chances of a lifetime that out of inertia, foolishness, or distraction I let go to waste. He was a fine fellow, a little too much of a barber and flute-player to suit me, but none the less, his attachment was touching. During the first days after my arrival in exile from prison in Rome, after I had paid an almost furtive visit to his barber shop, Antonino, thinking I might be in low spirits, came with two friends to play a serenade beneath my window. His flute, a violin, and a guitar, echoed in somewhat melancholy fashion in the silence of the night.

Riccardo was a sailor from Venice, who had been arrested, along with his shipmates, because when their ship came back to Trieste from Odessa, Communist propaganda leaflets were found aboard. He was tall, fair and athletic, a 500-yard swimming champion, with a faraway look in his blue eyes which were set up high on his forehead like those of a bird. The first time I saw him, I recognized his face from having seen it in a picture by De Pisis. Riccardo liked Grassano; he had married Maddalena, the sister of Antonino, and they were expecting a baby. He led a family life, as if he were a native of Grassano rather than a political prisoner. All those in compulsory residence at Grassano, as a matter of fact, enjoyed considerable liberty: they could walk anywhere in the territory of the township and had to report to the town hall only once a week, while the curfew regulations were enforced with laxity. Riccardo was a pleasant, affable sort and I enjoyed listening to his Venetian dialect. After these two came a group of their friends: shopkeepers, carpenters, one tailor, and a few peasants.

I knew fewer peasants at Grassano than at Gagliano. I had stayed there a shorter time and had not engaged in medical practice; moreover, they were in general far more reticent. At Gagliano the peasants for the most part owned their own bit of land, however small. Grassano, on the other hand, was divided into large holdings where they were merely tenants. They were equally poor in both places and worse living conditions would be difficult to imagine. The peasants of Grassano lived off advance payments for the crops, but when the harvest came around they were rarely able to pay back what they had borrowed. Every year their obligations grew and they were more and more entangled in a web of squalor and debt. At Gagliano, where they worked their own fields, they never produced enough to feed their families and pay their taxes, and whatever money they laid aside after a fat year went for doctors' bills and medicine for their malaria; hence they too were

168

underfed and had no prospect of moving elsewhere or of bettering their lot. The lives of both groups, in short, amounted to about the same thing. But while Gagliano was made up of two clearly divided classes, the gentry and the peasants, at Grassano there was a numerous middle class, consisting of tradesmen and skilled workers, mostly carpenters. I often wondered how there could be enough work to go around among the many carpenters of Grassano. Actually there was not enough, and the carpenters just managed to make a precarious living. The existence of this middle class gave a different complexion to the life of the village. The workers stood about all day at the entrance to their workshops, which were inactive in spite of their American machinery. The peasants, on the other hand, were to be seen only at sunrise and sunset and they seemed far away and relegated to a distant world of their own.

Antonino, as befits a good barber, was a source of news and gossip and he soon put me abreast of all that had been going on at Grassano. Not much had happened: several "Americans" had followed the example of the fellow with the gold teeth and accessories of whom we have spoken and lit out for New York; Lieutenant Decunto, the head of the local Fascist Militia, had gone as the only volunteer to Abyssinia; those who had enrolled to go as laborers had received no satisfaction and shared the discontent of their fellows in Gagliano; a new political prisoner had arrived, a Slovene from Dalmatia who was clever with his hands and made model ships and wax statuettes. My unexpected transfer of three months before was still a subject of discussion; like every other local event it had become a bone of dispute between the two factions into which the village was divided. The opposition charged the group in power with having reported me to Matera and brought about my removal because I was friendly with some of their adversaries, such as Signor Orlando and Lasala the carpenter. Those in power claimed, on the contrary, that the opposition had written anonymous letters about me to the authorities simply in order to accuse *them* falsely of causing me to be transferred. To both parties the circumstances of my departure constituted a grave breach of hospitality. In my opinion neither of the factional theories held water, but they had given rise to an embittered argument and served to swell the long standing hate and rivalry between the two groups.

These things did not interest me. I wished to take advantage of the remaining hours of daylight to go for a walk and see the landmarks I was so fond of, and I set out for this purpose with a group of my friends. Compared to Gagliano the no less appalling poverty of Grassano seemed almost like prosperity; the greater liveliness of the people and their rapid Apulian patter almost made me think I was in an up-to-the minute city. At last I could see shops, even if they were only holes-in-the-wall with hardly anything for sale; there were pushcarts in the square in front of the palace of Baron Collefusco, displaying cloth, razor blades, terra cotta jars, and kitchen utensils. One pushcart had a load of books, the same books I had seen in the hands of Capitano, his young friends, and the older peasants: lives of the Kings of France and brigand stories, a biography of Corradino, almanacs, and calendars.

A little farther on there was a café, a real café that had billiard tables in the back and old blown-glass bottles lined up on a shelf behind the bar, of the kind sought after by collectors, with faces of King Victor Emmanuel II, Garibaldi, and Queen Margherita, naked women balancing a ball, and a hand brandishing a pistol. A stroll up and down the few hundred feet between Prisco's inn and the café accounted for the social life of Grassano. To right and left, above and below, there were only alleys, paths, and flights of wide steps running between the peasant huts. These huts were even poorer and dirtier than those of Gagliano. Here there were no vegetable gardens or orchards around the houses, but they were all huddled together as if in mortal terror. The sheep and goats, even more numerous, ran up and down narrow streets choked with garbage, and half-naked, pale, puffy children chased one another among the rubbish. In Grassano the women wore neither veils nor peasant dress, but they had the same earthy, immobile, animal-like expression. Here, too, patience and resignation were written on both the faces of men and the desolation of the landscape. Because the outside world was a little nearer, there was in the air a stronger hankering after escape, although it was doomed to equal disappointment.

I went up alone, by familiar ways, to the wind-swept church at the summit of the village, to look once more at the wide view extending beyond the boundaries of Lucania. At my feet lay the houses of Grassano, below them the gray hillside and the Basento River bed; straight across from me were the Accettura Mountains, rising from the foothills that hid Ferrandina to the Dolomites of Pietra Pertosa where the Basento wound its way out of sight. On either side lay the sea of shapeless land, stretching beyond the Bilioso River, the caves of the brigands and gnomes, and Irsina high on its bristling hill. Everywhere distant villages stood out like scattered sails on this vast ocean. There were Salandra and Banzi, on whose burning sands it is hard to imagine the poet Horace's fountain, "more than crystal bright; none worthier to be sued with flowers and wine." Other villages, closer by, seemed to be setting their sails toward the home port of

Grottole straight across the way, behind St. Anthony's Chapel with its two lonely trees amid the desert. For some years these endless, dreary, rolling wastes had been sown with wheat of such a poor variety that it was hardly worth the expense and trouble of putting it in the ground. The first time I had looked out at them was in summer, near the harvest season. As far as the eye could see was an expanse of waving yellow grain in the sunlight, and the sound of threshing-machines throbbed through the silence. Now all was dull gray with no color to break the monotony.

I stayed for a long time, until dusk came and a few drops of rain began to fall, when I hurried down to the inn. Quite a few people were waiting for their supper: teamsters, peddlers, and Pappone. Raised above all the other voices I could hear from the street were those of Pappone and Prisco, the one shouting in Neapolitan and the other in Apulian dialect, as they played their favorite game of pretending to quarrel. Pappone was a fruit dealer from Bagnoli who often came to buy pears at Grassano; I had already met him during the summer. He and Prisco were the greatest of friends and they swore at each other all the time to show their devotion. "You old son of a . . . banker . . ." yelled Pappone. "That's right, with the devil's own tail, you stinker!" cried Prisco. And they went on from there, cursing, laughing, and rolling their eyes. Pappone was a former monk, greedy, fat, and, in his way, witty. He was a first-rate cook and he always banished Prisco's wife from the kitchen while he prepared a Neapolitan sauce for his own spaghetti. He invariably gave me a share of it and I can bear witness that it was the best I ever tasted. He possessed an even greater talent for telling the most extravagant stories, accompanied by highly expressive gestures. But their inspiration was so monkish and their subjects so salacious that I cannot repeat them, not even the one he told that

172

evening at table, which was perhaps the most innocent of his repertory.

At last I was having a meal with other people, and this simple pleasure made me feel like a free man again. Ever since my stay in Gagliano I have hated to dine alone and I have come to prefer even bad company to none at all. The plain supper seemed to me a feast, and Pappone's story far wittier than the most celebrated and boring tales of Boccaccio. While we ate, Prisco kept us company, with his shirt-sleeves rolled up, his elbows on the table, and a glass of wine in his hand, swearing and thundering oaths when he was not jumping up and down. A newly arrived guest soon joined us, a draper from Brindisi, whom I had seen at the inn before. He was an enormous hulk of a man, with the face of an ogre, a big nose, big eyes and ears, thick lips, and heavy jowls that shook noisily when he ate. He ate as much as four men together, but then this was his only meal of the day and he had spent a number of hours talking himself hoarse to persuade the women to buy his cloth. In spite of his jowls, the perspiration that ran down the furrows of his face, and his appearance of a deformed giant, he was the kindest of fellows and almost as entertaining as his friend Pappone. We were a lively and happy group around the table.

Capitano, his brother, and their friend Boccia, a youth left slightly retarded by some childhood disease, who worked at the town hall, were in one corner of the room poring over an old issue of the *Gazzetta dello Sport*. The ogre from Brindisi looked askance at their infatuation and he lashed out at Capitano in stentorian tones:

"Capità! Nothing but sport these days, eh? War and sport! You've no thought for anything else! What is there to this sport business, anyhow?" Capitano tried to defend himself: "Carnera," he said, "is world heavyweight champion!" The draper laughed so hard that the glasses on the table trembled.

"Your Carnera is just like Garibaldi," he said. This statement was so definite that Capitano could find no answer, and the giant went on:

"They're both fakes. Carnera wins because everything is fixed in advance. Just like Garibaldi, I tell you; it's the same old story. Of course they pass off a lot of tall tales on you in your schoolbooks, but the truth is something else again. When King Franceschiello had to leave Naples and went to Gaeta, Garibaldi and his Red Shirts set out to attack him, gay, proud and brave as lions. From the walls of Gaeta the soldiers fired cannons at them, but the Red Shirts paid no attention; they advanced as if they were going to a wedding, with a flag and drums and fifes stepping out ahead of them. When King Franceschiello saw that the cannons were having no effect he said to himself: 'Either they're madmen or there's something strange about the whole thing. I'll set off a cannon at them myself.' No sooner said than done. He chose a fine cannon ball, had it loaded into the barrel, and fired it himself. Boom! When they saw what was happening Garibaldi and his Red Shirts turned tail and fled, without waiting for a second shot from the King's hand. The other shots, of course, were blanks. Garibaldi, you see, like Carnera, had fixed everything in advance. When the King fired a real shot, Garibaldi said: 'Nothing doing here at Gaeta, boys. Let's go to Teana.' And so they did."

Pappone, Prisco, the teamsters, peddlers, and the rest all laughed. Garibaldi was not popular in these parts and that evening the reputation of Carnera was thoroughly discredited. Capitano acknowledged his defeat, and only Boccia, whose meningitis had left him a bit slow at catching on to what was said around him, kept his own counsel. Because of his affliction he had been given the job of filing away papers and acting as a general factotum at the town hall. The crippled were well treated hereabouts and cared for by their own townsmen. As often happens in such cases, Boccia made up for his slowness with a phenomenal memory, which was limited, however, to the objects of his ruling passions: sport and the law. He knew by heart the names of the members of every soccer team in Italy for several years past, and he used to recite them to me like litanies, his eyes shining with joy. His other passion was even stronger. Law, lawyers, and lawsuits filled him with delight. He knew the names of all the lawyers in the province and extracts from their most famous pleadings. In this he was not unique, for there is a widespread admiration for legal eloquence in this part of the country. An event of two or three years before was the most important and blissful of his existence. A provincial court had held hearings in Grassano for some petty lawsuit connected with fences and the boundary line between two pieces of property, and Latronico, a famous lawyer from Matera, the best known of the region, came to plead it. Boccia knew the whole of Latronico's peroration by heart and never a day went by that he did not repeat it, fired with admiration for its purple patches. "Wolves of Accettura, dogs of San Mauro, crows of Tricarico, foxes of Grottole, and toads of Garaguso!" Latronico had exclaimed, and to Boccia these appellatives were the highest flight of oratory every achieved by man. "Toads of Garaguso!" he would mutter to himself, in a tone of triumph or pity, depending on the mood of the moment. "Yes, *toads*, because Garaguso is in a swamp, surrounded by water. What a speech *that* was!"

For supper, besides spaghetti with Pappone's sauce, we had some ham, lean, tasty, and cut in thick slices, of a flavor quite different from what we have in the North, and in my opinion delicious. I sang its praises to Prisco and he told me that it was mountain ham which he bought himself from peasants living in the highest and most remote villages. The hams were very small and they cost two lire a pound. When I told Prisco that in the city they would be at least five times as expensive, his lively mind immediately conceived the idea of our going into business together. He proposed that we should form a company, and while he went about the mountains buying up hams, I should appoint sales agents among my city friends. He could guarantee quite a supply and perhaps in future years production could be stepped up.

Probably because I have no business head, his proposal seemed to me to be a very fine one. I observed that, apropos of Garibaldi, I should be following in his footsteps, because in a condition similar to mine he took to selling candles, a commodity not far removed from hams. Having accepted Prisco's offer I wrote in a flush of enthusiasm to a friend who traded in a variety of things with the strangest countries imaginable. Some time later he wrote back that the hams did not interest him because the public was not accustomed to their flavor and the small production did not justify the setting up of a sales organization. He advised me to see if I could lay my hands on broom, for making dyes, a product much sought after in this period of attempted economic self-sufficiency. Broom is practically the only flower that blooms in this desert; it grows everywhere among the bushes and is the favorite food of the goats. But by this time my enthusiasm for promoting business in Lucania had died down, and nothing further came of it.

This first evening in company slipped away swiftly, with business schemes, jokes, and the debunking of Garibaldi. The ogre from Brindisi went out to sleep in his truck, in order to be sure that no one stole his cloth during the night, and the teamsters set out in the dark for Tricarico. Pappone and I were Prisco's only overnight guests, and so each of us had a room to himself. I wanted to get up early the next morning. My plan was to go down almost to the Basento and to paint Grassano as I had seen it in the afternoon from the railway station, high up like a castle in the air. Antonino had offered to go with me and at dawn he was waiting at the door, with a mule to carry my easel and canvases, and a group of friends who wanted to go along. There were Riccardo, Carmelo, the road-mender and cyclist who had seen the gnomes, a carpenter, a tailor, two peasants, and several boys.

The weather was gray and windy, but there was hope that no rain would fall. In the vague, cold light of the clouds the landscape stood out more clearly and its monotony appeared somewhat less mournful than under the blazing rays of the sun. It was just the weather that I wanted for my picture. Prisco's younger son joined us, while Capitano waved good-bye to us from the door, for the way was too long for his lame leg. With Barone in the lead, a frolicking standard-bearer, we started down a steep path which cuts out the curves of the winding road and makes the distance to the bottom of the valley only about five miles. I had gone by the same route and in almost exactly the same company one August day to swim in a lonely stagnant pond formed by the Basento River, surrounded by a few poplars, anomalous in these surroundings, as if they had taken root by some strange error. We had plunged quite naked into the river in the hot air of the midsummer afternoon. Using only their bare hands, my companions had tried to catch the fish lurking in the mud along the banks, and with these primitive tactics they had actually caught quite a few. Fishing was forbidden in these rivers, because the fish were supposed to destroy mosquito eggs, but no one paid any attention to the law. The poor people of

Grassano had so little to eat all the year around that a plate of fish was a gift from the gods. Later we dried ourselves to the singing of grasshoppers and the buzzing of mosquitoes, under the hot sun reflected by the clay earth around us. Today the air was cool, but the landscape was unchanged except that it was gray instead of yellow. When we reached a spot I thought good to work in, we made a halt. Antonino stayed with me for the privilege of handing me my tubes of paint, and a boy kept watch over the mule which was browsing on stubble. The others went down to the river hoping for a miraculous catch, and I began to paint.

The view from where we stood was as little picturesque as possible, which was why I liked it. There was not a single tree or hedge or rock upon which to center a painting. In this landscape there was no rhetoric of mother nature or of man and the soil, only a monotonous expanse of waste land and, above, the white village. In the gray sky a little white cloud hanging low above the houses, had somewhat the shape of an angel.

My companions came back from the river empty-handed. They stood around my canvas, surprised to see Grassano where there had been nothing before. I had often noticed that because the peasants have not the preconceived ideas of the half-educated they have a good eye for painting, and I usually asked their opinion of my work. While I went on with my picture, my friends lit a fire to heat the food we had brought with us, and then we sat down on the ground to eat it, looking at the canvas on my easel which we had tied to stones so that the wind should not blow it away. After we had eaten it began to rain and there was nothing to do but go home. My picture was nearly finished. We wrapped it in a blanket, loaded it on the mule, and started to walk back under a gentle drizzle.

Chapter Eighteen

IN THE VILLAGE A GREAT SUR-
prise awaited us. A small troupe of actors had just arrived in a
wagon pulled by a thin white horse. They planned to stay
several days and to give performances. Their wagon, with a
waterproof cover draped over it, stood in the square, and in it
were their scenery and curtain packed in long rolls. The actors
themselves were bustling about in search of lodgings in the
peasants' houses, so as not to have to pay for rooms at the inn.
The troupe was a family one: the father, a comedian; the
mother, his leading lady; two daughters under twenty with
their husbands and a few other relatives, all of them Sicilian.
The head of the family came to Prisco for something hot to
give his wife, who was laid low with a fever. She could not
perform that evening, and perhaps not even the next day, but
they would surely stay on longer. He was a middle-aged man,
somewhat stout, with pendulous cheeks and exaggerated ges-

179

tures patterned after the great actor Zacconi. When he heard that I was a painter, he asked if I would make him some badly-needed scenery, as his equipment was in very poor shape after jogging about in all kinds of weather in the wagon. He told me that he had belonged to high-class stock companies before he came with his talented wife and daughters to this wandering existence. Usually they traveled around Sicily, and this was the first time they had been in Lucania; they stopped in the largest and most prosperous villages, the length of their stay depending on their box-office receipts. But they were not making much money and were having a hard time of it; one of his daughters was pregnant and could not appear on the stage much longer. I was quite willing to paint scenery for him, but nowhere in the village were we able to find canvas or paper or the right sort of paint, and so unfortunately there was nothing I could do about it. He then invited me to attend the performance to be given two days hence and introduced to me the members of his company. The father was the only one of the family who looked like an old actor. The women were not actresses but goddesses in human guise. The mother and her two daughters closely resembled each other; they seemed to have issued forth from the earth or to have stepped down from a cloud. They had enormous black eyes, opaque, and empty like those of statues; immobile, marble-like faces, accented by thick black eyebrows and full red lips; and their necks were white and sturdy. The mother was full blown and opulent, with the lazy sensuality of a Juno; the slender and graceful daughters were like woodland nymphs strangely rigged out in fancy dress.

I hastened to go to the local office of the *carabinieri* to obtain permission to stay out late on the evening of the performance. Dr. Zagarella, the mayor of Grassano, unlike Don Luigi, had no taste for the role of a policeman and he left the *carabinieri* in full charge of political prisoners. He was an able and cultivated man and thanks to him and another physician, Dr. Garaguso, of excellent reputation, Grassano was the only place in the province where successful efforts were made to fight malaria. The two were exceptions for these parts, where most medical men were on the order of the two specimens at Gagliano. In fact, one of the objects of my visit was to ask their advice and to profit by their long experience. The advice they gave me was very precious and they showed me their statistics to boot. For some years preventive measures and land reclamation had been undertaken at Grassano, even without encouragement or financial assistance from the provincial authorities. Now there were very few deaths from malaria and in the last two years the number of new cases had greatly diminished.

In this region malaria is a scourge of truly alarming proportions; it spares no one and when it is not properly cared for it can last a lifetime. Productive capacity is lowered, the race is weakened, the savings of the poor are devoured; the result is a poverty so dismal and abject that it amounts to slavery without hope of emancipation. Malaria arises from the impoverishment of the deforested clayey land, from neglected water, and inefficient tilling of the soil; in its turn it generates in a vicious circle the poverty of the peasants. Public works on a large scale are necessary to uproot it. The four main rivers of Lucania: the Bradano, the Basento, the Agri, and the Sinni, besides a host of lesser streams, should be dammed up; trees should be planted on the mountainsides; good doctors, hospitals, visiting nurses, medicines, and preventive measures should be made available to all. Even improvements on a limited scale would have some effect, as was proved to me by Zagarella and Garaguso. But a general apathy prevails and the peasants continue to sicken and die.

Autumn was in the air. It rained during the three days before the theatrical performance and I could not paint out of doors. I walked about the village, went to see my friends, and worked a bit in my room. Prisco went hunting and came back with three red foxes and a river bird. I painted these and did a portrait of Capitano. One day, while I was painting the foxes, I stopped work for a moment and looked out through my window over the street. It was early afternoon, everyone in the inn was taking a siesta, and there was complete silence. I heard a scurry of bare feet on the staircase and saw Prisco, in his shirtsleeves and without his shoes, leap into the street, burst into a doorway across the street and come out again, still silent, with a knife in his hand. I threw open my window and heard loud voices. Across the way was a barn where teamsters put up. Prisco had been asleep in his own room, but with one eye open and on the alert for the slightest sound, and he realized that all was not well on the other side of the street, where the teamsters were playing the game of *passatella*. He saw something shiny, and quick as a flash, without pausing to slip on his shoes, he noiselessly entered the barn, just in time to snatch a knife from the hand of a fellow who had drawn it with murder in his eyes.

Passatella is the most popular game in this part of the country, and a particular favorite among the peasants. On long winter evenings and holidays they play it for hours in the taverns. It often ends in violence; if not with drawn knives, as on the occasion I have just described, at least with quarrels and scuffling. *Passatella* is not so much a game as it is a peasant tournament of oratory, where interminable speeches reveal in veiled terms a vast amount of repressed rancor, hate, and rivalry. A brief session with the cards determines a winner, who is then the King of the *passatella*, and his assistant. The King holds sway over the wine, for which all the players have paid their share, and he fills the glasses or leaves them empty according to his fancy. His assistant holds the glasses out to be filled and has veto powers, that is, he can prevent the would-be drinker from downing his wine. The King and his assistant alike must justify both their choices and their vetoes, and this they do in the form of a cross-examination carried out in long speeches, replete with irony and concealed passion. Sometimes the game has an innocent character and does not extend beyond the pleasantry of piling up all the drinks on one man who is notoriously unable to hold them, or denying them to the keenest drinker at the table. But more often the arguments proffered by the King and his assistant reflect the feuds and conflicting interests of the players, expressed with all the slowness, roundabout ways, astuteness, mistrust, and deep conviction characteristic of the peasants. Cards and bottles of wine alternate for hours on end, until tempers boil from the effect of drink and heat and the re-kindling of smouldering passions, which are in turn sharpened by vindictive words and yet lulled by drunkenness. Even if a fight does not develop, all those present are aware of the bitterness latent in what has been said during the exchange of veiled insults. Prisco knew well this sole diversion of the peasants and was on the alert.

After the episode of the knife and when I had finished painting the foxes, I went out for a short walk. The rain was over and the air was filled with the odor of burned meat, coming from tripe broiled on braziers set out on the street and sold in sandwiches at a penny apiece. I climbed up a series of wide steps toward the higher part of the town until I came to the house where I had lived in the days just before my departure for Gagliano, when I had left Prisco's inn with the hope of settling down to stay. I had rented from a Nea-politan widow a large room with two windows on the second floor. Below me, on the ground floor, there was a carpenter shop. The carpenter's wife, Margherita, who did my washing and cleaning, was a good friend. When she saw me coming now she ran to meet me and welcome me with joy. "Have you come back? Are you going to stay here with us?" She was sorry to hear that I had to go away again.

Margherita was an old woman with an enormous gnarled goiter and a kind face. She was considered one of the best educated women in the village because she had gone through the fifth grade of school and remembered everything she had ever learned. When she came to clean my room she recited to me the poems she had memorized at school, the "Expedition to Sapri" and the "Death of Ermengarda." She said them in a singsong voice, standing erect in the middle of the room with her arms hanging down at her sides. Every now and then she stopped in order to explain to me the meaning of some difficult word. Margherita was of a mild and affectionate nature. Often she said to me: "Don't be sad because your mother is far away. You've lost one mother and found another, for I'll be a mother to you."

With her goiter and all, Margherita had a truly maternal instinct. She had two sons, now grown up, one of them in America. She spoke of them often with tenderness and showed me photographs of her grandchildren. When I asked her one day if she had had any other children she began to cry for the loss of her third and favorite boy, and told me his story. Of her three boys he was the handsomest; when he was eighteen months old he talked well, understood everything that was said to him and had beautiful dark curls and sparkling eyes. One winter day when there was snow on the ground, Margherita gave him to a friend and neighbor to look after, who took him with her while she went to gather some firewood in the country. That evening the neighbor came home alone and beside herself. She had left the child, who was barely able to walk, for a few minutes while she picked up some sticks along a woodland path, and when she returned he was gone. She had searched everywhere without finding the slightest trace. A wolf or some other wild animal must have carried him off and he would never be found. Margherita and her husband, with a group of peasants and *carabinieri*, searched every square foot of the countryside all night long and during the following days with no success, and after three days they gave up.

On the morning of the fourth day Margherita, who was wandering alone and disconsolate through the country, met at a turn in the path a tall handsome woman with a black face. It was the Madonna of Viggiano, who said to her: "Margherita, you mustn't cry. Your child is alive. He is there in the woods in a wolf's lair. Go home and get someone to go with you and you'll find him." Margherita ran off and later, followed by the peasants and *carabinieri*, she came to the spot described by the Madonna. In the wolf's lair, amid the snow, her child lay asleep, warm and pink-cheeked in spite of the cold. His mother embraced him and woke him up while the others all wept, even the *carabinieri*. The child told her that a woman with a black face had come for him and kept him with her for four days in the wolf's lair, nursing him and keeping him warm. When they came home Margherita said to her husband: "This is no ordinary boy. The Madonna of Viggiano gave him her own milk in the wolf's lair. Who knows what he may become? Let us go see the fortuneteller at Grottole."

"At Grottole," Margherita told me, "There was a fortune-teller who had made a name for himself. We went to him, paid him a lira and he told us all that had just happened, as if he had seen it with his own eyes. Then his face darkened and he said the child would fall on a stairway and break his neck when he was six years old. Alas, this turned out to be true. When he was six my poor boy died as the result of a fall . . ." And Margherita burst into tears.

Other children were known to have vanished into thin air and to have been found again through the merit of the Black Madonna. A lost baby a few months old was found on top of one of two trees flanking Saint Anthony's chapel, five miles or so from Grassano, about halfway to Grottole. A devil had carried him there, and Saint Anthony took him under his protection. But the only case where I personally knew the family concerned was that of Margherita's child.

At last the evening of the play arrived. The rains had blown over and the stars were shining when I made my way to the improvised theater. No public hall existed and choice fell upon a sort of cellar or grotto, partly underground, with benches from the school set on the hard earth floor. At one end a small stage had been erected, closed from view by an old curtain. The place was full of peasants, waiting with wonderment for the show to begin. The play was *La Fiaccola sotto il Moggio, The Light Under the Bushel,* by Gabriele d'Annunzio. I expected to be bored to tears by this romantic drama, played by second-rate actors. I had come to see it because under the present circumstances an evening at the theater was an unaccustomed diversion. But I was agreeably surprised. The female divinities, with their large, empty black eyes and attitudes charged with motionless but passionate intensity, played their parts to perfection and, on the stage not more than four yards wide, they stood out most impressively. All the rhetoric, affectation, and pomposity of the tragedy vanished, leaving just what d'Annunzio's drama should have been in the first place: a bare tale of immutable passions against the background of a land that knows no time. At last one of his works seemed to me good, and free of sham aesthetics.

Soon I realized that this sort of purification was due not so much to the actresses as to the audience. The peasants took part in the play with the liveliest interest. Its villages, mountains and streams were not far from Grassano; they knew exactly what they were like, and every time the names came up they murmured assent. The spirits and devils that enter into the story were the same spirits and devils that lived in the clay caves of this region. The plot was true to life, for the audience endowed it with its real atmosphere, that of the closed, hopeless, and mute world of the peasants. This performance, stripped by actors and audience together of its "dannunzianism," had a rough and elementary content which the peasants felt to be a part of their own experience. The whole thing was an illusion, but it demonstrated a truth. D'Annunzio was of peasant origin, but when he became a literary figure he was bound to betray them. His beginnings were in a mute world like this one, among the Abruzzi Mountains, but he sought to superimpose on it the many-colored coat of contemporary verse, which is primarily wordy, sensual, and haunted with a sense of time. In so doing he degraded this world to a mere instrument of rhetoric and its poetry to futile verbal acrostics. His efforts could only result in betrayal and failure; from such a hybrid combination only a monstrosity could be born. The Sicilian actresses and the peasants of Grassano reversed this: they tore away the layers of counterfeit and grasped in their own fashion the peasant core of the drama. It was this that moved them and fired their enthusiasm. The two worlds which d'Annunzio had vainly tried to weld into an empty aestheticism flew apart, as if aware that

they could not fit together, and beneath the flow of super-
fluous words there stood forth to the view of the peasants the
images of Fate and Death.

The next day I was asked to lunch by a certain Signor
Orlando, brother of a well-known journalist who lived in
New York. He was a tall, melancholy man who lived very
quietly in a large house of his own in an isolated part of the
village. As he was an adversary of the clique in power he took
as little part as possible in local affairs. We had come to know
each other because I had designed the jacket for a book his
brother had written about America, and he had been most
hospitable. In his house the old Lucanian customs were observed: his wife did not come to the table with us, but left
us to ourselves.

We spoke of the peasants, malaria, agriculture, and various
problems of the South. That morning I had talked with a
political prisoner, an accountant from Turin, who had formerly been employed by the Fascist trade unions. He had
been arrested, according to his story, as a scapegoat for his
superiors, who had pilfered the funds entrusted to them. Here
in Grassano he had found a job keeping the books of a large
landed estate, and he let me examine them. By government
order nothing was raised on this estate but wheat. In the fat
years, with hard work and quantities of fertilizer, the wheat
harvested came to only nine times the cost of the seed; in the
lean ones it amounted to much less, sometimes as little as
three or four times the cost. In other words, it was folly to
insist on raising wheat. This land was better suited to almond
and olive trees and the best thing of all would be to turn it
back into forests and pastures. The peasants received starvation wages. I remember seeing, on the day I first arrived in
Grassano, endless lines of women coming up from the fields
along the Basento with sacks of wheat balanced on their

heads, sweating like the damned in hell under the pitiless noon sun. For every sack they brought up to the village they got one lira. And in the fields where they worked malaria was rampant. Orlando and I agreed on the fallacy of the common theory that the root of all these evils was the existence of large estates and that the only cure would be to divide them up among the peasants. The small landowners at Gagliano were no better off than the tenants here; in some respects they had an even harder time of it. What, then, was to be done?

"Nothing," said Orlando, with his profound Southern melancholy, echoing the hopeless slogan of Giustino Fortunato, one of the best and most humane thinkers of the region, who was wont to call himself a "do-nothing politician." I could not help thinking how many times every day I heard this same word on the tongues of the peasants. "*Ninte*," as they say at Gagliano for *Niente*. "What did you eat today?" "*Niente*." "What are your prospects for tomorrow?" "*Niente*." "Well, what shall we do?" "*Niente*." Always the same answer, and they roll their eyes back toward heaven in a gesture of negation. The other word that recurs most often among them is "*crai*" from the Latin *cras*, tomorrow. Everything that they are waiting for, that is due to come, that should be remedied or attended to is "*crai*." But "*crai*" means "never."

Orlando's despair, so widespread among those men of the South who give serious thought to the problems of their country, stemmed from a deep-seated sense of inferiority. Because of it they can never fully understand their own country and its problems. Their point of departure is, quite unconsciously, a comparison that should never be made, or at least should not be made until the problems have found a solution. Because they consider the peasant world inferior to the world outside, they are bogged down by a feeling of either impotence or revenge. And impotence and revenge have never created anything living.

My few days at Grassano were occupied in painting, the theater, and good company, and went by like a flash. The time came for me to go. Early one gray morning the car waited for me in front of the door. With loud and hearty farewells from Prisco and his family, Antonino, and Riccardo, I left this village to which I have never since returned.

Chapter Nineteen

GAGLIANO SOON ABSORBED and closed around me again as the green waters of a swamp overtake a frog that has lingered to sun himself on the bank. The village struck me as more remote and lonely than ever; no echo of the outside world penetrated so far; no strolling players or peddlers came to break the monotony. The witch was waiting for me on my doorstep, just as I had left her, with her tall, dark, ageless body; Don Luigi was waiting for me in the square, happy to have me once more in his clutches, and my patients lay waiting in their huts, more numerous than ever after my week's absence. Once more the days passed by in endless procession.

The weather was turning cold. The wind came up in cold spirals from the ravines; it blew continuously from every direction, went straight through a man's bones, and roared away down the tunnel-like paths. Alone in my house at night I listened: it was a ceaseless cry, a wail, as if all the spirits of the earth were joined in chorus to lament their dire imprisonment. There were long, heavy rains; the village was covered with a white mist that lay as though stagnant in the valleys below, and the mountain tops stuck out of this weary pallor like islands in a shapeless ocean of vapidity. The clay was beginning to break up and slide slowly down the hillsides, a gray torrent of earth in a liquefied world. The metallic sound of the raindrops beating on the terrace above my room as if it were a drumhead, joined with the whistling and howling of the wind, made me feel as if I were in a tent in the desert. A gloomy, unsteady light came in through the windows; the surrounding hills appeared to lie in a sorrowful, uneasy sleep. But Barone frolicked happily outdoors in the dampness, sniffing the wet ground and shaking the water out of his soaked coat of hair when he leaped back into the house. The violence of the wind blew smoke back down into the chimney, spreading through every room the fragrant, bitter smell of the juniper and pine branches which an old peasant woman brought to me from the woods on her donkey. I had a choice between freezing and weeping; hours went by while my eyes watered and grew red, and the world just beyond my door melted away in the rain. Then came the snow; the women's hands were red with frostbite and they draped heavy black wool shawls over their white veils. A stillness and a silence thicker than before settled down around the lonely mountain wastes.

One evening after a raging wind had momentarily cleared the sky, I heard the rumble of the town crier's drum and the sound of his trumpet, while his strangely pitched voice repeated on one high, prolonged note: "Women, hear: the pig doctor is here. Come to the Mound by the Fountain tomorrow morning at seven o'clock with your pigs! Women, hear, the pig doctor!"

The next day the weather was unsettled but there were scraps of blue sky among the low clouds. The snow was almost all melted; there were only clumps of it here and there where it had been piled up by the wind. I got up early to see what was happening.

The Mound by the Fountain was a large, almost flat, clearing amid the rolling clay near the old spring just outside the village, to the right of the church. It was not yet daylight when I arrived, but the place was already crowded. Almost all the women, old and young were there, most of them leading a pig on a leash as if it were a dog. Those who had no pigs came along for the adventure. White veils and black shawls fluttered in the wind and a loud murmur of talk, shouts, and laughter, together with grunts on the part of the pigs, resounded in the icy air. The women were in great agitation, red in the face and filled with mingled fear and expectation. Children were running about and dogs were barking; everything was in motion.

In the center of the Mound stood the pig doctor, a well-built man about six feet tall, with a ruddy complexion, red hair, blue eyes, and a thick, droopy moustache, which made him look like an ancient Gaul, a Vercingetorix who had stumbled by chance upon this land of a swarthy race. His mission was to castrate the young sows, or such of them as were not needed for the perpetuation of the species, thereby making them fatter and more tender to eat. In the males this operation is not difficult and the peasants perform it themselves while the animals are still young. But in the females the ovaries have to be removed and surgical skill is required. The pig doctors, who carry out this rite, are a cross between priests and surgeons; there are few versed in this art and it is handed down from father to son. The pig doctor whom I saw upon this occasion was famous in his profession; he made the rounds of all the villages of the region twice a year. In spite of his reputed ability and the fact that very few pigs died under his knife, the women, who were attached to their own beasts, could not but tremble at the risk involved.

The red-headed man stood stalwartly in the center of the clearing, sharpening his knife. In order to leave his hands free he held in his mouth a heavy upholsterer's needle; the string looped through its eye hung down over his chest. He was waiting for the next victim, while each of the hesitant women around him pushed her friends and neighbors ahead of her with loud expostulations and a sudden respect for formality. The sows, too, seemed aware of what lay in store for them; they dug their feet into the ground or pulled at the ropes around their necks in a vain effort to escape, squealing all the while in their almost human voices like panicky girls. A young woman stepped forward with her animal, and two peasant assistants of the pig doctor took hold of the pink young sow, which struggled and gasped with fright. They tied its four legs to stakes driven into the ground and laid it down on its back. While the sow screamed with terror the woman made the sign of the cross and said a prayer to the Madonna of Viggiano, to which the other bystanders murmured assent.

Then the operation began. The pig doctor, with a sure swift stroke of his curved knife made a deep incision down to the abdomen. Blood spurted out over the surrounding mud and snow, but the red-headed man did not pause for a single second. He thrust his hand up to the wrist into the opening, seized one ovary, and pulled it out. A sow's ovaries are attached by a ligament to the intestine; when he had pulled out the left one he still had to go after the right one without making a second incision. He did not cut the ovary he had already extracted but stitched it with his heavy needle to the skin of the sow's stomach. When he had anchored it there securely, he took hold of the intestine with both hands and pulled it out, unraveling it as if it were a ball of wool. Yard upon yard of intestine emerged from the wound, rose, purple and gray, with blue veins and clusters of yellow fat at the conjunction with the omentum. And still it came, as if there were no end to it, until finally the right ovary appeared, attached to the intestine like the left one. Then, without making use of his knife with one powerful tug the man tore both of them away, and without turning around he threw them over one shoulder to his dogs. These were four enormous white sheep dogs, with thick tails, fierce red eyes, and collars bristling with nails to protect them from the wolves. The dogs were poised, ready for his gesture; they caught the bloody ovaries on the wing and then licked up the blood strewn on the ground. The pig doctor did not pause. When he had disposed of the ovaries he began to push the intestine back into place with his fingers, using considerable force when, inflated like a rubber tire, it entered with difficulty. When everything was back in place he took the threaded needle out from under his thick moustache and with a few stitches and a surgical knot he deftly closed the incision. The sow, released from the stakes, lay for a moment uncertainly, then got up, shook itself and ran squealing across the clearing, followed by the women, while its owner, freed from anxiety, dug the two lire fee for the pig doctor out of a pocket beneath her skirt. The whole operation lasted only three or four minutes; already the assistants had tied another victim to the stakes and stretched it out on the ground, ready for the sacrifice.

One after another, the whole morning long, the sows were castrated. Daylight came and a cold wind blew ragged bits of cloud about the sky. A smell of blood lay heavy in the air; the dogs had had enough of the raw meat. The snow ran red with blood; the women's voices were shriller and the sows, operated and unoperated alike, squealed in unison whenever one of them was laid out on the ground, sympathetically answering each other's laments like a chorus of mourners. But the onlookers were happy; it seemed as if not a single animal would die. When twelve o'clock came the miracle man stood up straight and announced that he would finish with the few remaining sows in the afternoon. The women drifted away, chattering, with their sows on their leashes. The pig doctor counted his earnings and went off, followed by his dogs, to the widow's house for his dinner, and I left after him. For several days there was talk of little else in the village. The women were still afraid that some post-operative complications might bring about the death of one of the sows, but all went well, they were reassured, and in the end all their fears were dispelled. The pig doctor with the red whiskers of a Druid priest and the sacrificial knife went away the same evening, showered with the blessings of the village, to Stigliano.

The days were now short, and I spent long, melancholy evenings by the crackling, smoky fire while Barone pricked up his ears at the howling of the wind and the baying of wolves in the distance. The peasants had less and less to do; in bad weather there was no use going to the fields, so they stayed at home beside their meager fires or met in the wine-cellars where they played endless games of *passatella*. Even Don Luigi was a devotee of these oratorical tournaments. He spent entire afternoons at them, with his fellow schoolteacher, P., the lawyer and perennial student, four or five other landowners, and, to make a show of democracy, the local constable or the "American" barber. He would not emerge until late in the day, with bleary eyes, barely able to stay on his feet, and there was little danger of meeting him in the square. He had lost his boon companion and strong right arm, the inseparable and irreplaceable partner in his political power. The sergeant of the *carabinieri*, having squeezed some forty thousand lire, according to local gossip, out of the impoverished citizenry of Gagliano, had succeeded in being transferred to new and greener pastures.

His successor was a diametrically opposite type, a boyish, fair-haired, blue-eyed young fellow from Bari. He was just out of training school and this was his first post; he brought to it zeal, conviction, and a real desire to serve the cause of justice. Idealistic and shrinking from venality, he felt himself to be the appointed guardian of widows and orphans, and it was not long before he realized that he had fallen into a den of wolves. After a few days of acquaintance with the village gentry, with their feuds and rivalries, and the scorn they displayed toward the poor benighted peasants, he understood that there was little he could do to combat the network of established interests built up on the impunity of one class and the passivity of the other. When we met in the square he looked embittered and disconsolate. "Merciful God, Doctor, what a place this is!" he said. "There are only two honest men in the village —you and myself." I cheered him up as best I could: "There are more than two, Sergeant. Besides, two just men would have sufficed to save Sodom and Gomorrah from the wrath of heaven. A lot of the peasants are honest; you'll see. And there's Don Cosimino."

Don Cosimino stood behind the window at the post office in a long black linen smock that covered his hump. He listened to what everyone had to say, looked out at the world with keen, sorrowful eyes, and smiled with disillusioned kindliness. On his own initiative he had begun secretly to give out incoming letters addressed to political prisoners before they were censored.

"There's a letter for you, Doctor," he would whisper from behind the window. "Come for it later when there's no one about." And he would slip it to me concealed in a newspaper. He was supposed to forward all our mail to Matera, whence it returned to Gagliano after a week's delay. But as things were I scanned postcards on the spot and gave them straight back to Don Cosimino; my letters I took home and opened with care. If the envelopes were still intact I took them back to the post office the following day in order that the censors should not be alarmed by a sudden dearth of correspondence. No one ever asked the kindly hunchback for this favor; he did it from natural kindness and of his own free will. At first I hesitated to take the letters for fear of compromising him; he thrust them into my hands and forced them upon me with an authoritative smile. Outgoing letters, too, had to go by way of Matera, with the same unfortunate delay, but here, in spite of his good will, Don Cosimino could be of no assistance.

At about this time the censorship rules were changed. The police in Matera, perhaps because they had too much to do, authorized the mayor to censor the outgoing mail, a step which vastly increased the power and prestige of his office. Letters were no longer given to Don Cosimino to be forwarded to Matera, but they were taken to the mayor, who first read them and then sent them on their way. The new rules were supposed to speed up the mail, but this gain was outweighed by the annoyance of having to submit to local tyranny, of confiding one's most private and intimate affairs to an inquisitive and childlike individual whom one ran into on the street a dozen times a day. There was scant hope that Don Luigi would be content with merely glancing at the letters before he sent them on. His duties as a censor were a real honor, a new and unhoped for means of satisfying his sadistic tendencies and his detective-story imagination. A new prisoner had just arrived, an important oil merchant from Genoa, who had been arrested on account of a run-in with business competitors rather than for political reasons. He was an old man, with a serious disturbance of the heart, accustomed to comfort, practical and sentimental at the same time. Homesickness and the inconveniences of Gagliano at first caused him considerable anguish. He had been forced to leave his very complicated business at a moment's notice and hence he sent instructions by mail to those who were left in charge. His letters were full of conventional business terms and abbreviations, such as: "In ans. to yrs. of the 7th inst., etc.," and of dates, check numbers, payments due and so on. They were the most innocent letters possible, but Don Luigi did not know the jargon of business, and the mantle of his new authority sat heavily upon his shoulders. He immediately imagined that these elliptical phrases and numbers made up a secret code and he thought that he was on the verge of uncovering a very important conspiracy. He did not mail the letters for a number of days while he tried in vain to decipher them. Finally he sent them to Matera and kept close watch on the old man in the meanwhile. One day he could contain himself no longer and he indulged in a violent outburst of temper against his prisoner, threatening him in a most mysterious way. It took a long time for him to calm down and I am sure he was never fully persuaded that his suspicions were groundless.

In my case things were quite different. Don Luigi took my outgoing letters home and read them attentively. For several days afterwards, whenever I met him in the street, he praised my style to high heaven: "How well you express yourself, Don Carlo. You're a real writer. I read your letters very slowly and enjoy every word of them. The one you wrote three days ago is a masterpiece; I'm making a copy of it now." Don Luigi made a practice of copying all that I wrote; I never knew whether his motive was literary admiration or official zeal or a combination of both. The fact was that it took up a great deal of his time, and my letters never seemed to get off.

Chapter Twenty

E were well into December and the snow lay thick on the deserted fields. The peasants were all in the village and the streets were unusually crowded. In the evenings, amid the smoke from the chimneys which swirled through the dark alleys, there was a hum of voices and a patter of footsteps. Bands of children darted about sounding the first strident notes on their *cupi-cupi*.

The *cupo-cupo* is a crude instrument made of a saucepan and a tin can with a top opening covered by a stretched skin like that of a drumhead. A wooden stick is set into this skin and when it is stroked vertically with one hand there issues forth a low-pitched, tremulous rumble. During the fortnight before Christmas all the boys and girls made themselves *cupi-cupi* and banded together to intone a repeated singsong motive to this single-note accompaniment. They sang long meaningless refrains, not without a certain charm, but their chief activity was the singing of serenades interspersed with improvised complimentary verses at the doors of the gentry. Those whom they thus honored were supposed, in return, to give them presents: dried figs, eggs, cakes, or small change. Every day as soon as it was dark, the same verses could be heard over and over again. The air was filled with the prolonged lament of childish voices to the grotesque rhythm of the *cupi-cupi*. I could hear them from far away:

> *Aggio cantato alla lucente stella:*
> *Donna Caterina è una donna bella;*
> *Sona cupille si voi sunà.*

> *Aggio cantato dal fondo del core:*
> *Il dottor Milillo è 'nu professore;*
> *Sona cupille si voi sunà.*

> By the light of the stars I sing:
> Donna Caterina is a beauty;
> Ring, bells, ring.

> From out of my heart I sing:
> Dr. Milillo is a learned man;
> Ring, bells, ring.

And so they went on, from door to door, with a melancholy clamor. They came to my house as well and sang an interminable string of verses ending with:

> *Aggio cantato sovra 'nu varcone:*
> *E Don Carlo è 'nu barone;*
> *Sona cupille si voi sunà.*

> From a balcony I sing:
> Don Carlo is a baron;
> Ring, bells, ring.

These primitive verses accompanied by the *cupi-cupi* resounded in the dark streets like the roar of the ocean in a seashell. They rose up under the cold winter stars and were lost in the Christmas air laden with the smell of hot buns and a sort of mournful festivity. "Once upon a time shepherds came to the village with their bagpipes," Giulia told me. "Every Christmas they played 'The Christ Child Is Born' in the church. But for some years now they have not come this way."

Just before Christmas one shepherd did come with his bagpipes and a boy, but he stayed only long enough to see some old friends and went away the same evening without playing in the church. I met him in the house of old Maria Rosano, the mason's mother, who had screwed up her courage to come pay me a visit alone. She was entertaining that evening and as I passed by she asked me to come in for cakes and wine. The furniture had been cleared away, and twenty or more young peasants, in some way related to their hostess, were dancing to the plaintive sound of the bagpipes. Their dance was a sort of *tarantella*; the dancers circled around each other, barely touching fingers, as if in a sort of harmonious courtship. Then they all stopped while one young peasant and his betrothed, Maria Rosano's daughter, came hand in hand to the center of the room. She was a strong, tall, rosy-cheeked girl, who worked for her brother the mason. I often saw her in the street balancing enormous weights on her head: bags of cement, buckets of bricks, and even big ceiling-boards which she carried as if they were twigs, not even steadying them with her hands. While the others looked on in silence, the piper struck up a new, nasal, bleating, wild *tarantella*. The two lovers had an instinctive feeling for the dance as a sort of religious rite: they stepped out cautiously at first, sidling up and then turning their backs to each other, wheeling about without ever meeting, beating their feet in time to the music with looks and gestures indicative of reluctance and refusal. Then they quickened their steps, brushed against each other, took hands and spun around like tops; they danced faster and faster in ever smaller circles until they collided and finally they stood face to face, dancing with their hands on their hips, as if the pantomime of amorous skirmish and simulated hesitation were over and a love dance were to follow. Instead, the onlookers clapped their hands, the bagpipes ceased playing, and the two dancers, red-cheeked, bright-eyed, and short of breath, sat down with the rest of the company. Wine passed around, there was talk by the flickering light of the fire, and then the bagpiper went his way. This was, as far as I know, the only dance given in Gagliano during the year I spent there.

It was Christmas Eve and the forsaken land was piled high with snow. The wind carried the funereal tolling of the church bell, which seemed to come down from the sky. From every doorway good wishes and blessings were called down upon my head as I went by. Bands of children made their last rounds with the *cupi-cupi*, and the peasants and their women took gifts to the gentry. Here the ancient custom prevails that the poor pay homage to the wealthy; their gifts are received as a matter of course and are not reciprocated. I, too, on Christmas Eve, had to accept bottles of oil and wine, eggs and baskets of dried figs; the donors were surprised that I did not treat them as well-deserved tributes, but tried to evade them or at least to make some simple return. What strange sort of gentleman was I, not to countenance the reversal of the story of the Three Wise Men, but rather to welcome those who came to his house empty-handed? If the Wise Men's wealthy successors among the gentry had followed a star in order to lay their riches at the feet of a carpenter's son, it would have been a sign that the end of the world was near. Here, where Christ had not come, the Wise Men, too, had never been seen.

Don Luigi generously sent word that because of the holiday we could stay out late and, if we wished, attend midnight mass. On the dot of midnight I was in front of the church, amid the crowd of villagers, all of us stamping our feet in the powdery snow. The sky was clear, with a few stars, and the Christ Child was about to be born. But the bell failed to ring, the church door was padlocked, and of Don Trajella there was no sign. We waited half an hour in front of the locked door with mounting impatience. What was the matter? Was the priest ill or, as Don Luigi loudly insisted, drunk? Finally the mayor decided to send a boy to the priest's house to call him. A few minutes later Don Trajella appeared, coming down the path in high snow-boots with a big key in his hand. He went up to the church door, muttering some excuse or other for his lateness, turned the key in the padlock, and hastened to light the candles on the altar. We all poured into the church and the mass began, a poor, hurried mass, without music or singing. At the end of the mass, after the *Ite missa est*, Don Trajella came down from the altar, walked in front of the benches where we were sitting, and went up into the pulpit to preach the sermon.

"Beloved brethren!" he began. "Beloved brethren! Brethren!" Here he stopped and began to search in his pockets, while incomprehensible mumblings issued from his lips. He put on his spectacles, took them off, put them on again, pulled out a handkerchief, wiped the perspiration from his face, raised his eyes to heaven, let them rest on his hearers, sighed, scratched his head in an agony of embarrassment, exclaimed "Oh!" and "Ah!", clasped and unclasped his hands, murmured a *pater*, and at last remained silent, with a look of despair. A murmuring rustled through the crowd. What was happening? Don Luigi turned red in the face and began to shout:

"He's drunk! And on Christmas Eve!"

"Beloved brethren!" said Don Trajella again. "I came here, as your pastor, to talk to you, my beloved flock, on the occasion of this holy day, to bring you the message of a devoted shepherd, *solliciti et studiosi pastoris*. I had prepared if I may say it in all humility, a fine sermon. I meant to read it to you because my memory is poor. I put it in my pocket, and now, alas, I can't find it; it's lost and I can't remember a single word of it. What can I do? What can I say to you, my faithful flock, you who are waiting to hear me? Alas, I have no words at all to say." At this point Don Trajella relapsed into silence, with his eyes fixed dreamily on the ceiling. The peasants waited, uncertain and curious.

Don Luigi could no longer control himself; he got up angrily.

"It's a scandal! A desecration of the house of God! Fascists, come here!" The peasants did not know which way to look.

Don Trajella, as if awakened from a trance, knelt down in front of a wooden crucifix set on the edge of the pulpit and prayed with folded hands:

"Jesus, my Jesus, see into what a plight my sins have led me! Help me, Lord! Jesus, come to the rescue of Thy servant!" Then suddenly, as if he were touched by grace, the priest leaped to his feet, snatched up a piece of paper hidden at the foot of the crucifix and shouted: "A miracle! A miracle! Jesus has heard me; Jesus has succored me! I lost my sermon and He has helped me to find something better. What value could there have been in my poor words? Listen, rather, to words from afar!" And he began to read from the paper he had just found by the crucifix. But Don Luigi was not listening. He had let himself go in a tempest of icy anger and outraged religiosity.

"Fascists, come here! It's a sacrilege! Drunk in church, on Christmas Eve! Here, to me!" And beckoning to the seven or eight Fascist Scouts from the school among the congregation he began to sing "Little Black Face."

The mayor and his boys sang, but Don Trajella appeared not to hear them and went on reading. The miraculous paper was a letter from Abyssinia, written by the conscript from Gagliano, who had been raised by the monks and was known to all the village.

"These are the words of one of you, a son of this village, the dearest of all my sheep. My poor sermon was nothing in comparison. Jesus performed a miracle when He sent me this letter. Listen to what it says: 'Christmas is coming and my thoughts travel back to Gagliano and to all my friends there. I can imagine them at mass in our little church. Out here we are fighting to bring our holy religion to the savages, to convert these heathen souls to the true faith, to bring them peace and eternal happiness . . .'" The letter went on interminably in this vein and ended up with messages to all and sundry, naming many of those present in the church. The peasants listened with satisfaction to the heaven-sent epistle from Africa. Don Trajella took the letter as his text and preached a sermon on war and peace. "Christmas is a day of peace and we are at war. But as the letter we have just read says so well, the war we are fighting is a harbinger of peace, a war raged for the Cross, which is the symbol of the only true peace men can find here below. . . ." The sermon was drowned out by a veritable pandemonium. Don Luigi and his boys went from "Little Black Face" to the Fascist anthem, *Giovinezza* and from *Giovinezza* back to "Little Black Face." When the peasants failed to follow him and the priest went on talking as if he were oblivious of what was going on, the mayor made for the door, shouting:

"Out of the church, every one of you! The church has been desecrated! Fascists, come with me!" Followed by the Scouts and a few of his friends he went out and led his followers around and around the church singing "Little Black Face" and *Giovinezza* in turn. This they kept up until the end of the sermon. Don Trajella, meanwhile, went on and on; he seemed to be the only person in the church quite at his ease; the only unusual thing about him was the presence of two bright red spots on his wan cheeks.

"*Pax in terra hominibus bonae voluntatis*, beloved brethren. *Pax in terra*, this is the divine message, to which we must listen with particular contrition and devotion in this year of war. The Christ Child was born at this very hour in order to bring us this message of peace. *Pax in terra hominibus*; we must cleanse ourselves, if we are to be worthy, we must examine our consciences and find out whether we have fulfilled our duty, if we are to listen to the word of God with pure hearts. You have done evil, you are all sinners, you never come to church, you never say your prayers, you sing wicked songs, you blaspheme the name of the Lord, you don't baptize your children, you don't come to confession or communion, you have no respect for the Lord's ministers, you do not render unto God that which is His due, and there is no peace in you. *Pax in terra hominibus*. You don't know Latin; what then do these words mean? *Pax in terra hominibus* means that on this Christmas Eve you should have observed the custom of bringing a young kid to your pastor. Because you are unbelievers you did not do your duty, you are not *bonae voluntatis* or men of good will and there is no peace on earth for you and no blessing of the Lord upon your heads.

Take heed of what I have said and bring a young kid to your pastor, pay off the mortgage on his land which you owe him from last year. Do these things if you wish God to look mercifully upon you, to pour his blessings upon you and send peace to your hearts, if you wish for peace on earth and an end to the war which makes you tremble for the fate of your dear ones and our beloved country . . ."

And so he went on, with a medley of witticisms, threats, and Latin quotations. The strains of "Little Black Face" drifted in through the door, underlining phrases of the sermon, while the boy bell-ringer, obeying a sign from the priest, tried to override the mayor's singing with the deathlike tolling of the bell. Amid this noise and general consternation the sermon came to an end. Don Trajella came down from the pulpit and without looking either to the right or to the left he went out of the church, followed by the congregation. Outside Don Luigi was still singing. A peasant in a black coat waited in front of the church, holding the halter of a mule with a saddle on its back. He had come to take the priest to Gaglianello, where he had another midnight mass to say. Don Trajella locked the door of the church, put the key in his pocket, and, with a hand from the peasant, he mounted the mule and went his way. He had a two hours' ride ahead of him on the snowy path through the ravines, and this year the Christ Child must have come to Gaglianello about four o'clock in the morning. There Don Trajella repeated his miracle, and because in this lonely settlement there was neither mayor nor gentry, all went well. The peasants were delighted with his sermon and for once the poor priest was treated with the honor due him. He had all the wine he wanted and got drunk in earnest, with the result that he did not come back to Gagliano until three days later.

I made haste to leave the gathering in front of the church where there was a buzz of comment on the happenings of the night. All the gentry, with the exception of Dr. Milillo, who shook his head in disapproval of his nephew's behavior, were on the mayor's side and they agreed to report the priest to the authorities. "At last we can get rid of him," shouted Don Luigi. "This is the chance we've been looking for." No one will ever know whether Don Trajella planned the entire miracle, starting with his theatrical late arrival in the Stendhal tradition and going on to the loss of his prepared sermon and his apparent embarrassment in the pulpit merely in order to produce a more edifying effect upon his hearers with his oratorical virtuosity, or whether at the same time he did not intend to ridicule both himself and the enemies who had so long persecuted him. It is quite certain that he was not drunk; if he had imbibed a little more than usual, his wits were all the sharper as a result. But Don Luigi was convinced that the drunkenness and the loss of the sermon were genuine and a cause for scandal, and his anger brought about the poor old priest's downfall. Although the next day was Christmas and a holiday, anonymous letters were despatched to the prefect, the police, and the bishop. Soon afterwards two priests arrived from Tricarico to make an investigation. Probably I was the only one among all those they questioned to stand up for the old man, but my words carried little weight. The bishop sentenced Don Trajella to take up residence in Gaglianello, which was his real parish, and forbade him to present himself as a candidate for the church at Gagliano. But all this happened later.

Christmas Day was cold and gray and the peasants slept late in the morning. A greater volume of smoke than usual came out of the chimneys; perhaps goat meat was cooking in the pots swung between the andirons. This was the chief holiday of the year, a day for the simulation of peace and prosperity. Above all it was a day when things could be said and done that were impossible on any other day of the year. Giulia arrived at my house with her face clean and shining, her shawl spotless, her veil freshly ironed, and her child less ragged than usual and wearing a pair of shoes several sizes too large for him. I waited for her impatiently; a considerable part of her witchcraft could be imparted to me on this day and this day alone. Although she had taught me all sorts of spells and incantations for the inspiration of love and the cure of disease she had steadfastly refused to acquaint me with death magic, or the art of bringing about the illness and death of an enemy. "Such things can be told only on Christmas Day and then in strict secrecy. He who receives enlightenment must swear never to communicate what he has learned except on the feast of Christmas. On any other day of the year it is a mortal sin." Yet I had to coax and beguile her into telling me the secret; even on Christmas Day its communication was not entirely sinless, and I had to bind myself to discretion with a solemn oath if we were to escape the mockery of the devil. At last she made up her mind to reveal to me the awesome spells whose mere pronouncement ravages a man in his vitals and gradually dries him up until he is ready for the grave. Shall I, then, in turn reveal some of these fearful exorcisms, which might be so useful to my readers in the times in which we are living? Alas, no. It is not Christmas and I am bound by a solemn oath.

The end of the year was at hand. I wished to wait for midnight according to the time-honored custom, so I sat alone in front of my sputtering kitchen fire while a storm of wind and snow raged outside. I had a glass of wine, but what toast could I make? My clock had stopped and no bells rang in the new year in this land where time did not pass. Thus, at an indeterminate moment, ended the truly tiresome year of 1935, and 1936, its successor, started to repeat the familiar, impersonal, indifferent cycle of things past and things to come. It began most inauspiciously, with an eclipse of the sun.

Chapter Twenty-One

THE ECLIPSE WAS A PORTENT in the heavens. A plague-ridden sun looked through half-closed eyes at a world that had entered upon a war of dissolution. A sin lay beneath it all, and not merely the sin, committed in these very days, of massacre by poison gas, something the peasants shook their heads over because they knew that no sin goes unpunished. No, the sin was deeper yet and of the kind that all pay for alike, the innocent along with the guilty. The face of the sun was darkened in warning: "The future holds only sorrow," the peasants said.

The days were cold and bleak; the sun was pale and seemed to rise with difficulty over the white mountains. Driven by hunger and cold, wolves closed in on the village. Barone smelled them from far away, instinctively, and fell into a state of unusual restlessness and excitement. He ran through the house growling with his hair standing on end, and clawed at the door to go out. When I let him go he disappeared into the night and didn't turn up again until morning. I never knew whether his excitement over the wolves was based on hate and terror or on love and desire, whether his midnight outings were hunts or appointments with old, old friends in the heart of the forest. This much is certain: on the nights he went out the north wind swept echoes of tumult and loud baying through the valleys. Barone came back in the morning worn out with his wanderings, wet and caked with mud. He stretched out near the fire and looked up at me from one half-open eye.

A few wolves came through the village, leaving their tracks in the snow. One evening I saw one myself from the terrace, a great, lean, doglike creature, emerging from the darkness to stand for a moment in the light of a lamp swinging in the wind and to sniff the surrounding air, then slowly fading away into the shadows.

This was a good season for hunting. Some of the men went off to hunt boars beyond Accettura, where they were said to abound, although none came near Gagliano this year. The peasants took advantage of their vacation from the fields to go out in their corduroy jackets with their shiny guns after rabbits and foxes, and often they brought back a considerable bag. The bone of the right hindleg of a buck rabbit, after the marrow had been burned out with a red-hot iron, was made into a cigar-holder. The old men used these holders with religious care not to let the cold air crack them, until they took on a fine black gloss. One old peasant whom I cured of some affliction or other insisted on presenting me with his cigar-holder, endowed by age with a splendid patina. When it became known in the village that I appreciated this gift the peasants began to vie with each other in offering me both finished holders and rabbit bones, and I, too, by dint of perseverance, blackened them by smoking cheap cigars as I strolled up and down the main street.

The mail stopped coming because the roads were piled high with snow, and the island among the ravines lost all contact with the rest of the planet. One day differed from another only in its cloud formations and the quantity of sunshine; the new year did not appear to progress, but lay dormant like the fallen trunk of a tree. In the monotony of the passing hours there was place for neither memory nor hope; the past and the future were two separate unrippled pools. The entire future, as far as the end of the world, was merging for me too into the vague *crai* of the peasants, with its implications of futile endurance, remote from history and time. How deceiving are the contradictions of language! In this timeless land the dialect was richer in words with which to measure time than any other language; beyond the motionless and everlasting *crai* every day in the future had a name of its own. *Crai* meant tomorrow and forever; the day after tomorrow was *prescrai* and the day after that *pescrille*; then came *pescruflo, maruflo, maruflone*; the seventh day was *maruflicchio*. But these precise terms had an undertone of irony. They were used less often to indicate this or that day than they were said all together in a string, one after the other; their very sound was grotesque and they were like a reflection of the futility of trying to make anything clear out of the cloudiness of *crai*. I, too, began to lose hope that anything new might come forth from *maruflo* or *maruflone* or *maruflicchio*. Nothing broke the solitude of my evenings in the smoky kitchen except an occasional visit from the *carabiniere* on duty, who stopped in for the sake of routine and stayed to drink a glass of wine. The landlord had warned me that I should often be disturbed by the noise of the oil press just below my ground floor; it was set up in a cellar to which there was access through a little door beside the steps leading into the house. The press, he told me, would work at night. When the old millstone was drawn around in a circle by a blind-folded donkey the whole house shook and a continuous roar came from below. But this year the olive crop was so meager that the millstone operated for only two or three days; then it was still and silent as before and my evenings were to-tally undisturbed.

Once, after supper, the new sergeant and P., the lawyer, came to play cards with me. They said that they knew I was alone and thought I might enjoy a bit of company; in fact, they proposed to come often to while away the·hours. I trembled at the idea that their visit might come to be a daily event and oblige me to waste my time at stupid card games, for I much preferred to work or read alone.

> To rede and dryve the night away
> For me thoughte it better play
> Than plyen either at chesse or tables.

However, in appreciation of their good intentions, I made the best of it and we spent the evening over an endless game of rummy. But they never came back. Don Luigi heard almost immediately from one of his acolytes of their visit. To me he said nothing but he made a scene with the sergeant in the public square, accusing him of fraternizing with political pris-oners and threatening to report him to his superiors and have him transferred to another post. After this no one except my patients, and the peasants, who were free to come and see me because they were not considered human beings, dared to cross my door. The only exception was Dr. Milillo, who had a taste for independence and, as an elderly uncle, did not stand in awe of his nephew, the mayor.

And so I was free to dispose of my time and my person. If I did not have the company of the gentry I had that of the children. There were many of them of all ages and they knocked at my door at every hour of the day. At first they were attracted by that childlike and marvelous creature Barone. Then my painting struck their fancy; they never ceased to marvel at the images that appeared, as if by magic, on my canvas, of the houses and hills and faces they knew so well. We became good friends, and they went in and out of the house freely; they posed for me and were proud to see themselves in paint. They would find out when I was going to work beyond the village, and a band of twenty or more would call for me. They came to blows over the honor of carrying my paint box, easel, and canvas, until I made a distribution from which there was no appeal. First place went to the paint box, whose weight made it an object of value and desire; its chosen bearer stepped out with it as gaily and proudly as a squire of old.

One ten-year-old boy, Giovanni Fanelli, a pale little fellow with big, black eyes, a long, slender neck and an almost girlish complexion, had a particular enthusiasm for painting. All the children begged for my discarded tubes and brushes to play with, and Giovanni got his share of these, but he put them to a better use. Without so much as a hint to me he made secret attempts to become a painter. He watched very carefully everything I did, from sizing the canvas to stretching it on a frame. Just because I did these simple things they seemed to him no less fundamental than the actual laying on of color. He picked up sticks and made them into irregular frames; then on these he stretched odd bits of old shirting and covered them with some sort of sticky substance in lieu of size. When he had done this much he thought that the worst was over. With what was left in my used tubes of paint, an old palette, and worn brushes he tried to imitate my exact strokes. He was a timid, blushing boy and he would never have summoned up the courage to show me his work. I happened to see it only at the prompting of his young friends. His would-be painting was not the usual sort of childish thing, nor was it a mere imitation. He made shapeless masses of color, which were not altogether without charm. I do not know if Giovanni Fanelli had it in him to become a painter, but I have never seen another boy with his faith that a spontaneous revelation would come out of his labor, that the practice of a technique would work like magic, and that his efforts would bear fruit as certainly as a field that has been plowed and sown.

These boys, who had made the rounds at Christmas with their *cupi-cupi* and who ran through the streets like a bevy of birds ready to take flight, had no leader such as Capitano at Grassano. They were lively, wide-awake, and sad. Most of them were clothed in badly patched rags, wearing jackets handed down by their older brothers with the cuffs turned up; they had bare feet or wore heavy men's shoes with holes in them. They were thin and pale, often yellow from malaria, with deep-set, empty black eyes that had an expression of fixed intensity. There were all sorts among them—naïve and quick-witted, sincere and hypocritical, all of them endowed with a precocious vivacity, which was doomed to decline with the passing of the years in the monotonous imprisonment of time. I saw them move silently all around me, full of mute loyalty and unexpressed desires. Everything I owned or did filled them with ecstatic admiration. The merest trifles that I threw away, such as empty boxes or scraps of paper, were treasures whose possession they fought over. They ran to do me unsolicited favors of every kind. They gathered for me from the fields bunches of wild asparagus or fibrous and tasteless mushrooms, which are eaten in those parts for want of anything better. They went as far as Gaglianello to fetch me bitter wild oranges, the only ones in the neighborhood, for a still life. Friendly as we were, they remained shy and diffident, given to silence and the concealment of what was in their minds, immersed in the elusive, mysterious animal world in which they had their being, like timorous and swift-footed little goats.

One of them, Giovannino, who had round black eyes, white skin, and a look of perpetual astonishment under the man's hat that tumbled over his forehead, was inseparable from a tawny, yellow-eyed nanny goat that followed him like a dog everywhere he went. When he came to my house with the other children, Nennella the goat traipsed after him into the kitchen, sniffing about for salt, of which she was inordinately fond. Barone learned to respect her, and when we went on a painting expedition Nennella leaped after the line of children, while Barone ran on ahead, barking with joy over his unrestricted liberty. When we came to a halt Giovannino watched me work with one of his arms around Nennella's neck until she suddenly cut loose and went off to nibble at a tuft of broom. Eventually I would send the children away to prevent them from disturbing me. They wandered off reluctantly and came back toward evening when swarms of mosquitoes had begun to buzz around me and the last rosy rays of the sun fell upon my finished canvas, which they bore triumphantly back to the village.

Now that the ground was covered with snow, our processions were over, but the children came to see me at home; they warmed their hands at the kitchen fire or asked if they might go up to play on my terrace. Three or four of them hung about me continually. The littlest of them was the son of La Parroccola, who lived in a hut a few yards from the house. He was five years old, with a large, round head, a short nose, thick lips, and a frail body. His mother, who owed her name to the fact that the size of her head made her look like the knobbed walking stick of the parish priest, was one of the local witches, the ugliest, kindest, and least pretentious of them. Her enormous face, with its wide, flat nose, crooked mouth, and rough, yellowish skin, and her sparse, stringy hair made her quite monstrous-looking; her body was short and squat, bundled up in rags beneath her flowing veil. She was a good soul who earned her living as a laundress and was not averse, if need be, to granting her favors, in a bed as large as the public square, to one of the *carabinieri* or young peasants. I saw her every day in the doorway almost across the street and for a joke I used to say that I had taken a fancy to her and hoped she would not refuse me. La Parroccola blushed to the extent that her thick rind of a skin permitted, and answered: "I shouldn't do for you, Don Carlo; I'm just a rough countrywoman!" Rough as she was, and in spite of her ogress' face, she was known for her kindness. The little boy, who looked like his mother, was the only one left of her children; the others were all dead or far away.

Another one of my faithful followers was Michelino, a boy of about ten, who was alert, greedy, and melancholy. His opaque black eyes seemed to be the heritage of generations of tears and to mirror the desolate land in which he lived. My closest hangers-on, however, were the tailor's children, especially the youngest, Tonino. He was a wee slip of a boy, quick of mind and body in spite of his shyness, with dark close-shaven hair and keen eyes like black pinheads. The father, who was devoted to his children, tried to bring them up better than the rest; he was proud of his trade and of the fact that he had practiced it in New York. But what was he to do, now that he had come home again and everything had gone wrong and he was no richer than the peasants? His boys were growing up no different from their playmates and he thought bitterly as he plied his needle that there was no hope of raising their station in life; he had not even the means to take care of their swollen tonsils and adenoids. And Tonino, although he was as lively as a gnome, already seemed to share his father's disappointment.

There was something unusual about all these children, a mixture of young animal spirits and precocious maturity, as if they had received as soon as they were born a consciousness of sorrow and the patience to bear it. Their games were not those of city tenement children, which are the same the world over; they had only the animals for company. They were self-contained and knew how to be silent. Beneath their childish ingenuousness there was something of the impenetrability of the peasant who scorns trivial consolations and something, too, of the reserve with which he manages to defend his inner self against a hostile world. As a general rule they were further advanced, both mentally and physically, than city children of the same age. They were gifted with insight, a thirst for learning, and ready appreciation of all the wonders of the outside world. One day when a group of them saw me writing they asked me to teach them the art. They learned precious little at school with the inspiration of Don Luigi's cane, cigars, and patriotic speeches; although attendance was obligatory they came out as illiterate as when they went in. Of their own free will some of them came in the evening to practice writing in my kitchen. I am sorry, as I look back, that my aversion for all that smacks of the didactic prevented me from giving them more time and attention. No teacher could have asked for more eager pupils.

The carnival season, just preceding Lent, came around quite unexpectedly in these strange surroundings. There were no particular festivities at Gagliano in its honor and I had forgotten its existence. One day when I was walking beyond the square I saw three white-robed ghosts appear at the lower end of the village and dash up the main street. They were jumping and shouting like maddened beasts, drunk with their own hue and cry. These were peasant masqueraders. Their carnival fancy dress consisted of these white robes, on their heads white knitted caps, or stockings with white feathers stuck in them, and whitened shoes. Their faces were covered with flour and they carried dried sheepskins in their hands, rolled up like sticks, which they brandished threateningly and brought down about the head and shoulders of anyone who failed to get out of their way. They seemed like devils let loose, bursting with savage joy at this brief moment of folly and impunity so different from their usual humdrum and browbeaten existence. I thought of the feast of San Giovanni in Rome when boys go around knocking passers-by over the head with enormous cloves of garlic. But that night is one of collective phallic pleasure, celebrated with plates of steaming snails, songs, fireworks, dancing, and love-making under the kindly warmth of the midsummer sky. The masqueraders of Gagliano were alone and lonely in their forced and gloomy folly; they were trying to make up for hardship and enslavement with a parody of freedom, exaggerated, but reflecting their repressed ferocity. The three ghosts beat without mercy anyone that came into their grasp, no matter who he might be; on this occasion the barriers between gentry and peasants were down. They leaped diagonally from one side of the street to the other, shouting as if they were possessed by evil spirits, their white feathers shaking in the air, like savages run amuck or the performers of a sacred dance of terror. Almost as quickly as they had appeared they disappeared again behind the church.

In the following days the children began to run about with blackened faces and moustaches made with burnt cork. One day twenty or more of them in this array came to see me, and when I said that it would be easy to make them real masks, they begged me to do so. I set to work and made every one of them a cylinder of white paper with holes to see out of, big enough so that the whole face was covered. The memory of the peasant ghost masqueraders or else the *genius loci* of Gagliano unconsciously inspired me to make the masks all alike, in black and white. They came out as skulls, with black holes for the eyes and nose and bared teeth. The children were not in the least frightened; they gaily hurried to put them on, slipped one onto Barone and ran back to their houses. When evening came, these apparitions charged shouting into dim kitchens lit by a fire or a swinging kerosene lamp. Their mothers fled from them in terror, because here every symbol is a reality and to them the masked children stood for a triumph of death.

CHAPTER TWENTY-TWO

THE DAYS WERE SLOWLY BEginning to grow longer; the season had changed and the snow gave way to rain and sunshine. Spring was not far away and I thought it a good time to take every possible measure to stave off the dread malaria before the return of the mosquitoes. Even with the limited means available in the village there was a great deal that could be done. We could ask the Red Cross for some Paris green to disinfect the few pools of stagnant water near by, pipe off the drippings from the old fountain, and lay in a stock of quinine, atabrine, and plasmochin—with some candy for the children—in order to be ready for the hot weather. These were simple precautions and, according to law, they were compulsory. I mentioned them over and over again to Don Luigi, but I soon realized that although he approved of my plans he took care to do nothing at all about them. In order to hold him to his responsibility I decided to write a memorandum of twenty pages or so with a detailed list of everything to be done, including both the requirements that could be met locally and the items that would have to be requested from Rome. The mayor read the memorandum, expressed satisfaction, praised my efforts, and informed me with a broad smile that on the following day, when he went to Matera, he would show it to the prefect, who was in a position to help us. As soon as he came back from Matera he hastened to tell me that His Excellency was enthusiastic about my suggestions, that everything I had asked for to fight malaria would be forthcoming and that, incidentally, the other political prisoners, as well as I, would benefit from the project. Don Luigi was glowing with pride that I should be under his jurisdiction and everything seemed for the best.

Three or four days after the mayor's return a telegram came from the police in Matera to the effect that I was forbidden to practice medicine in Gagliano, under penalty of prison. Whether or not this sudden ban was a direct result of the excess of zeal betrayed by my memorandum I never found out. As the peasants would have it: "We're saddled with our malaria and if you try to do anything about it they'll drive you away." Others were of the opinion that the local doctors had conspired against me, and in my own mind there was a suspicion that the police were afraid I might become too popular, because my reputation as a miracle man was growing by leaps and bounds, and patients came from remote villages to consult me.

The telegram from Matera was delivered to me by the *carabinieri* one evening. The next morning at dawn, when no one in the village yet knew of the ban, a man on horseback knocked at my door.

"Come quickly, Doctor," he said. "My brother's ill. We

live down near the Bog, three hours away. I've brought this horse for you to ride."

The Bog was a distant and lonely district near the Agri River. There was one big farm in it and the peasants lived there on the spot, far from any settlement. I told the man that I couldn't possibly come, first, because I was not allowed to go beyond the village limits and second, because I had been forbidden to practice medicine. I advised him to consult Dr. Milillo or Dr. Gibilisco.

"Those tenth-rate fellows? Better have no one at all." With which he shook his head and went away.

There was a mixture of rain and sleet in the air. I stayed home all morning to write a letter to the police, objecting to the ban and requesting its annulment. I asked them in the meantime, until they should receive new orders, to authorize me at least to continue the cases at present under my care and to pursue, for the welfare of the population, my plans for the drive against malaria. To this letter I never received a reply.

I was just getting up from my dinner at about two o'clock in the afternoon when the man on horseback returned. He had been down to the Bog again; his brother was much worse and I must try at any cost to save him. I told him to come with me to ask the mayor for a special permission. Don Luigi was not at home, he had gone to have a cup of coffee at his sister's, where we found him stretched out in an armchair. I set my case before him.

"Impossible. Orders from Matera have to be obeyed. I can't take any such responsibility. Stay here, Doctor, and have a cup of coffee."

The peasant, who was an intelligent and determined fellow, would not take no for an answer and Donna Caterina, my protectress, took our part. The edict from Matera threatened to upset all her plans by clearing the way for her enemy, Gibilisco. She deplored it loudly and finally exclaimed:

"This comes of anonymous letters! Who knows how many they've written? Gibilisco himself went to Matera last week. The police don't know that you're a godsend to us here. But leave it all to me; we have some influence ourselves in the office of the prefect and the ban will be lifted. What a perfect shame!" And she tried to console me with cakes and coffee.

But the problem was an immediate one, and in spite of the fact that Donna Caterina was on our side, Don Luigi could not be budged.

"I can't do it; I have too many enemies. If the thing were to be known I'd lose my job. I have to keep in line with the police."

Don Andrea, the old schoolteacher, agreed with him, between a cat-nap and a mouthful of cakes, and our discussion dragged on without coming to any conclusion. The mayor, who liked to pose as a friend of the people, was reluctant to refuse the peasant's plea, but fear won the day.

"After all, there are other doctors. Try them."

"They're worthless," said the peasant.

"He's quite right there," shouted Donna Caterina. "Your uncle is too old, and as for the other, well, let's not even mention him. And then in this weather, with the roads wet, neither of them would want to go."

The peasant got up.

"I'll go to look for them," he said and went away.

He stayed away almost two hours, while the family council continued the discussion without any concrete result. In spite of Donna Caterina's backing I could not overcome the mayor's fears; there was no precedent for the case, and too much responsibility was involved. At last the peasant came back with two sheets of paper in his hand and on his face the satisfied look of a man who has succeeded after a long struggle.

"Neither doctor can come; they're both sick. I have signed statements from both of them. Now you'll have to let Don Carlo come. Just look at these . . ." And he thrust the papers in front of Don Luigi.

After tremendous efforts of persuasion, with possibly a few threats thrown in for good measure, the peasant had got both doctors to state in writing that because of the bad weather and their age and health they simply could not go to the Bog. In the case of Dr. Milillo, this was indeed true. Now it seemed as if there could be no further obstacle to my going, but the mayor was not won over, and he went on debating the pros and cons. He sent for the village clerk, the brother-in-law of the widow with whom I had lodged, a good fellow who thought I should be allowed to go. Dr. Milillo himself came, somewhat out of sorts because he was spurned in his professional capacity, but not opposed to my going.

"Just make sure you're paid in advance. All the way to the Bog? No, I shouldn't dream of it, even for two hundred lire."

Time was passing, fresh cakes and coffee were brought in, and still we were making no progress. Then I suggested calling in the sergeant; if he were willing to take upon himself the responsibility for my trip the mayor might consent to it without compromising himself too seriously. And so it came about. As soon as he heard the story the sergeant told me to go, saying that he trusted me and would not send any of his men along to escort me. A human life, he added, should be above every other consideration. There was relief on every side; even Don Luigi appeared to be pleased by the decision, and to show his good will he sent for a heavy coat and boots which he said I should need down in the valley. Meanwhile, darkness had come; they had to authorize me to spend the night at the farm and to return the following morning. Finally, with advice and good wishes all around, I set out with the peasant and his horse and Barone.

The weather had cleared; the rain and sleet had stopped. A brisk wind was sweeping the sky and a bright, round moon peered out among the broken masses of scurrying clouds. As soon as we had left the steep paved village street, near the Mound of the Madonna of the Angels, my companion, who had been leading his horse by the bridle, stopped and signaled to me to mount. I had not ridden horseback for a number of years and among these ravines in the dead of night I preferred my own two legs. I told him that he should ride his own horse while I walked along at a good clip. He looked at me with astonishment, as if the whole world were topsy-turvy: a peasant on horseback and a gentleman on foot?—perish the thought! I had quite a time to convince him, but at last he reluctantly took my advice. Then we began a real race toward the Bog. I strode down the steep path with the horse right at my heels; I could feel his hot breath and hear his hoof-beats in the mud just behind me. I coursed over the unfamiliar ground like a man pursued, buoyed up by the night air, the silence around me and my own motion. The moon filled the entire sky and seemed as if it would overflow onto the earth. The terrain we were covering might, indeed, have been the surface of the moon, as it lay white in the silent moonlight without any vegetation, not even a blade of grass, belabored by the everlasting flow of the waters which had wrinkled, pierced, and roughened it. The stretches of clay slanted steeply down to the Agri in a series of cones, caves, mounds, and other irregularities which stood out in varying degrees of light and shadow. We wound our way without speaking through this labyrinth made by time and earthquakes. I felt as if I were floating over the ghostly landscape like a bird.

After more than two hours of our race the barking of a dog from below broke the silence around us. We came out of the clay and found ourselves in a sloping meadow; in the background, behind a rise in the ground, appeared the outlines of the white farmhouse. Here, far from any human habitation, lived my companion and his brother with their wives and children. At the door we were greeted by three hunters from Pisticci, who had come the previous day to hunt foxes down by the river and had stayed out of sympathy for their friend. The two wives, sisters, also from Pisticci, were tall with large black eyes and noble faces. Their beauty was set off by the peasant dress of their village: long skirts with black and white flounces and black and white ribbons among the veils on their heads, which made them look like some strange sort of butterflies. They had prepared the best foodstuffs at their disposal: fresh milk and cheese, which they offered me as soon as I arrived with that old-style hospitality, devoid of servility, which puts all men on the same footing. They had waited for me all day long, as for a savior, but I soon discovered that there was nothing I could do. The man had a ruptured appendix; he was in his death agony and not even an operation, had I been able to perform one, would have been of any avail. There was nothing I could do but soothe the patient's pain with injections of morphine and wait for the end.

The house was made up of two rooms, which were joined by a wide door. In the farther room were the sick man, his brother, and the women who were watching over him. In the first room a fire was lit in the fireplace and around it sat the three hunters; a high bed with a soft mattress had been made ready for me in the opposite corner. Every now and then I went to see the dying man, then I came back and talked in a low voice to the hunters beside the fire.

About midnight I climbed into the bed for a rest, without

taking off my clothes, but I could not sleep. I lay in the high
bed, which was like a theater box suspended in mid-air. Hung
on the walls all around me were the bodies of newly killed
foxes; I could smell their gamey odor and see their sharp muz-
zles outlined against the flickering red flames. I had only to
stretch out my hand to touch their skins, which had something of woods and caves about them. Through the door I
could hear the dying man's continuous wailing, like an endless litany of pain: "Jesus, help me; Doctor, help me; Jesus,
help me; Doctor, help me," and the whispered prayers of the
women. I looked at the dancing flames, the long, wavering
shadows, and the dark figures of the three hunters with their
hats on their heads, motionless in front of the fire.

Death was in the house: I loved these peasants and I was
sad and humiliated by my powerlessness against it. Why,
then, at the same time, did a great feeling of peace pervade
me? I felt detached from every earthly thing and place, lost in
a no man's land far from time and reality. I was hidden, like
a shoot under the bark of a tree, beyond the reach of man. I
listened to the silence of the night and I felt as if I had all of
a sudden penetrated the very heart of the universe. An immense happiness, such as I had never known, swept over me
with a flow of fulfilment.

Toward dawn the sick man's end was very near. His muf-
fled calls for help changed into a death rattle and this in turn
became weaker and weaker in the final struggle until it ceased
altogether. He had hardly finished dying when the women
pulled the lids down over his staring eyes and began their
lament. Those two gentle, reserved butterflies with their
black and white ribbons were suddenly transformed into fu-
ries. They tore their veils, pulled their clothing out of place,
scratched their faces until blood came and began to dance
with long steps around the room, beating their heads against

the wall and singing on one high note the death story. From
time to time they put their heads out the windows, still crying
out on the same single note, as if to announce the death
to the countryside and to the world; then they drew back into
the room and went on with the wailing and dancing, which
were to last forty-eight hours without stopping, until the
funeral. This single note was long drawn-out, repetitious and
agonizing. It was impossible to listen to it without being overcome by an irresistible feeling of physical anguish; it brought a
lump to the throat of the hearer and made its way straight to
the pit of his stomach. To avoid bursting into tears I hurriedly
took leave and went out with Barone into the light of the
early morning.

The weather was calm. The meadows and the ghostly
stretches of clay of the previous evening lay before me bare
and lonely in the still gray light. I was my own master
among these silent wastes and I still felt some of the happiness of the night just past. Of course I had to go back to the
village, but meanwhile I wandered through the fields, twirling
my stick and whistling to my dog, who was highly excited,
perhaps by the presence of some invisible game. I decided to
go home by a roundabout way, passing through Gaglianello,
which I had not yet been able to visit.

Gaglianello is a group of houses, without even a street con-
necting them, on a low, barren hill near the malaria-ridden
river. Four hundred people live there without a doctor, a
midwife, a *carabiniere*, or any other representative of the
State. Even so, the tax collector with the flaming initials on
his cap passes time and again their way. To my astonishment
I saw that I was expected. The people knew that I had been
to the Bog and hoped that I might stop by on my way back.
The peasants and their women stood outside to welcome me
and persons afflicted with the strangest kinds of diseases had

themselves carried to the doorways so that I should see them as I went by. The scene was reminiscent of a medieval court of miracles. No doctor had set foot in the place for who knows how many years. Old afflictions which had received no treatment except incantations had piled up in the peasants' bodies, spreading in strange forms like mushrooms on rotten timber. I spent most of the morning going from hut to hut among emaciated victims of malaria, ancient ulcers, and gangrene, giving what advice I could, since I was no longer allowed to write prescriptions, and drinking the wine offered me as a token of hospitality. They wanted me to stay all day, but I had to go on, and so they walked with me for a piece of the road, imploring me to return. "Who knows?" I said to them, "I'll come if I can." But I never did. I left my new friends from Gaglianello by the wayside and began to climb up the path among the ravines toward home.

The dazzling sun stood high in the sky; the irregular terrain through which the path wound its tortuous way shut off my view. All of a sudden the sergeant, with one of his men, came around a curve on his way to meet me, and I joined forces with them on the homeward climb. Big blackbirds, perching on clumps of broom, took off into the air as we passed by. "Would you care to take a shot, Doctor?" said the sergeant, holding out his rifle. The feathers of the bird I hit fluttered down to the ground, but the large shot must have shattered the body into a thousand pieces and we did not linger to look for it.

As soon as we reached Gagliano the expression on the peasants' faces told me that something was brewing. During my absence everyone had heard about the ban upon my practice of medicine and about the time wasted the previous day before I could obtain permission to go down to the Bog. News of the sick man's death had already arrived by some mysterious underground wireless. The villagers all knew and cared for him, and he was the first one of those I had attended in all these months to die. For this reason they were convinced that if I had been able to reach him earlier I could surely have saved his life. When I told them that in all likelihood, even if I had arrived a few hours sooner, my restricted knowledge of abdominal surgery, the lack of instruments, and the difficulties of transportation even to Sant' Arcangelo, would have kept me from doing very much, they shook their heads incredulously. In their opinion I was a miracle man and nothing would have been beyond my powers if only I had reached the spot on time. The whole incident was proof to them of the evil intent back of the ban, which from now on would stand in the way of my helping them. The expression on the peasants' faces was one I had never seen before. Despair mingled with grim determination made their eyes look blacker than usual, and they came out of their houses with guns and axes on their shoulders.

"We're dogs," they said to me, "and in Rome they want us to die like dogs. One Christian soul took pity on us, and now they want to take him away. We'll burn the town hall and kill the mayor."

Revolt was in the air. The peasants' deep sense of justice had been outraged and, gentle, passive, and resigned as they were, impervious to political reasoning and party slogans, they felt stirring in them the old spirit of the brigands. These downtrodden folk have always been given to wilful and ephemeral explosions. Some human mischance arouses their age-old repressed resentment and they may set fire to a tax office or a barracks or cut the throats of their over-lords. For a brief moment a sort of Spanish ferocity is awakened in them, and they break loose in search of a freedom to be bought only with bloodshed and violence. Then they are led off to jail in stony indifference, like men who have released themselves in a single second from the burden of centuries.

That day, if I had wished, I might have put myself at the head of several hundred brigands and have either laid siege to the village or fled to the wilds. For a moment I was sorely tempted, but in 1936 the time was not yet ripe. Instead, after considerable effort, I managed to calm the peasants. They took home their guns and axes, but the anxious look did not leave their faces. Rome and the State had wounded them to the core; one of their own had been struck down. Under the heavy weight of death they had felt the hand of the faraway government and they rebelled against its iron vise. Their first impulse was to wreak immediate vengeance upon the symbols and the emissaries of Rome. If I dissuaded them from taking this course, what was left for them to do? As always, nothing. But to this eternal "nothing" for once they were of no mind to resign themselves.

The next day the peasants came in small groups to see me. Their anger and bloodthirstiness had somewhat subsided; they had refrained from staging a massacre and when the moment for release through vengeance has gone by without fulfilment, its red-hot temperature goes with it. Now their only wish was that I should be allowed to carry on my medical practice lawfully among them, and they had decided to circulate a petition on my behalf. Their enmity toward a foreign and hostile government went hand in hand (paradoxical as it may seem) with a natural respect for justice, a spontaneous understanding of what Government and the State *should* be, namely the will of the people expressed in terms of law. "Lawful" is one of the words they most commonly use, not in the meaning of something sanctioned and codified but rather in the sense of genuine or authentic. A man is "lawful" if he behaves as he should; a wine is "lawful" if it is not watered. A petition which they all signed seemed to them truly lawful, and as such possessed real effectiveness. They were quite right, but I had to explain to them something of which they were already better aware than I: namely, that they were up against a strictly unlawful power against which legal arms were of no avail, that not only were they too weak to prevail by violence but that the undermined and disarmed state of legal justice blocked their way, and that, in short, the only result of their petition would be my removal to some other place of confinement. Let them go ahead with the petition, I said, if they were convinced of its efficacy, but let them cherish no illusions that it would lead to anything but my departure. They understood my argument all too well.

"Just as long as Rome controls our local affairs and wields the power of life and death over us we shall go on like dumb animals," they said. And so the petition was given up. But the incident had touched them too deeply to go by without protest. Where violence and law had failed them, they had recourse to art.

One day two young men came to see me and asked very mysteriously for the loan of my white doctor's jacket. I was not to ask them what they wanted with it, for their purpose was a secret; the following day everything would be made clear to me and they would bring it back that evening. The next day, while I was strolling through the square I saw people hurrying toward the mayor's house where already a small crowd had gathered. I went along with them and the onlookers made way for me. Right in the middle of the street a play, without benefit of stage or scenery, was going on, surrounded by an eager circle of men, women, and children. Every year at the beginning of Lent, as I was later to learn, the peasants put on an unrehearsed comedy of their own devising. Occasionally they chose a religious subject, sometimes they told the deeds of knights or brigands, but usually they parodied scenes of everyday life. This year, while they were still upset by the incident I have just described, they gave poetic vent to their feelings with a piece of satire.

The actors were men, even those who took the part of women, all of them peasant friends of mine, but I could not recognize them under their extraordinary make-up. The play consisted of one simple scene, and the players made up their parts as they went along. A chorus of men and women announced the arrival of a sick man, and in he came on a stretcher, his face painted white with dark circles under his eyes and black spots to hollow out his cheeks as if he were already dead. The sick man was accompanied by his weeping mother, who said nothing but: "My son! My son!" over and over again as a monotonous, sad accompaniment to the entire drama. Summoned by the chorus, there appeared beside the sick man a fellow in my white jacket who was just about to heal him when he was interrupted by an old codger in a black suit and wearing a goatee. The two medical men, one white and one black, representing the spirits of good and evil, fought like an angel and a devil over the sick man on the stretcher, exchanging volleys of witty and bitter words. The angel seemed about to bear away the victory when suddenly an emissary from Rome, with a fierce and monstrous face, appeared on the scene and chased him away. The man in black, Dr. Bestianelli (named for the famous surgeon Bastianelli, who was known even in these parts), was left master of the situation. Pulling a knife out of a bag, he began to operate. He pretended to cut through the sick man's clothing and with a rapid motion of his hand drew out of the wound a pig's bladder which was hidden there. Then he turned triumphantly toward the chorus, which was murmuring words of horror and indignation, brandished the bladder and shouted: "Here is his heart!" He pierced the heart with a big needle until blood spurted out, while the mother and the chorus began to intone a dirge, and the drama came to an end.

I never found out who wrote the play; perhaps there was no single author but all the participants thought it up together. The improvised dialogue centered about the burning question of the day, but peasant cunning saw to it that the references were not too direct; they were both pertinent and pointed without crossing the danger line. The peasant actors were carried away less by the satirical voicing of their grievance than by genuine artistic fervor. Every one of them lived his part: the weeping mother seemed the desperate heroine of a Greek tragedy or Madonna by Jacopone da Todi; the sick man had a truly deathlike countenance; the charlatan in black drew blood from the heart with savage joy; the Roman was a horrible monster representing the State itself in the form of a dragon, and the chorus made its commentary and interpretation with the patience of despair. Was this classical form the reminiscence of an ancient art, descended to a popular level, or was it an original and spontaneous re-creation in a language natural to this land, where the whole of life is a tragedy without a stage?

As soon as the play was done the dead man got up from his stretcher and the actors hurried down a lane toward the house of Dr. Gibilisco, where they acted out the play again. In the course of the day it was given many times, at Dr. Milillo's house, the church, the barracks, the town hall, in the square, and here and there in the narrow streets of Upper and Lower Gagliano. When evening came the angel's white jacket was brought back to me in triumph and all returned to their homes.

Chapter Twenty-Three

THIS POETICAL RELEASE OF their feelings did not entirely calm the peasants' spirits nor do away with their resentment. They saw no sense in the ban and so they ignored it. They came to me for treatment just as before; the only difference was that they came after dark and looked cautiously up and down the street before knocking at my door, to make sure that no spies were about. So great were their needs and so pressing their insistence that I simply could not turn them away. I had complete faith in their loyalty and discretion; they would have died rather than betray me. Nevertheless my activity was curtailed; all I could do was to give advice and dole out such medicines as I had in stock. I wrote out prescriptions only for those of my patients who had relatives in Naples and could get them filled there and sent by mail. I could not put on bandages or perform minor operations whose traces would be visible to the public eye and reveal what I was doing.

This need of secrecy kept up the general agitation. The village was temporarily freed from boredom, for the ban came like a stone thrown into the stagnant waters of the tedious existence of the gentry. Dr. Gibilisco was triumphant. Whether or not he was the *deus ex machina* of the whole affair, he was radiantly happy. Old Dr. Milillo's feelings were complex and contradictory. The loss of my competition gratified his professional pride and added to his earnings, but as an old liberal and former admirer of Nitti he could not but disapprove of the police's high-handed behavior. His position was rather a happy one and afforded him double satisfaction. On the one hand he gained financially, while on the other he indulged in the expression of sincere moral indignation over the misdeeds of the government and in friendliness toward me. For Donna Caterina the incident was a serious defeat; her plans were thwarted and she was humiliated in her ruling passion before her enemies. She was highly incensed and went so far as to say:

"If that weak-kneed, silly brother of mine doesn't do something I'll go to Matera myself and speak to the prefect."

While Donna Caterina remained my chief ally, Don Luigi was uncertain as to what attitude he should take. The influence of his sister and of public opinion inclined him to take action and bring what pressure he could to bear for "the good of the village," but he feared that by taking my side he might antagonize the authorities and this fear confined him to purely verbal support of Donna Caterina and her friends. The gentry, then, came to be divided into two factions, like the Guelphs and the Ghibellines; one of them took up the cause of the common people while the other stood alone, but upheld by the Holy Roman Empire of Matera. Don Luigi

240

steered a prudent course among conflicting opinions. He was the mayor and the appointed guardian of whatever passed for law, but his conception of the law was a strange one.

One evening he sent a maidservant to summon me to his house; his little girl had a sore throat and he was afraid that she had diphtheria. I sent word that I could not come because I was forbidden to. He sent the girl back with a message to the effect that it was permissible for me to come to him because he was the mayor and hence above the law. I said that I would look at his child on condition that he authorize me to give the same care to any peasant who might call upon me. To which he replied that I was first to look after his child and then we should see; he could not give me an outright authorization but he might close an eye. The little girl's diphtheria, of course, turned out to be just another of her father's imaginary ailments. Thus there came to be established a permanent *modus vivendi* by virtue of which I carried on a halfway medical practice under a halfway and far from explicit dispensation which was to last only as long as I kept everything secret. I should have preferred to give up the whole thing and to concentrate on my painting, but this was impossible for the length of my stay in Gagliano. Naturally the illegality and secrecy of this situation had various disadvantages, and other incidents took place which threatened to rekindle the public fury which had been so difficult to contain.

One evening a young peasant with a bandaged arm came up from Gaglianello with several companions. He had hurt himself with a scythe and when I took off the bandage, blood spurted out against the wall. He had cut an artery and the stump had to be located with a pair of pincers and tied up. I could not perform the operation because its traces would be too apparent. I therefore sent the fellow to Dr. Milillo with a note in which I offered my services as an assistant; my intention was that he should give me the protection of his name and let me do something I feared was beyond his powers. But the old man took offense and answered that he could handle the case without my help. Early the next day the young peasant came back on a donkey, along with his older brother. He was pale as wax, having lost blood all during the night. When I looked at his hand I saw that the old man had simply taken a stitch or two without making any effort to locate the stump of the artery. An operation which would have been comparatively simple the previous evening was now difficult, and with the ban hanging over my head I could not interfere with the case of another practitioner. Since the peasants were unwilling to go back to Milillo or to consult Gibilisco there was nothing for them to do but to take the "American's" rattling car and look for a better doctor in Stigliano or beyond. Before they set out, the older brother, a man of daring and resolution, called together a crowd of peasants in the square in front of the town hall and held forth loudly upon the subject of his grievances, hurling defiance at the gentry, the mayor, and the authorities in Rome, to the applause of his audience. The scene was memorable and the day another very troubled one.

Giulia attached little importance to the ban.

"Just do as you like," she said. "What can they do to you in return? If they won't let you be a doctor, you can heal the sick all the same. You can be a sorcerer. You now know all the secrets of the trade. And there's nothing they can do to stop you."

During the past months, thanks to the teachings of Giulia and the other women who came to the house and the things I saw with my own eyes at my patients' bedsides and in the homes of the peasants, I had, indeed, become a master of magic and its applications to medicine. I could easily have followed Giulia's advice, which she gave quite seriously, resting her malicious, listless, cold eyes upon me as she said: "You ought to be a sorcerer." Just as seriously, whenever she heard me sing, Giulia would say: "Too bad you're not a priest; you've such a fine voice." To her a priest was an actor worthy of magnifying God by virtue of his singing. As a combination of priest, physician, and sorcerer, I might in Giulia's mind have possessed all the powers of Rofè, the Oriental medicine man.

Magic can cure almost any ill, and usually by the mere pronouncement of a spell or incantation. There were formulas for specific ailments and others for general application. Some of them were, I believe, of local origin; others belonged to the *corpus* of classical lore which came to these parts who knows when and how. The most common of all was the abracadabra. When I went to visit the sick I often found hung around their necks a tiny roll of paper or a metal plate bearing the triangular inscription:

```
              A
            A B
          A B R
        A B R A
      A B R A C
    A B R A C A
  A B R A C A D
A B R A C A D A
A B R A C A D A B
A B R A C A D A B R
A B R A C A D A B R A
```

At first the peasants tried to hide their amulets or apologized for wearing them, because they knew that doctors despise such superstitions and deplore them in the name of reason and science. This is all very well where reason and science can take over the role of magic, but in this remote region they are not yet, and perhaps never may be, dieties which enjoy popular worship and adoration. I respected the amulets, paying tribute to their ancient origin and mysterious simplicity, and preferring to be their ally rather than their enemy. The peasants were grateful for my respect, and perhaps the abracadabra really did them some good. Anyhow, magic as it was practiced in Gagliano was harmless enough and the peasants considered it in no way in conflict with official medicine. The custom of prescribing some medicine for every illness, even when it is not necessary, is equivalent to magic, anyhow, especially when the prescription is written, as it once was, in Latin or in indecipherable handwriting. Most prescriptions would be just as effective if they were not taken to the druggist, but were simply hung on a string around the patient's neck like an abracadabra.

Besides the abracadabra, there were many other different objects with general curative properties: cabalistic and astrological signs, images of the saints and of the Madonna of Viggiano, old coins, wolves' teeth, the bones of toads, and so on. The cures for specific ailments were more picturesque. Children were freed from worms with the following incantation:

> Holy Monday
> Holy Tuesday
> Holy Wednesday
> Maundy Thursday
> Good Friday
> Holy Saturday
> Easter Sunday
> Worms-on-the-run-day.

244

Then backwards:

> Holy Saturday
> Good Friday
> Maundy Thursday
> Holy Wednesday
> Holy Tuesday
> Holy Monday
> Easter Sunday
> Worms-on-the-run-day.

This incantation was pronounced three times in succession, forwards and backwards, in front of the child. The worms were exorcized and died, and the child was cured. This is certainly a very old formula, a degeneration of a late Roman exorcism, one of the first Latin texts with Christian symbols.

The peasants called jaundice *male dell' arco* or rainbow sickness, because it makes a man change his color to that which is strongest in the spectrum of the sun, namely, yellow. And how does a man catch jaundice? The rainbow walks across the sky with its feet on the ground. If the rainbow's feet step on clothes hung out to dry, whoever puts them on will take on the colors of the rainbow, with which they have been impregnated, and fall ill. They say, too (but the first theory is better founded and enjoys wider belief) that one must be careful not to urinate in the direction of the rainbow, because the curved jet of the urine resembles and reflects the curved bow in the sky and the whole man may be turned into an image of the rainbow. The cure for jaundice was to carry the sick man at dawn to a hilltop outside the village. A knife with a black handle was applied to his forehead, first vertically, then horizontally, making a sort of cross. The knife was then applied with slightly different gestures, but still in the sign of the cross, to every joint of the body. This operation was repeated three times over, without skipping a single joint, for three consecutive mornings. Then the rainbow faded away, one color at a time, and the sick man's skin was white again.

The spell to cure erysipelas required the accompaniment of a piece of silver. The peasants kept an old silver crown in their houses for this particular purpose, and I never saw a man stricken with this rather common affliction who did not have a thick coin applied to his swollen red skin.

There were spells for mending broken bones, for curing toothaches, stomach-aches, and headaches, for throwing off the influence of the evil eye or of a bewitchment. At this point there was less concern with the art of healing than with its opposite, the art of causing a man to sicken and die. Another very important branch of magic was, of course, the inspiration of love or liberation from it. I often witnessed the practice of this magic and perhaps even more often I was its object or victim. Even if at the time I noticed nothing out of the way it may well be that the spells that were cast over me and the potions I was given to drink brought about my later unfortunate capacity for passion. Meanwhile I had to defend myself from the direct attack of witches like Maria C. She used to call me to look after her supposedly sick child when her husband (who had already been in jail for murder motivated by jealousy) was in the fields. This was the woman who had caused the death of my widow-landlady's husband, and he was said to be the father of her child, a pretty, innocent little thing. The mother, on the other hand, was a truly fearsome creature. She was short and stubby, with a forehead so low that her smooth blue-black hair, which she wore parted in the middle and wound about her head in two bands, came down almost to her thick dark eyebrows. The pale face that peered out from this jungle was filled by her enormous, wide-open, faraway, blue-green, mad eyes, which looked like lakes surrounded by dangerous quicksands in a setting of rotten tropical foliage.

"You ought to be a sorcerer; you know our way of healing . . ." I secretly went on with my doctoring, taking care not to run afoul of magic. Here where magic and magnetism underlie every relation of one thing to another, medicine, too, derives its power from magic, no matter how orthodox and rigorously scientific the physician may be, without the least bit of mystery about him. Quinine, alas, has lost its efficacy, because in the eyes of the peasants it belongs to a discredited, incomprehensible, and pretentious body of science. Severe orders had to be given them to take it and because of their reluctance it did them little good. I preferred to prescribe newer drugs, more powerful and possessed of greater magic, such as atabrine and plasmochin. These were doubly effective, both because of their chemical composition and the sway they exerted over the imagination. All medicines except quinine were gladly received by the peasants, but they were usually out of stock or too costly, and often doctors and druggists exploited the needs of the sick. In the few dust-covered pharmacies of these villages one could never be sure whether a prescription would be accurately compounded or whether it would come out, with good luck, as a mixture of harmless powders. It was generally better to make use of prepared or patent medicines and these had the disadvantage of being expensive.

La Parroccola's little boy had a malignant pustule. Anthrax is frequent in the proximity of so many animals, and I saw many cases of it. I went to see him toward evening. As my small stock of serum was exhausted and there was none to be had in the village, I told the mother to hurry by short-cut to the pharmacy in Sant' Arcangelo for more. "Have you money?" I asked her. "Thirty lire. The *carabinieri* have just paid me for the week's wash." I knew that the vials cost eight and a half lire each; so she had enough to buy them. "Get three, just for safety." Anthrax is an ugly thing and only generous hypodermics will cure it. It was dark and La Parroccola did not dare set out by night. "There are spirits along the path and they wouldn't let me by." She did go, none the less, long before dawn, and anxiety lent wings to her stocky, misshapen legs. Five miles there and five miles back; when morning came she was home again. But she brought with her only two vials. I expressed my surprise and then she told me that the druggist had asked her how much money she had. "Thirty lire." "Then you can have two. Can you read? They're fifteen lire each; it's printed on the label." On the label was printed eight lire and a half. This is how the middle class perpetuates its feudal rights? Fortunately the two vials were sufficient.

La Parroccola was very poor; she had no earthly possessions other than her enormous bed and her peasant charms. She should have had free medicines and the services of a doctor, and she should have been on a list of persons of her condition. Such a list did exist, tucked away on a shelf somewhere in the town hall, but in spite of the widespread poverty, it contained no more than four or five names. A multitude of excuses were found for ruling ineligible all those that applied for a dole of any kind. Otherwise who would have been left to pay tribute to the doctors and druggists, who were among those who drew up the list? This was another one of the ancient evils of this land, sanctioned by custom until it seemed inevitable that it should be tied up with the authority of the State, to which there was no appeal. "If we knew how to read and write they couldn't rob us like this.

Now they've built schools, but they teach us nothing. Rome wants us to remain like dumb animals."

These over-taxed peasants would make a day's journey on foot from Senise to sell two lire worth of celery or to carry all the way from Metaponto a basket of fine oranges which had cost the lives of some of those who grew them down near the sea, where a fatal form of malaria prevails. Yet, when the government asked for the donation of wedding rings and all other objects in gold to supply funds for the prosecution of the war with Abyssinia, they responded in full measure. There was not very much gold left in the region. Every year gold merchants went all over the countryside, usually in May or June just before the harvest, when the peasants were short of food, in debt, and at the end of their rope. When the government's gold collection took place they were given to believe that contributions were obligatory, that severe punishment awaited evaders, and that the Pope himself had ordained the sacrifice of all the gold in the churches. And so, resigned to this new imposition, they gave all they had to their country. Even Giulia and La Parroccola stripped themselves of their wedding rings, reminders of their marriages long ago and of the husbands who had disappeared across the sea.

Giulia's husband had gone with their son, the first of her seventeen children, to Argentina, and nothing more was ever heard of them. But one day Giulia received a letter and brought it to me to read to her. It was written in a mixture of Italian and Spanish and mailed from the port of Civitavecchia. The boy who had been lost to her for twenty years while he was growing up in Buenos Aires, wrote that he had volunteered for service with the Italian army in Abyssinia. He did not speak of the father, but said that he hoped to have a furlough before leaving Italy so that he could come to visit his mother. The furlough did not materialize, but the boy sent a photograph of himself and every now and then he wrote to her from Africa and I answered him, at Giulia's dictation.

At last a letter came in which he said that the war would soon be over and he begged his mother to find him a wife in Gagliano. The choice was up to her, and as soon as he came he would marry the girl. As in so many cases America had had no effect upon this boy, although he had left the village when he was far too young to preserve any memory of it. And he intended to return to a place he had never seen and to marry a strange girl chosen for him by his witch-mother, of whom he remembered only her name. Giulia, who knew all there was to know about every girl in Gagliano, chose for her son a peasant bride, healthy and shy rather than beautiful, who lived almost across the street from me, and the two of them settled down to await the boy's arrival and the wedding day.

Chapter Twenty-Four

APRIL WAS A CAPRICIOUS month with sun and rain and wandering clouds. In the air there was a faint tremor which perhaps in faraway places was a harbinger of Spring. But here there was none of the stir of renewed life, none of the budding and tumescence of the happy lands of the North, when they shake off their burden of snow and breathe in the warm sunshine and new vegetation. The cold was over and there were fresh breezes, but no grass grew on the hillsides, nor violets, nor any other flowers. Nothing in the landscape was changed, and the wastes of clay were the same gray as before. A vital part of the revolving year was missing and its absence saddened the heart. As the weather improved the village streets were once more empty, for the men were away all day long in the distant fields. The children splashed in puddles with the goats. I walked about in my corduroy suit or painted from my terrace. From the peasants' houses came alternately the sound of women's voices and the squeals of the piglets as they were lathered and washed and curried, according to local custom, while they protested just like rosy babies shrinking from the water.

Late one afternoon I was going home up and down the familiar way between Upper and Lower Gagliano, stopping every now and then to gaze mechanically at the mountains, whose every wrinkle and blemish I knew as well as we know the faces of those close to us, which we hardly see any more at all because we have looked at them so long. I was gazing thus, without seeing anything in particular, into the wind-swept grayness, as if I had lost all my senses and slipped out of time into the waters of eternity from which there was no return. I had sat down for a moment near the fountain, which was deserted at the moment, and was listening to the echo of this ocean, when I was overtaken by the letter-carrier. This was a sickly, old, emaciated woman, racked with coughing, who struggled around the narrow village alleys with the mail pouch on her head. She had a telegram, which had been held up by the censors, telling me of the death of a close relative. I went on home and a little later I was informed that, at the urgent request of my family, the police would allow me to return for a few days under strict guard to my native city. I was to leave at dawn to catch the bus and Don Gennaro, the local constable, would take me as far as Matera.

Thus I was torn away from a succession of listless days and found myself once more in motion, on a road, in a train, among green fields. The trip was such a sad one that I have almost completely forgotten it. From a distance I saw the barren crest of Grassano and the prosaic village so near to heaven; then we went through a part of the country which was new to me, between the Basento, the Bradano, and the Gravina rivers, beyond Grottole and Miglionico, in the direction of

Matera. At Matera there was a wait of several hours while arrangements were made for my police escort. I had time to see the town and then I understood my sister's horror, although at the same time I was struck by its tragic beauty. Finally I boarded the train, along with a guard, and traveled night and day the whole length of Italy. I stayed for only a few days in Turin, shadowed by two policemen, who were supposed to watch over me even when I was in bed, but who, instead, slept in a small room which I put in order for them in my house.

My visit was a melancholy one, quite apart from its mournful motive. I had expected tremendous enjoyment from seeing the city again, talking with my old friends, and taking part, if for only a moment, in the busy and complex life with which I was once so familiar. But when I got there I felt isolated, faraway, and unable to adapt myself to the places and persons I had longed to see. Many of my acquaintances avoided me for the sake of their own safety, others I myself kept away from in order not to compromise them. Some, braver or less exposed to risk than the rest, did come to see me without fear of the daily report drawn up by my guards, but even with them I found relations difficult. Part of me seemed by now foreign to their interests, ambitions, activities, and hopes; their life was no longer mine and it no longer touched me. After a few days, which passed in a flash, I set out again, with no regret, in the company of two new guards. These two had gone to some pains to get the job of escorting me because they hoped by shortening our traveling time to squeeze in a visit to their families. One of them, a lean Sicilian, had a wife in Rome, where we had to wait several hours for a train connection. He asked me not to tell on him if he stopped over to see her instead of going the rest of the way. I told him to go ahead and enjoy himself as his companion was quite able to watch over me alone. He said goodbye and disappeared.

The other guard, De Luca, went with me as far as Gagliano. He was a dark, well-dressed young fellow, who was already beginning to be bald. He expressed considerable shame for his present occupation and told me that he came from a good family of Montemurro in the Agri Valley. I heard later in Gagliano that all he had said was true. His father had been a very rich blind man who was known all over the province. He had land in various remote parts of Lucania and everyone recognized him when he rode alone, with his famous horse as a guide, to visit his scattered properties, which were often twenty-five or more miles apart. He had eight sons and all the older ones had university degrees. When the father died, the family affairs immediately went to pieces. Young De Luca's brothers all had good positions but he was still in school. He had had to give this up, and all that custom allowed him to do was to join the police. He hated his job and was anxious to go back for a high school diploma and then find a better one. In the course of this confession of his troubles he asked if I could recommend him. His brothers and his uncles were all employed in government offices in Rome and he wanted to go and see them; since he could not leave me alone he asked me to go with him. Thus it came about that I called upon several government employees and was introduced to them as his friend; in every house where we went we had coffee and I had to give evasive answers to questions about my personal history. De Luca was so ashamed of his profession that he did not want even his family to know about it. He told them that he had a good job in the North and that I worked in the same office with him.

Soon the train carried us beyond Rome toward the South. It was night and I could not sleep. As I sat on the hard seat

254

I meditated upon the past few days. I thought of my feeling of strangeness, and of the complete lack of understanding among those of my friends who concerned themselves with political questions, of the country to which I was now hurrying back. They had all asked about conditions in the South and I had told them what I knew. But although they listened with apparent interest, very few of them seemed really to follow what I was saying. They were men of various temperaments and shades of opinion, from stiff-necked conservatives to fiery radicals. Many of them were very able, and they all claimed to have meditated upon the "problem of the South" and to have formulated plans for its solution. But just as their schemes and the very language in which they were couched would have been incomprehensible to the peasants, so were the life and needs of the peasants a closed book to them, and one which they did not even bother to open.

At bottom, as I now perceived, they were all unconscious worshipers of the State. Whether the State they worshiped was the Fascist State or the incarnation of quite another dream, they thought of it as something that transcended both its citizens and their lives. Whether it was tyrannical or paternalistic, dictatorial or democratic, it remained to them monolithic, centralized, and remote. This was why the political leaders and my peasants could never understand one another. The politicians oversimplified things, even while they clothed them in philosophical expressions. Their solutions were abstract and far removed from reality; they were schematic halfway measures, which were already out of date. Fifteen years of Fascism had erased the problem of the South from their minds and if now they thought of it again they saw it only as a part of some other difficulty, through the fictitious generalities of party and class and even race. Some saw it as a purely technical and economic matter. They spoke of public works, industrialization, and domestic absorption of the plethora of would-be emigrants, or else they resurrected the old Socialist slogan of "making Italy over." Others saw the South burdened with an unfortunate historical heredity, a tradition of enslavement to the Bourbons which liberal democracy might little by little relieve. Some said that the question of the South was just one more case of capitalist oppression, which only rule by the proletariat could supplant. Others spoke of inherent racial inferiority, considering the South a dead weight on the economy of the North, and studied possible measures to be taken by the government to remedy this sad state of things. All of them agreed that the State should do something about it, something concretely useful, and beneficent, and legislative, and they were shocked when I told them that the State, as they conceived it, was the greatest obstacle to the accomplishment of anything. The State, I said, cannot solve the problem of the South, because the problem which we call by this name is none other than the problem of the State itself.

There will always be an abyss between the State and the peasants, whether the State be Fascist, Liberal, Socialist or take on some new form in which the middle-class bureaucracy still survives. We can bridge the abyss only when we succeed in creating a government in which the peasants feel they have some share. Public works and land reclamation are all very fine, but they are not the answer. Domestic absorption of the emigrants might yield some results, but it would make the whole of Italy, instead of just the South, into one huge colony. Plans laid by a central government, however much good they may do, still leave two hostile Italys on either side of the abyss. The difficulties we were discussing, I explained to them, were far more complex than they realized.

There are three distinct sides to it, which are three aspects of one central reality; they can neither be understood nor resolved separately. First of all, we are faced with two very different civilizations, neither of which can absorb the other. Country and city, a pre-Christian civilization and one that is no longer Christian, stand face to face. As long as the second imposes its deification of the State upon the first, they will be in conflict. The war in Africa and the wars that are yet to come are in part the result of this age-old quarrel, which has now reached an acute point, and not in Italy alone. Peasant civilization will always be the loser but it will not be entirely crushed. It will persevere under a cover of patience, interrupted by sporadic explosions, and the spiritual crisis will continue. Brigandage, the peasant war, is a symptom of what I mean, and this upheaval of the last century is not the last of its kind. Just as long as Rome rules over Matera, Matera will be lawless and despairing, and Rome despairing and tyrannical.

The second aspect of the trouble is economic, the dilemma of poverty. The land has been gradually impoverished: the forests have been cut down, the rivers have been reduced to mountain streams that often run dry, and livestock has become scarce. Instead of cultivating trees and pasture lands there has been an unfortunate attempt to raise wheat in soil that does not favor it. There is no capital, no industry, no savings, no schools; emigration is no longer possible, taxes are unduly heavy, and malaria is everywhere. All this is in large part due to the ill-advised intentions and efforts of the State, a State in which the peasants cannot feel they have a share, and which has brought them only poverty and deserts.

Finally, there is the social side of the problem. It is generally held that the big landed estates and their owners are at fault, and it is true that these estates are not charitable institutions. But if the absentee owner, who lives in Naples, or Rome, or Palermo, is an enemy of the peasants, he is not the worst of the enemies they have to cope with. He, at least, is far away and does not interfere with their daily life. Their real enemies, those who cut them off from any hope of freedom and a decent existence, are to be found among the middle-class village tyrants. This class is physically and morally degenerate and no longer able to fill its original function. It lives off petty thievery and the bastardized tradition of feudal rights. Only with the suppression of this class and the substitution of something better can the difficulties of the South find a solution.

The problem, in all of its three aspects, existed before the advent of Fascism. But Fascism, while hushing it up and denying its existence, aggravated it to the breaking point, because under Fascism the middle class took over and identified itself with the power of the State. We cannot foresee the political forms of the future, but in a middle-class country like Italy, where middle-class ideology has infected the masses of workers in the city, it is probable, alas, that the new institutions arising after Fascism, through either gradual evolution or violence, no matter how extreme and revolutionary they may be in appearance, will maintain the same ideology under different forms and create a new State equally far removed from real life, equally idolatrous and abstract, a perpetuation under new slogans and new flags of the worst features of the eternal tendency toward Fascism. Unless there is a peasant revolution we shall never have a true Italian revolution, for the two are identical.

The problem of the South cannot be solved within the framework of the Fascist State nor of that which may follow it, under a different label. It will solve itself if we can create new political ideals and a new kind of State which will belong also to the peasants and draw them away from their inevitable anarchy and indifference. Nor can the South solve its difficulties with its own efforts alone. In this case we should have a civil war, a new horrible form of brigandage which would end, as usual, with the defeat of the peasants and a general disaster. All of Italy must join in and, in order to do so, must be renewed from top to bottom. We must make ourselves capable of inventing a new form of government, neither Fascist, nor Communist, nor even Liberal, for all three of these are forms of the religion of the State. We must rebuild the foundations of our concept of the State with the concept of the individual, which is its basis. For the juridical and abstract concept of the individual we must substitute a new concept, more expressive of reality, one that will do away with the now unbridgeable gulf between the individual and the State. The individual is not a separate unit, but a link, a meeting place of relationships of every kind. This concept of relationship, without which the individual has no life, is at the same time the basis of the State. The individual and the State coincide in theory and they must be made to coincide in practice as well, if they are to survive.

This reversal of the concept of political life, which is gradually and unconsciously ripening among us, is implicit in the peasant civilization. And it is the only path which will lead us out of the vicious circle of Fascism and anti-Fascism. The name of this way out is autonomy. The State can only be a group of autonomies, an organic federation. The unit or cell through which the peasants can take part in the complex life of the nation must be the autonomous or self-governing rural community. This is the only form of government which can solve in our time the three interdependent aspects of the problem of the South; which can allow the co-existence of two different civilizations, without one lording it over the other or weighing the other down; which can furnish a good chance for escape from poverty; and which, finally, by the abolition of the powers and functions of the landowners and the local middle class, can assure the peasants a life of their own, for the benefit of all. But the autonomy or self-government of the community cannot exist without the autonomy of the factory, the school, and the city, of every form of social life. This is what I learned from a year of life underground.

All this I said to my friends, and I was still thinking it over as the train slipped by night into Lucania. Thus began a series of ideas which I developed further in later years, after the experience of exile abroad and of war. And with such thoughts I fell asleep.

Chapter Twenty-Five

THE SUN WAS HIGH OVER-
head when I awoke, and we were already past Potenza, among
the steep slopes of Brindisi-in-the-Mountains. Something unusual was in the air which I had not yet fully taken into
account. We entered the Basento Valley, went past the
lonely stations of Pietra Pertosa, Garaguso, and Tricarico and
soon reached our destination, Grassano. Here we got off to
wait a few hours, as usual, for the bus. The station was deserted
and I walked up and down on the road outside, talking with
my guard. Grassano greeted me from its pinnacle, a friendly
apparition with which I was periodically blessed, but there was
a change in its appearance. Then I understood the strange
aspect of the landscape which had struck me earlier in the day
from the train window. The mountain rose up as before, with
its gradual rises and irregular crags, to the cemetery and the
village, but the earth which I had always seen gray and yellow,

was now an unexpected and unnatural green. Spring had suddenly burst forth during my brief absence, but the green, which elsewhere is a symbol of harmony and hope, here seemed artificial and violent; it was out of key, like rouge on the sunburned cheeks of a peasant girl. This same metallic green extended all the way along the mountain road to Stigliano; it was like the false notes of a trumpet in a funeral march. The mountains closed in after me like prison gates as we went down toward the Sauro Valley and up again toward Gagliano. In the sunshine little patches of green that were scattered over the white clay stood out even more intensely and strangely than before, like expostulations. They seemed the torn pieces of a mask, thrown down at random.

It was nearly evening when we reached the village. My guard, De Luca, was recognized by everyone. All that he had told me about himself and his family was true; the villagers welcomed the son of the blind man with the trusty horse as one of their own and many of them asked him to share their supper before he went his way. But he was in a hurry; he managed to borrow a horse and trotted off toward Montemurro, where he would arrive after a night of riding.

After my short stay in the city, Gagliano seemed smaller and sadder than ever in its changeless Bourbon atmosphere. Two more years here! The tedious, monotonous days of the future suddenly bore down upon me. I walked towards my house, among greetings and calls of "Glad to see you back!" from the doorways. Barone, whom I had left with Giulia, was in the center of the square like one of the gentry and ran to meet me, barking with joy.

I had expected to find Giulia waiting for me, but the house was empty, the fire was out, and there was no supper ready. I sent a boy to call her, but he came back with the message that she could not come and that I should not expect her the next day either. She vouchsafed no explanation. I learned later from Donna Caterina that during my absence the albino barber, Giulia's lover, had had a fit of jealousy—God knows how groundless—and had threatened to cut my witch's throat with a razor if she went back to me. He had terrified her to such an extent that she did not dare see me or even nod to me on the street. Only after some time had gone by and her terror had subsided did Giulia speak to me when we met, with a mysterious smile on her face and a reserved and almost smug expression. Even then she said nothing of her reason for leaving me.

Donna Caterina went to great trouble to find me another servant. "There's one even better than Giulia. Just now she's busy, but I hope to get her for you." In the meantime the few village witches came to see me, but I decided to wait for Donna Caterina's protégée. Among those whom I sent away was an old woman, in appearance about sixty years old, who was particularly insistent. I found out later, to my astonishment, that she was almost ninety, that she was the mistress of Don Luigi's eighty-two-year-old father and that she had taken quite a fancy to me. Without my ever realizing it, I had run the risk of being devoured by one of the oldest crones of my acquaintance.

Finally the mayor's sister sent Maria to see me. She was even more of a witch than Giulia, in fact she was exactly the sort one might expect to see fly away on a broomstick at any moment, but she had none of Giulia's animal dignity. She was about forty, thin, and of medium height, with a dry wrinkled face, a long, sharp nose, and a prominent pointed chin. She was very agile and both able and quick at her work. She seemed to be consumed by an inner fire, by an insatiable greed and a nervous and diabolical sensuality. She threw dark, flaming looks at me and I saw immediately that she had none of Giulia's ancient passivity and that I should have to keep her at a distance. In all the time that she was with me I was never in the least familiar with her. But she was an excellent servant.

Besides the flight of Giulia other events had taken place in the village during my absence. Don Giuseppe Trajella had been banished and sent to die among the malaria-ridden hovels of Gaglianello. The affair of Christmas Eve had borne fruit and Don Luigi had triumphed. The bishop had held a competition for the vacant parish of Gagliano and forbidden Trajella to take part in it. His successor, Don Pietro Liguari, had already arrived from Miglionico. He found a comfortable house on the main street, near the square, and had settled down there with his housekeeper and an extraordinary stock of provisions. I met him in the square the day after my return and he came up to me with a cordial smile. He said he had heard a great deal about me and was very happy to make my acquaintance; he invited me to come to his house for a cup of coffee. Don Pietro Liguari was the exact opposite, in both manner and spirit, of the old misanthrope who had been relegated to Gaglianello. He was a man of about fifty or so, fairly tall, thick-set and heavy, with a pale, yellowish flabbiness about him. His eyes were black and Spanish and full of cunning; he had a large face, a slightly hooked nose, thin lips, and black hair. I felt that I had seen him before or that he closely resembled someone I knew and, upon closer study, this impression grew stronger. The fact is that the new priest had a face typical of his generation of Italians. The type was that of an actor, a prelate, and a barber rolled into one, a cross between Mussolini and the stage figure, Ruggero Ruggeri. Don Pietro Liguari was from this part of the country and probably of a peasant family; he had a crafty expression on his face and his manner was devious. He walked with a certain dignity, his habit was clean, the red tassel on his biretta was bright and new, and on one finger he wore a ruby ring.

When I went into his house I was struck by the quantity of sausages, hams, cheeses, strings of dried figs, peppers, onions, and garlic hanging from the beams of the ceiling, the number of jars of jams and jellies and bottles of oil and wine on the cupboard shelves. No house of the well-to-do in Gagliano was stocked so abundantly. The door was opened by the housekeeper. She was a tall, thin woman of about forty, with a severe, impenetrable face, dressed in black with a white collar around her neck and no veil over her head. This austere creature, I was later informed, was a peasant from Montemurro, an excellent cook and the mother of four sons (fathered by various priests, so rumor had it) who were now scattered about in the religious schools of the province. Don Liguari showed me his house and his larder.

"You must come sometimes to do penance with me," he said, pointing to some fresh butter, a thing which did not exist in Gagliano and which I had not laid eyes on since I came there. "My housekeeper makes first-rate spaghetti. You'll see. But now let's sit down and have some coffee."

When we had emptied our cups the priest began to talk about the village, and drew me into an exchange of views.

"There's a great deal of work to be done here," he said, "a great deal; yes, everything, from the ground up. The church is in bad shape and the bell-tower has yet to be built. The tithes due to the clergy are forgotten or in arrears. Above all, there's very little religion. Many of the children are not even baptized and no one does anything about it unless they are ill and about to die. Only a few old women come to church at all; even on Sunday it's almost empty. No one comes to confession or communion. All this must change and it will change very soon, you'll see. The authorities don't move a finger; in fact, they do what they can to make things worse. They are materialists and all they talk of is war. They think they run the whole country with their Fascism, poor idiots! They don't realize that ever since the reconciliation between Church and State their power has passed to us, by virtue of our spiritual authority. That's the whole meaning of the Concordat, that we priests have taken over. If the mayor thinks he's the strong man of the village, he's mistaken."

Don Pietro Liguari stopped, as if he had said too much. But he knew that he could be as outspoken with me as he chose and there was no danger of my reporting him. Moreover he wished to be in my good graces. He began to talk about political prisoners and said that he felt it his duty to aid and comfort them, regardless of their religious beliefs and political opinions. This was all very fine, but his insinuating ways and unctuous tone of voice betrayed self-interest rather than charity. After this long preamble he finally came around to the real reason for his desire to see me:

"We must lead the people back to religion or else they'll fall into the hands of the atheistic pretenders to power. This much even those who are of a different faith must admit. . . ." And here he shot me a meaningful glance. "Besides, anyone may be touched by divine grace. . . . But to bring the peasants back to the Church we must make the services more attractive and see to it that they appeal to the imagination. The church here is poor and bare, and preaching is not enough to draw them. If the peasants are to return to the House of God we must have music. I had a harmonium brought over here from Miglionico and yesterday it was installed in the church. It's just the thing we need, but there's one difficulty: who's to play it? No one in the village knows how. Of course I thought of you; you're so educated and you can do so many things. . . . We're all God's children, you know. . . ."

. The reasons for which he had feared a refusal on my part had never even crossed my mind. I told him that I had studied the piano, but that I hadn't touched a keyboard for years. I was willing to try, and to help him out once or twice, but I couldn't promise to be a regular organist. If there was anyone to sing I should be glad to act as accompanist, but first of all I should have to send for some music. We walked up to the church to look at the instrument, which had been placed in plain sight at one side of the altar and had already aroused considerable curiosity among the children. The priest was happy; he had been afraid I would refuse, and my unexpected consent emboldened him to ask more. He pointed to the bare, peeling walls of the church:

"Here there's a real need for some painting."

The idea was not altogether displeasing.

"Perhaps some day I'll cover the walls with frescoes," I told him. "I've two years more to stay here and plenty of time to think it over. Too bad they're in such bad condition. But I shouldn't like to antagonize Mornaschi, who's such a very nice fellow."

The ceiling of the church had already been frescoed with gold stars on a blue background and decorative bands that separated it from the walls below. The work had been done several years before by Mornaschi, a fair-headed young painter from Milan, who used to go from village to village, carrying out church decorations and staying in one place until he finished his job there and went on to another. Here at Gagliano his vagabond life had come to an end. He had come only to do the ceiling, but he had been offered a lowly clerical position in the assessor's office. Leaving uncertainty for security and art for bureaucracy, he had laid down his paintbrushes and never gone away. He was a modest, reserved, courteous man, the only stranger who had ever settled down in Gagliano. I saw him from time to time and he was always very agreeable.

"Mornaschi can lend you a hand," said the priest, who was evidently already well up on local affairs and enthusiastic about the prospects of leading his wandering flock back to the fold. I, too, was a lost sheep and the good man let his imagination run away with him. He made allusions to another prospect, a solemn ceremony of adult baptism, in which the bishop himself—why not?—might take part. He did not state this hope in such clear terms to start with, although I could guess at his eagerness. Don Liguari was an astute diplomat, and he merely let drop a discreet hint that it was a shame for me to live in such a solitary fashion, that although I was still young it was time for me to think of marriage. Then, as we left the church he invited me to have dinner with him the following Sunday: "Come do penance, Doctor, with a poor priest."

The foodstuffs I had seen piled up in the kitchen gave me a notion that the penance would not be too arduous. The austere and maternal housekeeper from Montemurro proved herself to be no mean cook; indeed, I had not dined so well for a whole year. The greatest delicacy consisted of home-made sausages filled, according to local custom, with Spanish red peppers.

From this time on, the priest was inseparable from me. He came to my house and sat for a portrait which he hoped I would give him. Don Luigi was jealous of the priest's attentions, but Don Liguari had persuasive ways and probably quieted him with some evangelical pretext or other. One day he saw on my bedside table a Protestant edition of the Bible, and he started back in horror, as if it were a serpent. "Such books as you read, Doctor! Throw it away, I beg of you!" His manner with me was quite intimate, and every time he saw me he said with fatherly solicitude: "First a baptism and then a wedding. Just leave it all to me!"

One Sunday I returned his dinner invitation, straining to the utmost the ability of my witch, Maria, in order to keep the "penance" from being on this occasion a real one. It happened that Poerio, the white-bearded old man who had been ill for many months but could not consult me because he was a *compare di San Giovanni* of Dr. Gibilisco, had died two days before, on Friday. The funeral took place on Sunday, with two priests from Stigliano participating in the ceremony, and I had to include them in my invitation. One was big and fat, the other short and scrawny, but both of them were of the same general type as Don Liguari: wily, used to good living, and thoroughly versed in peasant ways. I quite enjoyed myself in the company of these three strange creatures, who deplored the fact that the majority of those who died were poor and a really fine funeral such as the one we had just attended took place only once every year or so.

Meanwhile I had got hold of some church music and had practiced on the harmonium. As soon as I felt up to rendering the mass without too many errors and dared to face a not overly critical public, I arranged with Don Liguari to assist him for just one Sunday. I had found out that the barber who extracted teeth knew how to play the piano by ear, and I was sure that he would make a better permanent organist than I. Although he was not very keen to set foot in the church, I intended to leave the job to him after the one mass I had promised.

That Sunday the church was full. The priest had spread

the news that I was to play and no one wanted to miss this unaccustomed spectacle. The women in their white veils were packed in all the way back to the doors and many could not get in at all. People came who had not been to church since time immemorial. Among them, with her sister, was Donna Concetta, the elder daughter of S. the lawyer, whom I often met in the square in the evening. Donna Concetta had been cloistered for almost a year on account of the death of her brother; in all this time she did not leave the house and I had never laid eyes on her. She had decided to end her vow with this Sunday's mass and she sat in the first row of benches. Donna Concetta was said to be the most beautiful girl in Gagliano and this reputation was entirely justified. She was about eighteen years old, very small, with the perfect round face of a Madonna, large, languorous eyes, thick, smooth black hair, a small red mouth, a slender neck, and an agreeable air of shyness.

This was the only time I ever saw Donna Concetta, amid the throng of veiled women, and I never heard her voice. But the peasants had their plans. "You are one of us now," they used to say. "You should marry Donna Concetta. She's the wealthiest and prettiest marriageable girl in the village, and just the one for you. That way you'll not leave us, but stay here always." This is why I was curious to see the cloistered bride whom they had chosen for me.

The women were enthusiastic about the service. "What a fine fellow you are," they shouted after me as I left the church. But the priest's confidence in the drawing power of music was mistaken. Although the barber was a better organist than I, the church was soon nearly deserted again. Don Liguari did not lose heart; he spent his days going from house to house and baptizing the children. Little by little he may have obtained some results.

The strange, ephemeral spring had gone by. The vivid greenery had lasted no more than ten days, like a preposterous apparition. Then it had shriveled up under the burning wind and sun of May, which brought summer suddenly upon us. The landscape returned to its usual monotonous, white, chalky appearance. Just as when I had arrived, long months before, the air vibrated with heat over the silent stretches of clay, and it seemed as if the gray shadow of the same clouds had forever hung above that desolate white sea. I knew every color, every fold and irregularity of the land.

With the return of the heat, life in Gagliano crawled at a slower pace than ever. The peasants were in the fields, the shadows of the houses stretched lazily across the street, and the goats stood still in the sun. The eternal idleness of the Bourbons lay upon this village that was built of the bones of the dead. I could make out every voice, every whisper, every sound, as if I had known it always, and had heard it, endlessly repeated, just as it would be repeated endlessly in the future. I worked at my painting and the care of the sick, but my mood was one of complete indifference; I felt like a worm enclosed in a nutshell. Far away from those I loved, hemmed in by an almost religious monotony, I waited for the years to pass. My life had no base but was hung ridiculously in the air, and the sound of my own voice startled me.

The war was drawing to a close. Addis Ababa had fallen, the Empire had ascended the hills of Rome, and Don Luigi attempted to bring it to the hills of Gagliano as well, with one of the usual sparsely attended and depressing public meetings. There would be no more battle casualties and soon the few local men who were in the army would return. Giulia's son wrote that he was coming soon and that he hoped to find his bride ready for him. Don Luigi felt more important than before, as if the imperial crown had passed over his head. As for the peasants, in spite of all that was promised, they saw no openings for themselves in the mythical and ill-gotten new land. The thought of Africa did not even cross their minds as they went down to the banks of the Agri.

One day at noon I walked through the square. The sun was blazing, the wind raised clouds of dust, and from the steps of the post office Don Cosimino waved his hand urgently in my direction. As I came closer I saw a look of affection and happiness in his eyes.

"Good news, Don Carlo!" he said, "I don't want to give you false hopes, but a telegram has just come from Matera authorizing the release of the prisoner from Genoa. I've just sent for him. The message tells me to stand by this afternoon for more names. I hope yours is among them. It seems that there's an amnesty to celebrate the fall of Addis Ababa."

A group of us stood about the post office all day. Every now and then we heard the click of the telegraph receiver, then Don Cosimino's face appeared at the window, wreathed in smiles, and he shouted a new name. Mine was the very last; it did not come in until nearly evening. All of us were freed except the two Communists: the student from Pisa and the worker from Ancona. The gentry gathered around to congratulate me upon the liberation accorded me without my having lifted a finger to obtain it. My unexpected joy soon turned to melancholy, and I called Barone and went home.

Everyone else left the next morning, but I could not bring myself to hurry. I was sorry to leave and I found a dozen pretexts for lingering on. There were patients I could not abandon, paintings I wanted to finish, and others I had to pack up, along with the rest of my belongings. I had to have packing-cases made and a box for Barone, because he could slip away from a leash and he was too wild to send loose in the baggage car. Thus I stayed on for another ten days.

The peasants came to see me and said:

"Don't go away. Stay here. Marry Concetta.. They'll make you the mayor. You must stay with us."

When the day of my departure drew nearer, they said they were going to puncture the tires of the car that was to take me away.

"I'll come back," I said.

But they shook their heads.

"If you go, you'll never come back. You're a Christian, a real human being. Stay here with us."

They wanted me to make a solemn promise to return and I made it in all sincerity, but I have not yet been able to keep it.

Finally I took leave of one and all: the widow, the grave-digger and town crier, Donna Caterina, Giulia, Don Luigi, La Parroccola, Dr. Milillo, Dr. Gibilisco, the priest, the gentry, the peasants, the women, the goats, the gnomes and the spirits. I left one of my paintings to the village as a memento. Then I saw my baggage loaded, turned the big key in the lock of my house door and gave a last look at the mountains of Calabria, the cemetery, the Bog, and the surrounding wastes of clay.

It was dawn, and the peasants were going down with their donkeys to the fields when I climbed with Barone into the "American's" car and went away. After we had rounded the curve below the sports field, Gagliano disappeared from view and I have never seen it since.

I had a pass for the railway and had to travel by slow trains; this prolonged my trip considerably. I saw again the rocky heights and the museum of Matera. Then we went across the plains of Apulia, studded with white stones like a graveyard, and through Bari and Foggia in the mysterious night. After this I proceeded northward by short stages. I went up to the cathedral of Ancona and looked out at long last upon the sea. It was a quiet day and from this height there was a wide view over the water. A fresh breeze was blowing from Dalmatia, making tiny whitecaps on the smooth surface of the waves. Vague notions floated through my head: the life of this sea was like man's fate, cast for all eternity in a series of equal waves, moving through time without change. I thought with affectionate sorrow of the motionless time and the dark civilization which I had left behind me.

Already the train was carrying me far away, through the checkerboard fields of Romagna, toward the vineyards of Piedmont and the mysterious future of exile, of war and death, which I could then but barely perceive, like an uncertain cloud in the boundless sky.

THE END

Florence, December 1943–July 1944

Library of Congress Cataloguing in Publication Data

Levi, Carlo, 1902-1975.
Christ stopped at Eboli.
Translation of: Cristo si è fermato a Eboli.
Reprint. Originally published: Time reading program
special ed. New York: Time Inc., 1964.
1. Basilicata (Italy)—Social life and customs.
2. Levi, Carlo, 1902-1975—Journeys—Italy—Basilicata.
I. Title.
DG975.B3L4813   1982   945'.77   82-10344
ISBN 0-8094-3748-1
ISBN 0-8094-3749-X (pbk.)